THE END OF
THE AGE OF INNOCENCE

Fig. 1 Edith Wharton in front of a railway car for
wounded soldiers. (Courtesy of Jacques Fosse)

THE END OF
THE AGE OF INNOCENCE

Edith Wharton and the First World War

Alan Price

St. Martin's Griffin
New York

Dedicated to the memory of my father,
Richard C. Price, 1916-1994

THE END OF THE AGE OF INNOCENCE:
Copyright © Alan Price, 1996, 1998.

ISBN 0-312-17677-5 paperback

Library of Congress Cataloging-in-Publication Data

Price, Alan, 1943-
    The end of the age of innocence : Edith Wharton and the First
World War / Alan Price.
        p.   cm.
    Includes bibliographical references and index.
    ISBN 0-312-12938-6 (cloth) ISBN 0-312-17677-5 (pbk)
    1. Wharton, Edith, 1862-1937—Biography. 2. Literature and history—
United States—History—20th century. 3. Women and literature—United
States—History—20th Century. 4. Women authors. American—20th
Century—Biography. 5. World War, 1914-1918—Literature and the war.
    6. World War, 1914-1918—civilian relief. I. Title.
    PS3545.H16Z78   1996
    813'.52—dc20
    [B]   95-38196
                                                           CIP
Book Design by Acme Art, Inc.

First published in hardcover in the United States of America in 1996
First St. Martin's Griffin edition: January 1998
10 9 8 7 6 5 4 3 2 1

CONTENTS

LIST OF ILLUSTRATIONS

ACKNOWLEDGMENTS

The following history of Edith Wharton's relief activities during the First World War draws heavily on her unpublished letters and the ephemeral records from her charities held in a number of archives and libraries. I am especially indebted to Ambassador William R. Tyler, residual legatee of the Edith Wharton Estate, for permission to quote from unpublished Wharton letters. I am grateful to the following institutions for permission to quote from unpublished archival sources: the Yale Collection of American Literature, the Beinecke Rare Book and Manuscript Library, Yale University; the Lilly Library, Indiana University; Department of Rare Books and Special Collections, Princeton University Libraries; the Houghton Library and the Harvard University Archives, Harvard University; the Harvard University Center for Italian Renaissance Studies, Villa I Tatti; Evergreen House, Johns Hopkins University; Manuscript Division, Library of Congress; and the Rockefeller Archive Center.

As a professor at a two-year campus of a major public university, my primary responsibility is teaching. However, Penn State University has granted me two sabbatical leaves and has supported me with office and library facilities during the fifteen years this project has been under way. In particular, the Hazleton Campus, the Department of English, and the College of the Liberal Arts at Penn State have offered timely support. Librarian Richard Tyce and interlibrary loan specialist Kathleen Stone at the Hazleton Campus Library answered every request I made. Two gifted, former students served as research assistants: Anna Sprague in Hazleton and Princeton in August of 1990, and Maria Sabatino in Florence in June of 1991.

Much of the additional financial support and intellectual stimulation for my research came from programs sponsored by the National Endowment for the Humanities. Two NEH Summer Seminars for College Teachers allowed me to study with outstanding scholars: Martha Banta's "Images of Women in American Literature: 1870-1920" (University of Washington, 1979) taught me not to be in a rush to simplify complexity; and R. W. B. Lewis and Alan Trachtenberg's seminar "Usable Pasts:

Versions of History in American Literature and Culture, 1900-1940"
(Yale University, 1986) gave me the opportunity in New Haven to
transcribe hundreds of important letters and documents from the Whar-
ton Papers in the Yale collection of American Literature at the Beinecke
Rare Book and Manuscript Library. An NEH Travel to Collections grant
(June 1991) permitted me to transcribe more letters from Wharton to
Bernard and Mary Berenson held at Villa I Tatti in Florence.

One of the many pleasant things about research on Wharton is the
willingness of fellow scholars to share materials, displaying a trustfulness
not universal among literary scholars. I want to thank Eleanor Dwight for
sharing Wharton's letters to Elizabeth Cameron held at the Library of
Congress. Shari Benstock caught several factual errors and remained
enthusiastic about my project during the writing of her own extensive
biography of Wharton. I had the opportunity to read draft chapters of the
war years from both Shari Benstock's *No Gifts from Chance: A Biography
of Edith Wharton*, and Eleanor Dwight's *Edith Wharton: An Extraordinary
Life*.

I am grateful to Wilma R. Ebbitt, whose careful copy-editing of early
drafts of the text smoothed the way for later readers. I value the friendship
and encouragement of Bruce R. Smith, who assured me that I had a story
to tell. Earlier drafts of the book were commented on by Alan Albright,
David Mallery, Bob Miller, Richard C. Price, and William Schneider.
Katherine Joslin, my coeditor on an earlier Wharton project, offered
helpful criticism. Judith L. Sensibar urged me to bring my own voice
forward and to reconceptualize whole sections of the book. My shaky
French was corrected by Jean Méral, Valérie Baudier, and Christiane
Verbeeck. My editor at St. Martin's Press, Jennifer Farthing, has supported
this project with efficiency and care.

Portions of the following chapters have been revised from articles
published in *Tulsa Studies in Women's Literature*, *The Princeton University
Library Chronicle*, and *Women's Studies*. I am grateful to the editors of
those journals for permission to use earlier published materials, much
altered, in the following chapters.

PREFACE

A LIFE PUNCTUATED BY WAR

EDITH WHARTON'S LIFE WAS BRACKETED BY WARS. SHE WAS BORN DURING A bitterly cold January week in 1862, when the line of military camps stretched from northern Virginia through Kentucky to Cairo, Illinois. She died in 1937, the year that General Francisco Franco and his insurgents waged war against the Spanish Republican Army, supported by the International Brigade with its scattering of American writers. Her friend Teddy Roosevelt fashioned his public reputation during his military exploits in the Spanish-American War. Wharton's own literary career was interrupted, almost bisected, by the First World War.

She was one of a number of American writers, primarily women, who became involved in war charities during the opening months of the conflict in Belgium and France, well before the United States abandoned its official policy of neutrality. Wharton was among the 25,000 American women who volunteered for war-related work in Europe, Serbia, China, and Russia.[1] During the four years and three months of the war, she witnessed a transformation that saw economic and political power shift from a Europe bled white by the war (more than 10 million dead) to a United States that got through relatively unscathed (115,000 dead).[2]

The first chapter of this book describes how Wharton's plans for a new novel and a leisurely summer at a rented estate in England were interrupted by the opening of the war (variously called the Great War, the European War, and the First World War) during the first days of August 1914. For the next year Wharton threw her energies into organizing and raising money for several large civilian war charities, many of which bore her name.

Wharton's relief efforts began simply enough, with a sewing room. The need was obvious. Several thousand working women in Paris had been thrown out of their jobs by the military mobilization in early August of 1914. With the mobilization, hundreds of shops, cafes, and small businesses in Paris closed, leaving previously employed women without a means of support. In her workroom Wharton offered employment to as many as ninety French women at a time. They received a nutritious lunch and a modest daily stipend. Wharton oversaw the work and secured orders from American friends. Some of the sewing women had worked for the famous couture houses on the rue de la Paix. Within a few weeks, Wharton's sewing room had established a reputation for producing fine lingerie as well as bandages for the hospitals and knitted socks and gloves for the men in the trenches.

By October and November Paris was flooded with refugees from Belgium and the invaded provinces of northern France. The French government could barely keep up with its own homeless, so the Belgians were forced to find shelter in railroad stations, in large sporting arenas, and on the streets. Again the need was obvious. With French, Belgian, and American friends, Wharton established the American Hostels for Refugees, a charity that provided housing, food, employment, medical services, education, and even Montessori classes for children of nursery-school age.

The second chapter follows Wharton to several locations on the French front, where she distributed medical supplies for the French Red Cross while collecting impressions for a series of evocative war essays that appeared first in Scribner's Magazine and were later collected in her book Fighting France (1915). By the summer she had begun another literary project, The Book of the Homeless (1916), an elaborately illustrated anthology with contributions from the leading writers, artists, and composers of the period. A detailed history of the creation and production of this gift book shows the breadth of Wharton's reputation as well as her extensive organizational skills.

Her charities continued to grow during 1915. The Belgian government, so impressed by Wharton's work with the adult refugees, asked if she could care for a small group of orphaned and abandoned children from Flanders. She said yes. With less than twenty-four hours' notice, she received sixty young girls. She had barely settled them when she received two hundred more. Soon the Children of Flanders Rescue Committee was caring for more than six hundred children and another two hundred aged and infirm Flemish refugees. Realizing that the children would return to Belgium after the war and would need to make a living, Wharton set up lace-making, gardening, and carpentry classes.

The work with the charities frequently left her exhausted. She began to take periodic rest trips in 1915 to get back to her writing. A cycle of exhaustion and recovery was soon established. She would perform administrative and fund-raising tasks for the war charities in Paris until she reached a point where ill health and fatigue would force her doctor to send her away, usually to the south of France, for several weeks. The rest cures, however, rarely accomplished their goal. Often she had barely gotten her first wind when the deaths of close friends or the needs of the charities would shatter her peace and drive her back to Paris more tired than when she had left.

The third chapter looks at how official recognition for her war work—the French Legion of Honor awarded in March of 1916—was quickly overshadowed by private griefs—the deaths of her dear friends Henry James and Egerton Winthrop. She was slowly able to get back to her first love—writing fiction. During the summer and the autumn she wrote the novella *Summer*, which with its passion she called her "hot Ethan."

Also in 1916 she could see that all of her humanitarian efforts would waste away in the scourge of tuberculosis unless something were done immediately, and on a large scale, to limit its sweep. Wharton had already established a number of convalescent homes to care for the ill among her own refugees, but the disease was rampant among the soldiers coming out of the damp, rat-infested trenches. She joined several other prominent Americans in France as a vice president for the *Tuberculeux de la Guerre*, a large charity with official French government sanction. She set up demonstration sanatoriums using the American method of fresh-air cures for tubercular French soldiers and civilians.

The fourth chapter details the coming of America into the war and Wharton's subsequent struggle with a charity octopus—the American Red Cross. While her salvation might have come with its arrival in the summer of 1917, it did not. Wharton never publicly revealed her disagreements with the organization. However, her unpublished letters, an especially rich source for understanding the politics of American relief aid during the First World War, reveal her growing frustration. Moreover, they make clear that Wharton's disillusionment with the American Red Cross after 1917 was representative of what other American women in France felt. Scores of private relief agencies organized and administered by American women during the first three years of the war were unceremoniously swallowed up in a vast centralizing wave. Fourteen months after America entered the war and only three weeks before the Armistice, Wharton told her sister-in-law Mary Cadwalader Jones, "the feeling against the Red Cross is not only as strong as it was but far stronger within the last two or three months . . . and apparently their purpose is to strangle all the independent war charities."[3]

The fifth chapter shows Wharton withdrawing increasingly from the management of the charities. She was still officially recognized: She had meetings with General John Pershing and Woodrow Wilson's representative, Colonel Edward M. House. But she moved to the Pavillon Colombe, a small estate in the village of St. Brice-sous-Forêt some twenty miles from Paris, and into a private imaginative space with her brief war novel *The Marne* (1918).

The conclusion of this book looks at the use Wharton made of the war in her later fiction. She regained her satirical edge to portray the frequently less than noble motives that prompted civilian volunteers to join war charities. The fiction she wrote during the war and that uses the war as a subject investigates themes of incest and social politics.

෨

Though Wharton's humanitarian war work was widely recognized—the Legion of Honor from the French and the Queen Elizabeth's medal from the Belgians—her writing from the war years has been largely dismissed by literary historians as an embarrassing passage during which she fell prey to propaganda. Blake Nevius, her first serious critic in the generation following her death, contends that Wharton's war fiction "adds nothing to her laurels; on the contrary, it proves that a novelist whose detachment was always precariously maintained could, when confronted with reports of German atrocities, lose her head as easily as the average newspaper reader."[4] Stanley Cooperman in his sweeping survey of American novels about the First World War contends, "Miss [sic] Wharton combined gentility with blood-thirst, the manners of the social novelist with the matter of the recruiting poster."[5] Even her most ardent admirers are left with uncomfortable questions: How did a sophisticated social satirist turn so quickly into a partisan war propagandist? What led Wharton, with her rich sense of irony, to turn her pen to sentimental fiction and propaganda essays?

This book first offers a historical context for Wharton's humanitarian and literary activities during the war. In addition, it probes her decision to adopt genres and literary voices she once condemned. We need to remember that the phenomenon of American authors turning from fiction to propaganda to sway a neutral American reading public and to aid war charities was not uncommon between 1914 and 1917. Dorothy

Canfield Fisher, Mary Roberts Rinehart, Gertrude Atherton, Alice B. Toklas, and Gertrude Stein participated in and wrote about relief activities in Belgium and France. Even that most detached of social observers, Henry James, wrote public letters to American newspapers and propaganda pamphlets urging support for the Norton-Harjes ambulance units in France and for the Belgian refugees in London.

For James and Wharton, the proposed imposition of German *kultur* (used by German intellectuals to justify the war) was an unconscionable violation of cultural boundaries. As expatriates and as writers of exquisite sensitivities, James and Wharton used their isolation from their native culture to heighten perception and contrast. For them the idea of Germany imposing a master culture on France or England or Italy was not just a political and military invasion, it was an assault on the cultural gradations that made their art possible.

Edith Wharton, it is true, wrote at the top of her voice during the early war years. She learned during the course of the war, however, to modulate her pitch and to hit and hold "the tremolo note" when its effects served her ends. The shift in rhetorical registers is instructive. When the war began, her dominant tone had been satire, with a strong secondary suit in irony. She and Henry James were swept uncritically into a total and totalizing condemnation of Germany, and in German *kultur* they foresaw "the crash of civilization." They quickly concluded that they could not remain silent in the face of wider American neutrality. Peter Buitenhuis in his study of the influence of British, American, and Canadian writers during the First World War concludes, "Expatriate American authors like Henry James and Edith Wharton were influential catalysts of American opinion."[6]

Both Wharton and James were aware of the shift in language generally and the dramatic dislocation in their own writing in particular. A few months into the war, James described the war's effect upon language. During a rare interview, where he insisted that his exact punctuation be taken down as well as his words, James asked the correspondent from the *New York Times* to consider the overwhelming fact that during a twenty-minute period, there had been as many as 5,000 casualties on the Western Front. James pondered the enormity of the statistic for a moment in a stunned silence. Then, anticipating by more than a dozen years Hemingway's statement in *A Farewell to Arms* about the decline of language, he continued: "One finds it in the midst of all this as hard to apply one's words as to endure one's thoughts. The war has used up words: they have weakened, they have deteriorated like motor car tires; they have, like millions of other things, been more overstrained and knocked about and voided of the happy semblance during the last six months than in all the long ages before, and we are now confronted with a depreciation of all our terms, or, otherwise speaking, with a loss of expression through an increase in limpness, that may well make us wonder what ghosts will be left to walk."[7]

With her keen sense of noblesse oblige, Wharton makes an especially illustrative case of the tension American writers felt between the disinterested code of their craft, on the one hand, and their sympathy for allies and the refugees, on the other. Wharton's unpublished correspondence with her editors from the war years reveals a writer who had previously rejected the subjects and techniques of popular fiction now testing the boundaries of her literary identity.

Part of Wharton's reaction to the cataclysm of the war was social and aesthetic. "Propriety," "social grace," "good breeding"—these are terms not in favor today. Yet for an understanding of Wharton's actions during the war, such terms are important. She felt very strongly that private things should be kept private and public things made public. An example from her daily life may help.

During the mornings she wrote in her bedroom. Sometimes she would break off from her business writing to pen a quick note to one of her frequent houseguests. Those unpublished, and unmailed, notes were carried along the corridors of her rue de Varenne apartment by maids or her butler to the guest's bedroom. Yet even these little notes, frequently setting luncheon appointments or suggesting afternoon diversions, which were scribbled in relaxed moments during her writing mornings, would be inserted in envelopes and carefully addressed to, for example, Bernard Berenson, Esquire. The notes within often showed her great sense of fun. But the envelopes themselves observed an outer courtesy and an attention to good manners.[8]

Wharton had a keen sense of rhetorical and literary registers. Her observation that she had to sound the "tremolo note" in her frequent appeals for money for her charities reflects her self-conscious attention to voice and tone, especially during times of financial and social stress. The phrase itself comes from a letter to Elisina Tyler, her able lieutenant in the war charities. In the letter Wharton describes her struggle to overcome her long-standing reluctance to showcase pathetic individual cases of need to raise funds. "The Report [an annual report on the charities] is exactly the contrary of what I approve in that line, but I always get money by the 'tremolo' note, so I try to dwell on it as much as possible."[9] The tremolo note, with its quavering pitch and its easy emotional appeal, initially stuck in Wharton's throat. Its obvious appeals to sentimentality and bathos struck her as inauthentic—it was making a private situation public. (In part, her objections to the literary modernism of James Joyce and D. H. Lawrence grew from what she saw as their inappropriate reversal of the private and the public.) Yet if stooping to a sentimental appeal would save the lives of the children and aged refugees for whom she had assumed responsibility, then Wharton could sustain a vibrato that would shake dollars from the pockets of a neutral American public.

It is easy to see how her appeals written during the war years have struck her readers as startlingly out of her literary character. Even during her best years, Wharton had a well-earned reputation for prickliness. Acquaintances, knowing her emphasis on propriety but missing her keen sense of fun and curiosity, were often overprotective. Those who knew her only by reputation were especially sensitive about offending Mrs. Wharton. F. Scott Fitzgerald, during a drunken pilgrimage after the war to her suburban home, could not bring himself to finish his story about the time he and Zelda mistakenly rented a room in a brothel on their first visit to Paris.[10] Even her friend the French novelist Paul Bourget stopped interrogating André Gide about homosexuality, for example, when Wharton entered the room.[11] Wharton, however, would have gladly listened to both conversations and participated. It was not the bawdy or sexual elements of life that offended her sensibility; it was the destruction of life and culture that she found blasphemous.

The war was an obvious assault on the order of life, on decorum. In a passage from one of her war essays collected in *Fighting France*, she describes the destruction of the Flemish city of Ypres. Aside from being gracefully written, the passage reveals the way the war had turned the public and the private worlds inside out:

> But Ypres has been bombarded to death, and the outer walls of its houses are still standing, so that it presents the distant semblance of a living city, while nearby it is seen to be a disembowelled corpse. Every window-pane is smashed, nearly every building unroofed, and some house-fronts are neatly sliced off, with the different stories exposed, as if for the stage-setting of a farce. In these exposed interiors the poor little household gods shiver and blink like owls

surprised in a hollow tree. A hundred signs of intimate and humble tastes, of humdrum pursuits, of family association, clung to the unmasked walls. Whiskered photographs fade on the morning-glory wall-papers, plaster saints pine under glass bells, antimacassars droop from plush sofas, yellowing diplomas display their seals on office walls. It was all so still and familiar that it seemed as if the people for whom these things had a meaning might at any moment come back and take up their daily business. And then—crash! the guns began, slamming out volley after volley all along the English lines, and the poor frail web of things that had made up the lives of a vanished city-full hung dangling before us in that deathly blast.[12]

Wharton was essentially a social and philosophical conservative, in the root sense of "one who conserves or maintains." As Shari Benstock, Wharton's most recent biographer, notes: "New wealth posed a dangerous threat to American society, she claimed, because it came 'without inherited obligations, or any traditional sense of solidarity between the classes.'"[13] Wharton believed in a general sense of fitness in life. She was not an obvious snob about family lineage or aristocratic titles, but she was a snob about breeding and learning. She preferred an oligarchy of taste and erudition, a meritocracy of learning. She favored a society that would protect, if not favor, the connoisseur: Walter Berry, Robert Norton, Royall Tyler, Bernard Berenson, John Hugh Smith, Percy Lubbock. She celebrated the past. After her trip to Morocco in the fall of 1917, she playfully insisted that her host, Bernard Berenson, should supply her nightstand with books on the history of North Africa. But with her interest in the past, it should be noted that she was no technological Luddite. She loved what the automobile had done for travel, and she embraced the telephone.

Wharton has been an obvious and, it would seem, easy target for those who resented her strong personality. Percy Lubbock, who early enjoyed her hospitality and support, characterized her as "one of the few people I have ever known who used to do what severe ladies used to do so regularly in novels: she 'drew herself up'—"[14] Shifting to nautical imagery, he remembered Wharton as a "full-rigged ship under sail, with an eye for every detail and time for every claim."[15]

Some of the most lasting characterizations of Wharton by her contemporaries were based on hearsay that was largely untested by fact. Take, for example, Janet Flanner's poisonous profile in the *New Yorker*

Magazine, which presented Wharton as a conqueror: "Later, still pursuing her policy of Continental expansion, she purchased a charming Cistercian monastery near Hyères on the Mediterranean, where she summers. Finally, for permanent residence, she acquired an eighteenth-century villa, the Pavillon Colombe, at Saint-Brice-sous-Forêt, about eighty motor kilometers from Paris. It was here she collected her half-dozen adopted war orphans, left from the six hundred she housed during the war when she gave her property to the government and devoted herself to French and little Belgian refugees with a patriotism of which only an expatriated American who dislikes children is capable."[16] This acid portrait of Wharton as an aloof, acquisitive aristocrat was largely unchecked by the facts. Wharton spent her winters, not her summers, in Hyères. It was earlier, not later, that she bought the Pavillon Colombe in St. Brice, which is thirty kilometers, not eighty, from Paris. She never turned over her property, either in Paris or elsewhere, to the government during the war. In fact, she owned no property in France at that time. She never adopted a half dozen of the remaining war refugees. Nor, as the evidence shows in a number of cases, did she dislike children.

Wharton entered one type of world and witnessed the emergence of another after the First World War. Even though England and France won the war, the world Wharton valued was largely lost. It was obliterated by the mass world, a world without taste, a world without an aristocracy of intellect. Finally, the convergence of historical forces that transformed Wharton from an ironic social satirist into a partisan war reporter provides one of the few periods in her life when she was not in control of what happened. The war was not just a shock; it was a catastrophe that threatened one's ability to make a world. For a novelist who made fictional worlds and for a woman who created aesthetic spaces (her houses and their gardens), the loss of control was potentially devastating. The First World War ushered in the true end of the age of innocence.

INTRODUCTION
THE SECOND GREATEST FOURTH

THE MORNING OF THE FOURTH OF JULY, 1918, DAWNED OVERCAST IN PARIS, with a threat of rain that could spoil the elaborate schedule of ceremonies planned for the day.[1] Raymond Poincaré, the president of France, had sent a formal greeting to Woodrow Wilson proclaiming that America's Independence Day would for that year become a day of national celebration in France as well. Later in the morning, in what might have been taken as a metaphor for the Allies' military progress during the previous six months, the sky cleared.

The day's events got under way at nine o'clock with a brief ceremony at Lafayette's tomb in Picpus Cemetery, followed at nine-thirty by the dedication of the new avenue du Président Wilson, formerly the avenue du Trocadéro. The broad, tree-lined street stretched from Place de l'Alma (where the Bâteaux Mouches and other excursion boats dock in today's Paris), turned sharply left and slightly uphill as it paralleled the Seine for six hundred yards, before reaching its destination at the aristocratic Place d'Iéna, all in the elegant sixteenth *arrondissement*, or district.

The equestrian statue of George Washington at the Place d'Iéna had been decorated with so many flowers and potted ferns that the pedestal looked as if it grew out of a flower garden. Washington, sword raised, emerged out of a small mountain of color. The Paris edition of the *New York Herald* commented, "Hortensias predominated and were arranged in that attractive fashion associated with French good taste."[2] Reviewing platforms flanked the statue. The more elaborate one on the right, covered with red velvet trimmed in gold fringe and cord and backed by a row of Allied flags, was reserved for the official group of Frenchmen, including Poincaré, Premier George Clémenceau, the presidents of the French Chamber of Deputies and the Senate, and the American ambassador, William G. Sharp.

After the closing speech by Monsieur Stéphen Pichon of the Ministry of Foreign Affairs, and just as the band was striking up the "Chant du Départ," two dust-covered automobiles pulled up in front of the reviewing stand. Out stepped British Prime Minister David Lloyd George and Italian Premier Vittorio Orlando. No one in the crowd knew they were even in France. Their dramatic appearance on the platform served as a further symbol of Allied solidarity, and the crowd applauded enthusiastically.

Following the official speeches, the parade of the Allies began. The American contingent of 3,000 soldiers represented an American force of more than 1 million troops in France. Their commander, General John "Black Jack" Pershing, had sent a message home on behalf of the troops, declaring their resolve was "quickened by sympathy for an invaded people of kindred ideals and the war challenge of an arrogant enemy."[3]

The procession moved off smartly down the newly inaugurated avenue to the Place de l'Alma, where several hundred spectators had been waiting since seven o'clock. Mounted police guarded the entrances to the avenues along the parade route. The crowd lining the route wore American flags and French tricolors in their coats and hats. Wounded French soldiers, some on crutches and others in rolling chairs with their attending nurses, from every hospital in Paris and from as far beyond as Le Raincy, waved small French tricolors and Stars and Stripes as the units passed in review. At the Place de l'Alma the parade turned left onto the avenue Montaigne, which led the half mile from the river up to the Rond-Point des Champs-Elysées. Upon reaching the Rond-Point the parade columns turned right onto the broad avenue Champs-Elysées and marched the final thousand yards to the Place de la Concorde, where there was to be a brief ceremony at the Strasbourg statue.

One of the estimated 50,000 thousand people waiting was Edith Wharton, the distinguished American novelist, who would follow the day's events from eight that morning until well after dark.[4] She had set out early for the large square because she had to decide whether to watch the parade with the crowd at ground level or to look on the wider spectacle from an elevated perch. She explained her choice to her sister-in-law:

I saw the show from a balcony of the [Hôtel] Crillon, my pictorial instinct having made me decide that I'd rather have the impression of that matchless ensemble than the "human interest" of getting closer to "the boys."

Since one *had* to choose, I don't regret my choice, for no doubt my eyes will never look on a sight at once so aesthetically and so symbolically splendid.[5]

Wharton saved her most vivid description of the parade for Mary Berenson, the wife of her dear friend, art historian Bernard Berenson. Mary was recuperating in England from problems relating to nerves and digestion, and Wharton's patriotic description full of rich imagery was partly meant to infuse the patient with some of her enthusiasm for the color and pageantry of life:

The crowd was immense, incalculable; the buildings were richly beflagged, and everybody in the streets had a little stars-and-stripes in hand or button-hole. The motors were covered with them, and the old cab-horses caparisoned like Paolo Uccello's cavalry!—The Pl. de la C. was never half as beautiful, or as vast. The crowds made it immeasurable. All the big stone Cities (except poor decorated Strasbourg) had their laps full of American soldiers and French poilus, joyously intertwined; and flags and handkerchiefs and straw-hats and roses butterflied about above the dingy-coated crowds with an immense effect of popular festivity.

And then they came! First, the tallest-ever Drum Major—then the biggest-ever Band, with the hugest wind-instruments all shining newly polished silver; and *then* the magnificent regiments, every man the same size, slim, tall, brick-red and fair haired, swinging along with a perfect rhythmic movement of their athletic bodies that simply amazed the French spectators. There never *was* such marching—it was really Pyrrhic!

After the two beauty regiments, fresh out of their camps, came the infantry and marines from Château Thierry in their trench helmets, like Greek shepherds—and the crowd understood and cheered louder.

But the climax of popular success was reserved for—the Red Cross nurses who closed the procession!! To see "La Femme" illimitably extended before his enterprising eyes was too much for the French male, and he roared like a young lion at such succulent prey! It was really funny, if one looked a little bit beneath the obvious sentimental surface.[6]

At noon Wharton's longtime friend and adviser Walter Berry presided over the American Chamber of Commerce's annual Fourth of July banquet held at the Hôtel du Palais d'Orsay. Berry's speech, as president of the chamber, was delivered in impeccable French. When he spoke of the American troops, however, he was momentarily upstaged by the impromptu remark of British Lord Derby: "After all, we've every reason to believe in your army, for you gave us the worst beating we ever had."[7]

The banquet was followed by a special performance of the Comédie Française with the American ambassador in attendance. At five that afternoon, the ambassador hosted a limited reception at the American embassy. (The previous Fourth, when he had opened the embassy to the entire American community in Paris to introduce General Pershing, more than 2,000 thousand people turned up.) The official day wound up at nine with a reception held by French Field Marshal Joseph Joffre. A gigantic entertainment of music and sport to honor America's wounded was held concurrently at the Gaumont Palace.

Some six hours later, New York City was the scene of a "monster parade," with bands and detachments assembling before nine in the morning and not finishing their march until late in the afternoon. "There were large groups representing Alsace-Lorraine, France, England and Italy: there were Poles, Greeks, Hungarians, Czechs and even citizens of German origin but of proven loyalty."[8]

Back in Paris, Wharton was writing up her impressions of the Fourth and reflecting on the fact that June had not been a productive month for her. Her usual hay fever had been compounded by a serious case of anemia that left her with barely enough energy to write. She had been spending a few days at a time recuperating at her friend Madame Béarn's château at Fleury, not far from Paris. There she had completed the first 8,000 thousand words of her short war novel, The Marne, reading it in the evenings to her cousin, LeRoy King, to check the accuracy of her military details. On the first day of July, however, she got stuck. After three days of sunshine and quiet in the French château, she experienced the "horribly Stygian sensation" of writer's block. It had happened before, three years earlier, when she had promised her publisher, Charles Scribner, an essay of her impressions of Paris during the opening days of the war. At that time she had gone to a leased estate in the English countryside and found that she could not write a word. Now she felt the same "hateful sensation of rattling at the locked doors of memory, imagination, creative activity, the life of any kind beyond the mollusk, and perpetually getting the same answer: 'No one there.'"9 Quoting a French jurist whose book of correspondence she had been reading, she told Berenson, "I search for myself and find no one."10

The same day, July 1, 1918, she returned to her apartment on the rue de Varenne on the left bank of the Seine in Paris. She still suffered from the exhaustion that had understandably plagued her from 1915 on. This time she did something about it: "I gave myself a good mental kick, pulled my 'author's pad' toward me, and attacked 'The Marne' again—with the result that I reeled off 2,000 words in no time!"11

Such swings between physical and nervous exhaustion and periods of literary productivity marked the four years of the war for Wharton. To capture the rhythms or cycles of this time, which was in many ways the darkest of her life—the death of Henry James, the First World War, the draining of France—and surely the most heroic, we need to begin at the beginning of 1914.

1

ॐ

A SEASON OF NEW BEGINNINGS: 1914

EDITH WHARTON STARTED THE YEAR 1914 POISED FOR NEW BEGINNINGS. SHE had recently divorced Teddy Wharton after twenty-eight years of an increasingly painful marriage. Teddy's mood swings between manic highs and depressive lows became more pronounced after 1910. Wharton's attempts to distract her husband with travel became less and less successful after their move to Paris in 1907. She arranged for Teddy to be treated at a sanitarium in Switzerland, but he returned to her Paris doorstep little improved. The final break came after Wharton discovered that her husband had been speculating with money from her trust funds.

In addition, Wharton's secret love affair with Morton Fullerton, begun in 1907 and alternating between brief periods of sexual passion and long periods of unexplained silence from him, was also over. *The Custom of the Country*, the novel she had worked on for more than five years, had finally been published the previous October.

Her next major project would be the much-delayed novel *Literature*. In February, full of ambition, she warned Charles Scribner that the projected novel would run 170,000 words—too long for serial publication in *Scribner's Magazine*. The novel was "to be a full and leisurely chronicle of a young man's life from his childhood to his end," Wharton said: "I want it to be my best and most comprehensive piece of work, and it must move slowly."[1] Two weeks later, having a better sense of the novel's shape, she thought that it should be no longer than the 125,000-word *The Custom of the Country*. At the end of March she told Scribner, "I hope there will be no difficulty about giving you the new novel by January 1916 (how far off it seems!)"[2] But before undertaking new projects, she was ready for a trip.

During April of 1914, accompanied by her secretary, her new maid Elise, and her chauffeur of ten years, Charles Cook, she traveled with Percy Lubbock through Algeria and Tunisia. The trip originally had been planned with French novelist Paul Bourget and his wife, but because Bourget got bogged down trying to finish his latest novel and because Minnie Bourget's health was poor, Wharton substituted Lubbock and Gaillard Lapsley. Even then Lapsley became ill with the flu and was obliged to turn back at Bougie.[3]

The trip was not without incident. At Timgad Wharton awoke during the night to feel a man hovering over her. She screamed and struggled with the intruder, but he escaped before her servants and the hotel staff could apprehend him.[4]

North Africa soon was suggested a literary project to her. Writing Edward Burlingame, one of her editors at Scribners, from the Excelsior Hotel in Rome, Wharton outlined "another story, a good deal longer, & rather different from anything I've done. It is called 'Peter Elsom,' & will be a sort of pendant to 'Ethan Frome'—at least in length! It's a wild embroidery, made out of the adventure of a game Englishman who goes to Tunisia soon after the French occupation to work in some phosphate mines in the interior and disappears."[5] Robert Bridges, editor of *Scribner's Magazine*, replied that the firm looked forward to the new story and accepted it in advance.[6] There was a snag, however. In late June she told Charles Scribner that for the first time she was blocked on a story because she was unable to recapture "the local atmosphere, so I fear I must put it aside till I get back to Africa next winter."[7]

Percy Lubbock believed that the trip restored to Wharton the energies she needed to cope with the demands of the war years: "It was again another Edith who was presently to be seen, active and ardent to new ends; she had taken her draught of rest before the storm, just in time."[8]

Meanwhile, through the winter and spring Wharton had been engaged in lengthy negotiations for a possible move to England. She had consulted her close friend Henry James, now a resident; and the two had visited country houses and discussed locations that might be suitable. James clearly enjoyed his role as real estate adviser, and together they narrowed the choices to three. Negotiations for the purchase of Coopersdale, an estate eighteen miles from London, were still under way in March when Wharton left for the south of France, en route to North Africa. She told Bernard Berenson that her plan to join him at his estate,

I Tatti near Florence, in mid-May was pretty well set: "The only thing that might alter this as far as I can see—is the possible acquisition of Coopersdale, with which I am still coquetting."[9] Her bid was unsuccessful, and soon she also rejected the possibility of leasing the more remote Sutton Courtney in Oxfordshire. Giving up plans to purchase property, she arranged to rent Stocks, the country estate of English novelist Mrs. Humphry Ward, for several weeks during the summer. It had been Wharton's "life-long dream" to spend a summer in England, and she set about coaxing friends such as Berenson and James to come and stay with her, promising long motor trips "to Scotland, to Wales, to all the places I had longed to see for so many years." Looking back, she added, "How happy and safe the future seemed."[10]

The Wards had for some time supplemented their family income by leasing their London townhouse on Grosvenor Place for part of the winter and renting Stocks, thirty-two miles northwest of London, for part of each summer. James, recalling a trip that Wharton and he had made together to Stocks in July of 1909, assured her that she had made the right choice: "You have seen it & known it for the passing hour—I memorably with you!—but the further impression coming from a few week-ends &c there in the past have determined my good opinion of its likelihood to 'do' for you for three months very sufficiently & amply indeed. It was much modernized & bathroomed some few years back—not, doubtless, on the American scale; but very workably & conveniently. And it's civilized & big-treed & gardened & library'd & pictured & garaged in a very sympathetic way—& in the midst of a country of the most pleasing radiations."[11]

In ordinary times Stocks would have been exactly the sort of restful country setting Wharton would have enjoyed. As James noted, the Wards had had their 120-year-old manor house completely renovated in 1907. The costs of those improvements (the house was found to need significant structural work) and the gambling debts incurred by the Wards' son Arnold meant that Mrs. Ward had to depend on her pen and her success in renting her homes to keep the family afloat. Situated on more than a thousand acres, Stocks was near the still larger Rothschild estate in Tring Park. Mrs. Ward occasionally took advantage of the special trains the Rothschilds ran between London's Euston and Tring stations.[12] Wharton, on the other hand, insisted that she would need her motorcar, a 50-horsepower Mercedes purchased three years earlier, in such an isolated spot.

Wharton's earliest intimation of the First World War came with innocent incongruity on a sunny June afternoon in 1914 at a garden party given by the painter Jacques-Émile Blanche. There, in the Paris suburb of Auteuil, amid festive tea tables and flowers in full bloom, a cloud momentarily passed over the gathering. The assassination of the heir to the Austrian throne, Archduke Franz Ferdinand, by a Serbian nationalist on June 28, 1914, was not, however, seen at first as a threat to European peace. Talk of the assassination mingled with reviews of the latest plays or the most recent exhibitions:

> I joined a party at one of the tables, and as we sat there a cloud-shadow swept over us, abruptly darkening bright flowers and bright dresses. "Haven't you heard? The Archduke Ferdinand assassinated . . . at Serajevo . . . where *is* Serajevo? His wife was with him. What was her name? Both shot dead."
>
> A momentary shiver ran through the company. But to most of us the Archduke Ferdinand was no more than a name; only one or two elderly diplomatists shook their heads and murmured of Austrian reprisals. What if Germany should seize the opportunity—? There would be more particulars in the next morning's papers. The talk wandered away to the interests of the hour . . . the last play, the newest exhibition, the Louvre's most recent acquisitions.[13]

Wharton had been invited to Blanche's home because she was well connected with the conservative French artistic scene, and later she could quote the murmured responses of the elderly diplomats present precisely because they were part of that circle.

While the conversation among other American expatriates at that time may have touched on art and drama, it was sure to include some comment on the recently announced imposition of a French income tax of 2 percent.[14] Americans living in Paris also turned out at a gathering on July 6 to say good-bye to the extremely popular ambassador, Myron Herrick, who, following Woodrow Wilson's election, was being replaced by William Sharp.[15]

With her plans for a summer in England firm, Wharton dispatched Alfred White, her English butler of more than twenty-five years, and her housemaids across the Channel to prepare for her arrival. In the meantime

Wharton, restless again, collected Walter Berry and set off in early July for a trip through Spain.

Berry and Wharton had been friends for many years, with Berry frequently serving as a valued adviser on her literary projects.[16] From his earliest job as counsel to the Italian and French governments in Washington, D.C., he was connected with international law and diplomacy, and these connections stood him in good stead during the war.[17] Berry and Wharton's intimacy apparently never extended to physical love, and in her letters to friends she occasionally commented in annoyance about Berry's dalliances with much younger and less intellectually inclined women. During the war years, however, they kept in close contact—how close is indicated by a casual remark in 1916; Berry, she wrote, "usually calls me up in the morning, but he didn't today."[18]

Because the trip to Spain had been hastily planned, the usually thorough Wharton had forgotten to book passage on the small boat that made the nightly crossing to Majorca. The travelers arrived in sultry Barcelona to discover that there was no space on the ferry for the next three weeks, so they quickly headed for the cooler, fresher Spanish Pyrenees.[19] (The following year Gertrude Stein and Alice B. Toklas would make the same journey, but they would be successful in crossing to Majorca—so successful, in fact, that they spent the next year, from May 1915 to June 1916, in a rented villa on the island.)[20]

Wharton wrote to Bernard Berenson from Burgos that the three-week trip "has been wonderful & beautiful, & Spain in July is the most delicious place imaginable." She complained, though, of Berry's forced-march regime. He insisted on starting in the car each morning at nine and sometimes not stopping until seven in the evening. When he and she viewed a motion picture travelogue in Bilbao loosely titled "What One Sees When Visiting a Town at a Gallop," she commented that upon leaving the theater, he had reminded her, apparently without irony, that they would have to begin the next morning at nine sharp.

At Altamira they visited the caves with their prehistoric drawings of "the big earth-shaking beasts, roaring & butting & galloping over the low-rock-roof." Standing up abruptly, the tall, thin Berry bumped his white linen hat against the ancient drawing, carrying off a souvenir of red marks.[21]

On July 26 the couple crossed into France and took a leisurely four days to reach Paris. For Americans in Europe there were few signs that this summer's events would be different from those of previous summers.

On the same day that Wharton and Berry crossed the border, for example, the European edition of the *New York Herald* reported Austria's ultimatum across the page from a story on the romantic effects produced by the Chinese lanterns hastily pressed into service at Mrs. Belmont's summer ball when the electric power plant at Newport, Rhode Island, failed.[22] At Poitiers on the evening of July 30, Wharton lay in her hotel bed listening to the crowds outside singing the *Marseillaise*. The next morning she and Berry said to each other, "What nonsense! It can't be war."[23] They stopped beside the road from Poitiers to Chartres for lunch under an apple tree in a field in the noonday quiet. The weather remained cloudy until four o'clock when they reached Chartres and found the cathedral suffused with sunlight. When they reached Paris at sunset, Wharton read the city imagistically—"like a princess guarded."[24]

The next day the capital was buzzing with rumors, but the only army of invaders that she saw was the usual flood of summer tourists. She planned to spend the night of July 31 at the Hôtel Crillon, as she had already closed her apartment at 53 rue de Varenne, and leave the next day for England. On the morning of August 1 she went to her dressmaker's, where the fitters were tired and looking forward to their month-long holiday. When the announcement of the mobilization came that afternoon, it was "like a monstrous landslide." Later, having dinner at a restaurant in the rue Royale, she watched tourists who by now looked like "puzzled inarticulate waifs caught in the cross-tides racing to a maelstrom."[25] This trope of the war described in pictures drawn from natural disasters indicates that Wharton had no other field of imagery to draw on to project the magnitude of the disaster.

The mood of those literary figures in France who had been getting more regular news of international events that last week of July was somber. The same day that Wharton and Berry were motoring from Poitiers to Paris, thinking only of what they had seen in Spain, André Gide was visiting his and Wharton's friend Jacques-Émile Blanche at the artist's summer home in the small Norman village of Offranville near Dieppe. When the fire alarm rang, everyone in the village, reflecting on Austria's ultimatum to Serbia published in the previous morning's papers, thought surely that it was a call to arms. "This morning the refusal of the delay requested by Russia increases the general nervousness," Gide wrote in his journal. "This is the only subject of conversation and J. E. Blanche has given way to the blackest misgivings." Gide's entry for the last day of July 1914 was prophetic: "We are getting ready to enter a long tunnel full of blood and darkness."[26]

When the mobilization notices went up on the afternoon of August 1, 1914, Wharton watched as Paris became a silent and disciplined city. She stayed only two nights at the Hôtel Crillon, just long enough for her housekeeper Catherine Gross and her personal maid Elise to take the muslin wraps off the furniture and to re-stock the kitchen at 53 rue de Varenne. By now her butler and housemaid had already been in England for three weeks, making necessary arrangements for her arrival. But civilian trains and boats between Paris and England were temporarily suspended, and bank accounts, even for Americans, after the mobilization were effectively frozen. With little money to pay further hotel bills at the Crillon, Wharton "moved back to my shrouded quarters in the rue de Varenne, and camped there until I could get a permit to go to England."[27]

She did not lack for company. Her favorite sister-in-law and one of her closest friends, Mary Cadwalader Jones, was also stuck in Paris. Mary Cadwalader Rawle of Philadelphia had married Wharton's brother Frederic in 1870, when Edith Jones was eight years old. The mature Edith Wharton became very attached to Minnie, as she called her sister-in-law, and to Minnie's daughter, Beatrix, born in 1872. When Frederic ran off with another woman and divorce was imminent, Wharton took her sister-in-law's side. As R.W.B. Lewis, Wharton's first biographer, notes, "In the course of time they became closer than blood sisters."[28] During the war Minnie became Wharton's able and efficient lieutenant in the United States, just as Elisina Tyler would become Wharton's right hand in France, overseeing the daily operations of the far-flung charities.

෧

For the moment no civilian was going anywhere. As Wharton noted, on August 2, "no trains stirred except to carry soldiers." The stranded American tourists in the luxury hotels of Paris had to contend with the "resounding emptiness of porterless halls, waiterless restaurants, motionless lifts." From the terrace of the Hôtel Crillon on the day after the general mobilization she felt "a first faint stir of returning life."[29]

Overnight Walter Berry had become a banker for stranded Americans, and he was able to help Wharton with some of her immediate expenses.[30] When Wharton referred in her letters to Berry playing banker to stranded American beauties, her satirical characterization was based on harsh economic truth. As early as July 30, nervous French bankers were refusing to change banknotes. Their frugal depositors, alarmed by the news, were already hoarding gold and silver, and making change was impossible.[31] The English journalist Pearl Adam witnessed the sudden disappearance of French currency: "Public confidence in the bank-note had never been a feature of the French character, and at the first breath of international disturbance (in those days people thought only of the possibility of war between Serbia and Austro-Hungary) every vestige of gold coinage fled into the obscurity of the *bas de laine* [the savings stocking] and was very shortly afterwards followed by the cart-wheel of the five-franc piece."[32] Edward Fowles, manager of the Paris office of the international art dealers the Duveen Brothers, noticed that "both the *louis d'or* (a 20-franc gold coin worth about $4 at this time) and the silver *écu* (5 francs) had quickly disappeared from circulation."[33] Nothing was available in the French capital unless one had the exact amount of one's purchase. Restaurants and cafés were accepting IOUs written on customers' calling cards. Bankers became suspicious of their customers as depositors waited in long lines to draw out their savings. Journalist Pearl Adam made an emergency trip to London "to bring back the hard bright golden sovereigns without which we could do nothing."[34]

Thomas Cook, the travel agency, was charging a 25 percent commission to cash its own checks, and tourists who had managed to reach England found that they could change their French currency only at a loss of 25 percent.[35] It was not only French money that disappeared from circulation. Wharton cabled her friend Frederick Whitridge at his home in Hertfordshire, asking him to give some money to her servants at Stocks. He wired back that he had no money either. Her first cabled request to her bank in New York for funds was greeted with the reply "Impossible." After repeated attempts she did manage to get $500, but only by paying another $500 for the transmission fee.

Her most immediate thought was to take the money and deliver it personally to the English merchants who had extended credit to her servants for a month. Her experience with suspicious French tradespeople led her to believe that soon her servants would be unable to get food or basic supplies. When she arrived in England, however, she was astonished to find that the local tradespeople had given her staff unlimited credit and probably would have gone on doing so until the end of the summer. Everyone expected a short war, and friends advised her that if she got to England to stay there until the end of the conflict, expected in October.[36]

Other Americans who were stuck in Paris and London during the first week of August found that, money or no money, there was simply no space available on ships that were heading west. Charles Inman Barnard, the Paris correspondent for the *New York Tribune* who had agreed weeks earlier to delay his retirement because "a quiet summer was expected," observed in his diary, "There are about three thousand who want to get home, but who are unable to obtain money on their letters of credit; if they have money, they are unable to find trains, or passenger space on the westward bound liners."[37]

Many Americans had a difficult time accepting the French bureaucracy and its security measures. Some demanded that officials accept their American identification papers without their having also to secure a *permis de séjour* issued by the local authorities. Estimates of Americans marooned in Europe ran as high as 40,000, with 7,500 in Paris and 1,500 of those without any financial means. The rector of the American Church in the avenue de l'Alma offered his sanctuary as a sleeping barracks to his homeless countrymen.

By the second week of the war the American embassy in Paris was able to advance small sums, averaging less than $17 apiece, to American tourists in need.[38] With powerful friends like Walter Berry, Wharton was fortunate enough to be spared days of what Pearl Adam described as "wild wrangles with passport-seeking crowds . . . , [and] in searching for provisions in all sorts of unlikely quarters of Paris, and in bathing our ankles, horribly swollen by too much exercise."[39]

Responding as quickly as it could, the United States government dispatched two armed cruisers to give financial relief to its citizens abroad. The *Tennessee*, carrying a cargo of gold, reached England on August 19. The next day the *North Carolina* arrived at Cherbourg with $200,000 in gold to aid needy Americans in France.

From a fully mobilized city, Edith Wharton cabled Scribner on August 4: "Detained in Paris . . . Extraordinary sights . . . Do you want impressions?" He did indeed want her impressions and immediately promised her space for 8,000 words in the October number of *Scribner's Magazine*. Unfortunately, his cabled reply, sent to her through her Paris bankers, never reached her.[40] When Barnard ran into her a week later, he noted that she "had made some valuable mental and written notes of what she has seen in Paris," but as of that date, Thursday, August 13, she was still planning to leave for England as soon as traveling was feasible. Barnard wrote in his diary: "Paris is no longer *la ville lumière*—it is a sad and gloomy city, where men and women go around with solemn, anxious faces, and every conversation seems to begin and end with the dreadful word 'War.'"[41]

During the first week, a number of prominent Americans volunteered their services to the French Red Cross. By the third day of August the American community, under the leadership of Ambassador Herrick and his wife, had organized the American Ambulance to operate out of the American Hospital in Paris. Wharton was a member of the executive committee. While she had had some experience on boards of charities—in 1906 she served on a committee of the New York City chapter of the Society for the Prevention of Cruelty to Animals that wrote new bylaws for the branch[42]—nothing in her background prepared her for the swell of work that was about to engulf her.

Wharton soon found herself engaged in a problem that at other times might have offered opportunities to a fiction writer. The government labor ministry was roundly criticizing the French Red Cross for sanctioning what Wharton criticized just as roundly: "The silly idiot women who have turned their drawing-rooms into hospitals (at great expense), & are now making shirts for the wounded, are robbing the poor stranded ouvrières of their only means of living."[43] At the request of the Comtesse d'Haussonville, head of one of the branches of the French Red Cross,[44] Wharton quickly organized a workroom for *midinettes*, or working women, many unmarried and from the provinces, who had been thrown out of their jobs by the mobilization. The most immediate need was to find something for them to do that would allow them to earn enough money to live on.

Contemporary newspaper reports give some idea of the financial crisis among the *couture* houses. Dresses normally costing 800 to 1,000 francs were selling at wartime prices of 200 francs. The last two weeks of August, usually the busiest season for shipping dresses to America, saw a decline to 25 percent of the usual number. Three-quarters of the shops on the normally busy rue de la Paix were closed, and the street itself presented "a long, gray expanse—broken only at intervals—of forbidding iron shutters."[45] The famous dressmaker Paul Worth responded to the drop in orders and the sudden availability of space in his rue de la Paix building by opening a hospital. The president of the *Syndicat de la Couture* announced on August 19 that since the closing of the Paris *salons de couture*, where the majority of them had been employed, more than 300,000 women were out of work.[46] Estimates of unemployment in Paris during the fall of 1914 ran as high as 44 percent, and the displacement was particularly hard on female workers.[47]

Wharton's first *ouvroir* (workroom) was part of a *foyer* (a loose collection of volunteered services to aid distressed civilians) located at 34 rue Vaneau.[48] Her *ouvroir* specifically served out-of-work seamstresses and secretaries from her own seventh and the neighboring sixth *arrondisse-ments*. Beginning with several pieces of calico dress material, as well as a budget of 2,800 francs raised from her friends, she established a workroom able to support twenty unemployed women. Each worker was given one franc a day plus a midday meal consisting of cabbage soup, fish and compote, or a meat stew with vegetables and fruit.

Wharton was assisted by two sisters, nieces of the French music critic Professor Jean Landormy, "who gave the aid of their quick wits and youthful energy."[49] From the beginning Wharton displayed keen executive and administrative talent. Her skills included an ability to organize groups from diverse backgrounds, an attention to detail, and a sympathy for individual suffering that did not cloud her understanding that to help increasing numbers of destitute civilians took large amounts of contributed money. The way in which she had approached complex literary projects earlier and the way in which she soon would meet the daunting challenge of helping thousands of refugees were not at all dissimilar. Years after the war, reflecting on the process of writing *The House of Mirth*, Wharton commented, "When the book was done I remember saying to myself: 'I don't yet know how to write a novel; *but I know how to find out how to.*'" Compare that statement in its can-do spirit, even its sentence rhythm, with the following on organizing war charities: "All this did not teach me how to run a big work-room, where we soon had about ninety women, but there was an ardour in the air which made it seem easy to accomplish whatever one attempted."[50]

Wharton claimed in her autobiography that her workroom was the first one established in Paris, but in truth it probably was neither the earliest nor the largest one aiding out-of-work women. In Versailles an *ouvroir* employing 80 women had opened on August 3, the day Germany declared war on France. And within Paris the *ouvroir* at rue de la Douane at Place de la République employed over 800 women and girls. At the end of the first six months of the war, 516 such *ouvroirs* operated in Paris.[51]

In an appeal to her friends and to the readers of the Paris edition of the *New York Herald*, Wharton pledged that if she could raise another 3,000 francs, she would be able to employ thirty women for three months or more. The early contributors' lists show donations in significant amounts from wealthy members of the Franco-American community as well as smaller contributions from Wharton's old friends. (Walter Berry contributed 200 francs, Mrs. Walter Gay, 100, and M. l'Abbé Mugnier, 20.)[52] An amended list of contributors noted a modest donation of 20 francs from Morton Fullerton, Wharton's former lover.

Once her work was publicized, contributions came from unexpected sources. A reader asked the Herald, "May I ask if this is the Miss [sic] Wharton whom we know as the novelist?" The editor answered yes and promised to forward the correspondent's check of $250 to Miss Wharton. Janet Scudder, a friend of Gertrude Stein's, offered her prized first-class ticket on the France, sailing on September 5 for New York, to the highest bidder. She promised that the "money made on the transaction will be devoted partly to . . . Mrs. Edith Wharton's excellent charity, in which I am very much interested." The ticket was sold immediately.[53]

Meanwhile Wharton delayed her own much shorter, but no less treacherous, crossing of the English Channel until her workroom was well under way. Before leaving Paris she made sure that its management was in smooth running order, and she notified contributors that during her absence donations should be sent to a Mlle de San Miguel at 34 rue Vaneau. Contributions of substantial amounts continued to flow in. As Wharton later told Sara Norton, it was only "after I had collected enough money to carry it on for three or four months, & seen orders pouring in from all sides [that] I decided to leave it in the very capable hands of the young woman who founded it with me, & come over here for a few weeks' rest."[54]

۶۵

Henry James had been waiting impatiently on the other shore scanning the horizon during July and early August. He had telegraphed Alfred White at Stocks to find out where Wharton was. White, who with some of Wharton's maids was preparing the country house for her arrival, expected her soon after July 30. Her lease ran from July 10, the very day she had departed with Walter Berry for Barcelona. (Wharton was less worried about exact arrivals than the frugal James.)

James finally learned where Wharton was and wrote her in Paris directly, expressing his "preference for the whereabouts, the actual, of your body." His preferences, expressed in a most Jamesian set of sentences, were "intensely in your getting over at the 1st moment you can do it with any comfort, though I call upon you too helplessly, I indeed feel, to make much of a figure as a cherished objective for yourself. If I could only reach out more brilliantly—but I feel all but unbearably overdarkened by this crash of our civilization."[55]

In spite of James's preferences, Wharton could not travel because the ferry link between France and England had been suspended shortly after the general mobilization. In fact, White was lucky to make it back to Stocks on August 4 after his brief visit to Paris. The first notice of a resumption of Channel ferry service was published on Friday, August 21. Two days later another sailing each way from Charing Cross via Folkstone was added. The travel crush had been accelerated by the American embassy, which was advising its noncombatant citizens to leave France as soon as possible. They left Paris at a rate of a hundred a day during the last two weeks of August. At the beginning of September the one crossing a day from Havre to Southampton was inadequate to handle the more than 1,500 Americans stacked up, waiting.[56]

On August 27 Berry accompanied Wharton to the coast in her car (she feared trains would be slow and uncertain), saw her off, and took the car back to Paris.[57] Wharton arrived that evening at Folkstone, where she was met by Henry James, and together they went to Lamb House in Rye for the evening. She found her *cher maître*, as she often addressed him, recovering from "a war-and-digestion attack" and guarded by "an armour-plated niece," Peggy James, with whom she quickly made friends.

Once comfortably settled at Stocks, Wharton was unhappy because the very isolation she had craved a few months earlier now cut her off from news of the war and what was happening in Paris. She had imagined the rooms full of friends, but she found herself deserted in "the big echoing rooms," and she had no heart to enjoy even the "gardens radiant with flowers." She tried to occupy herself by walking each day to the post office in the village to collect the London papers, which always arrived late, and irregularly at that. Even in the large library at Stocks, she found that for the first time in her life she could not concentrate on her reading. The few visitors she had—James for a day or two, Lubbock, Lapsley—did not stay long. Each day Mrs. Ward's upper housemaid (whose services came with the lease) filled every room with bowls of fresh flowers, but Wharton was miserable amid this "vain loveliness."[58]

She considered turning Stocks into a hospital for refugees and the wounded, then beginning to arrive in England in considerable numbers. There was a precedent. Mrs. Ward had long been a supporter and board member of London's Passmore Edwards School for Invalid Children. During the year the school regularly received hampers of fresh vegetables from the gardens at Stocks, and in the summer a large cottage on the estate was fitted out to take children from the school for a week at a time.

Aldous Huxley remembered visiting Stocks when children on crutches were hopping around the shrubbery and intimidating the Ward and Huxley children with their Cockney aggressiveness.[59]

Nothing came of Wharton's plans. Instead she turned her attention to returning to France as soon as possible and in the meantime lining up the support of her many influential American friends. She went to London in late August and had interviews with the American ambassador to Great Britain, Walter Hines Page, and with the French ambassador, Paul Cambon. Both were sympathetic with her urgent request that she be permitted to return to Paris, but they explained that even if she got across to Calais, she could not go farther because a big battle, perhaps the decisive battle of the war, was about to begin.[60]

Her sister-in-law, Minnie Jones, was also in England, visiting Henry James. Minnie was scheduled to sail for New York on the *Laconia* along with Wharton's old Boston friend Robert Grant, a probate judge and minor novelist of manners. On the last day of August, Wharton sent a letter to Grant by way of Minnie. Its tone reflected her impatience to return to France, "where the whole nation is rising to face this Black Death, and not playing cricket and philandering with girls like the British youth." Her eagerness was heightened by her general distaste for "the egoistic apathy" she found in the English countryside.[61]

The sharpness of her tone may be explained in part by the regret she felt over not having been at her workroom during the Battle of the Marne. On the evening September 2 the French government, facing a rapidly advancing German army, left Paris for Bordeaux under cover of darkness. Stranded in England, Wharton wrote Berenson, "I am simply sick & heart-broken at having left my work-room there at a time when I might have been of real use."[62] From September 5 to September 10, during the first Battle of the Marne, the German invasion was halted by the French Fifth and Ninth armies under the command of the unflappable Jacques Joffre, in concert with the British Expeditionary Force under the command of the quixotic general John French. At a critical moment, General Joseph-Simon Galliéni sent 5,000 soldiers from Paris in taxicabs and buses to reinforce the French lines. Wharton was happy for the victory, but she confessed to Sara Norton that being away from Paris during the climactic battle made her uncomfortable. She felt "like a deserter. . . . You can understand how I feel—as if my co-workers must think that I had planned my flight when I said I was going off for three or four weeks."[63]

Isolated at Stocks, she spent her time sharpening her propagandist's pen. She urged Grant to use his good name and his authority in Boston to "proclaim everywhere . . . what it will mean to all that we Americans cherish if England and France go under, and Prussianism becomes the law of life."[64]

Wharton had witnessed two invasions during her lifetime: The first was the invasion of the plutocrats into Old New York society in the 1870s and 1880s; the second was the threatened imposition of German *kultur* on her civilized and tasteful world of French and British culture. Like Henry James, she believed that the German attack threatened their ability to make a well-ordered world. To Wharton, the attack on French ways and their meaning was an attack on her own ability to make meaning imaginatively and to create habitable and elegant spaces. The war was turning intellectual ironists and satirists into emotional propagandists. And it was a big war, no doubt about that. The sweep of the German army through Belgium and into northern France gave James and Wharton an event, to paraphrase Fitzgerald, commensurate with their capacity to wonder.[65]

Her active mind also responded to her quarantine at Stocks by dwelling on widespread reports of German atrocities. She asked Minnie Jones to relay stories she had heard of German mistreatment of wounded civilians, and to Grant she insisted that "there are millions like it."[66]

Atrocity stories had great currency during the opening weeks of the war. In an article for the *New York Times*, the wife of the head of the Morgan Bank in Paris described a scene at the Gare du Nord railroad station, where she claimed that she "saw many boys with both of their hands cut off so it was impossible for them to carry a gun" and "mothers were vainly . . . begging for milk."[67] On the same day the *Times* report appeared, Wharton wrote privately to Sara Norton in Cambridge, "The 'atrocities' one hears of *are true*. I know of many, alas, too well authenticated. Spread it abroad as much as you can."[68]

She urged Norton to read *The Anglo-German Problem* by Charles Sarolea, "so far ahead of any other book I have seen on the subject that it ought to be known everywhere." Sarolea, Belgian consul in Edinburgh, had argued presciently in the first edition (1912) of his book that the German people were dominated by Prussian militarism and that their advance on France and England would come through his native Belgium. A popular American edition was published in 1915, and by then the author's predictions had made the book an international best-seller. With her evangelical zeal carrying her voice to the top of its range, Wharton insisted, "It should be known that it is to America's interest to help stem this hideous flood of savagery by opinion if it may not be by action. No civilized race can remain neutral in feeling now."[69] Whether Norton took Wharton's recommendations for reading and for propagandizing is not known, but on September 4 her father, Charles Eliot Norton, president emeritus of Harvard and an old friend of Wharton's, published a moderate letter in the *New York Times* recommending a continuing policy of neutrality but also pointing out the harsh effects of German aggressiveness.

Less than a month later, in another letter to Sara Norton, Wharton returned to the theme of German atrocities: "As to the horrors and outrages, I'm afraid they are too often true. —Lady Gladstone, head of the Belgian refugee committee in London, told a friend of mine she had seen a Belgian woman with her ears cut off. And of course the deliberate slaughter of 'hostages' in defenceless towns is proved over & over again."[70]

><

Wharton's isolation at Stocks was temporarily relieved when her chauffeur, Cook, managed to get her car across from Le Havre during the first week of September. It had taken all of Walter Berry's considerable diplomatic influence to ensure that the car could leave France. Such permission was unusual, for most automobiles, trucks, and horses were being requisitioned, no matter who owned them, as part of the general mobilization. Henry Huntington's car, for one, had been commandeered by the French military during the opening days of the war, and the American railroad mogul and his wife were reduced to using a dogcart to travel around their French country estate.[71]

When Mr. and Mrs. Humphry Ward visited Stocks briefly on September 5, they thoughtfully suggested that Wharton might be more comfortable and nearer to news in their London townhouse at 35 Grosvenor Place. The swap would take place on September 9. As Wharton told Minnie Jones, the new arrangement would be good for her. "In town I shall be a little nearer news, and shall be able to see people. Henry is coming up soon and that will be a joy. And it is impossible to go on sitting here, face to face with this vain loveliness." Far from insensitive to the charms of Stocks, Wharton had found that "this too lovely place . . . is made for such different hours."[72] She told Berenson that she was unable to "read or scribble" there,[73] and she insisted to Gaillard Lapsley, "You may imagine that I have only one thought—to get back to Paris!"[74]

After she moved to the Wards' townhouse, she could call more regularly on the American and French ambassadors. At first nothing could be done to expedite her getting to Paris. The American embassy told her that the last messenger it had sent expected to reach France in four days. And even if Wharton reached France safely, there would be further delays. Trains between Dieppe and Paris were heavily guarded and stopped at every station, making the normal four-hour trip into a ten-hour journey.[75]

Her determination was strengthened when she received a telegram from Berry saying that there was trouble at the workroom at rue Vaneau. When official word finally came that her visa was ready, she hastily took herself off to a photographer recommended by an overworked official at the embassy. She found an unprepossessing-looking photographer at what she thought was the right address. The confused man had her climb a ladder to the roof of an outbuilding and sit on a kitchen chair where, after much adjustment of his apparatus, he blurted out, "I'm so sorry madam; but the truth is, I've always specialized in photographing beasts, and this is the first time I've ever done a human being."[76] After a hearty laugh, Wharton told the man to go ahead with his work. She thought the result made her look like a wildcat robbed of her young, but the picture was a good enough likeness to get her back to Paris.

≥∙

Though the trip from London to Paris on Thursday, September 24, took Wharton twenty-two hours, she made it in relative comfort.[77] Paris seemed more interesting than London "because most of the fluffy fuzzy people have gone, & the ones left are working hard & seeing each other quietly."[78] She dined with Morton Fullerton and Victor Bérard, who told her amusing stories about the war. She could use the relaxation: Her first days back were filled with nervous strain and hard work. The complications at the *Foyer* at the rue Vaneau were indeed serious, and she was needed in Paris even more than she might have suspected.

During the German advance, the French government had provided free trains to evacuate women and children from Paris. Thousands left, among them the woman who managed the rue Vaneau workroom and her friend, the acting treasurer of Wharton's charity, who carried off all of the operating funds. Wharton later calmly described for a newspaper interviewer the chaotic situation that greeted her: "It was on my return that I learned that the directress had left Paris and closed the establishment. I immediately set about reorganizing the workroom, the necessity of which is undeniable."[79] Her private account of the "nasty and . . . very mysterious business," however, bristled with her characteristic irony and sarcasm: "I am back in Paris much sooner than I had expected," she told Sara Norton, "as the philanthropic lady in whose settlement I had established my work-room fled before the German approach and put her 50 compatriots into the streets! The situation was complicated by the fact that her manageress (and confidential friend) carried off ALL the funds (nearly $2000!), and that we got these back only through the intervention of the Red Cross, under whom I am working."[80]

In addition to recovering the operating funds, Wharton needed a new location for the workroom. She was immediately offered a room on the third floor of a new building owned by the Petit St. Thomas at the corner of rue de l'Université and rue du Bac. Both the original location of the workroom and the new site were within three blocks of her apartment at 53 rue de Varenne. The new workroom soon employed fifty women from a variety of backgrounds: "It was impossible to confine my aid to seamstresses when typists and accountants, nursery governesses and dramatic artists, cooks and concert singers were all pleading for help."[81] Before the war some had been earning as much as 200 francs a month as stenographers, but now a reporter from the Herald found them "busy, bright-faced and manifestly well satisfied" earning their one-and-a-half francs a day.

The daily work of organizing the orders, cutting out patterns, and supervising the sewing was overseen by Renée Landormy, who had been so indignant about what had happened at the Foyer on the rue Vaneau that she voluntarily took charge of the new workroom. Wharton's job of securing contributions and relieving her assistant a few hours each day allowed her to "feel the oppression of war much less than I did in England." She wrote Royall Tyler, "It is awful to be quiet a minute, and think of the crashing ruin all around us, and I am so glad to be absorbed in the price of sweaters and the cut of flannel shirts."[82]

Royall Tyler and his wife, Elisina, would soon play a major part in Wharton's life. He was a young art historian, working during the fall of 1914 in London. Elisina, born the Countess Palamidessi di Castelvecchio in Florence and educated at the Convent of Santa Anna in Pisa, had formerly been married to Tyler's English publisher, Grant Richards. In 1910 she left Richards and her children to be with Tyler. She had met Wharton in June of 1912 and, despite finding her personally somewhat intimidating, admired her published work. As she told Mildred Bliss a year later, "I like her as much as you could wish, and I hope I admire her work as much as she could wish, or at least some of her work. She lent us one of her first books, 'The Valley of Decision,' which is a most remarkable piece of art."[83] Elisina followed Wharton's production closely: "We've been reading that irresistible book 'The Custom of the Country'—and I have marveled again at the firm wrist and the easy mastery of its author. The craftsmanship is on a very high level. It's a novel of ways and means."[84]

One visitor to the sewing room discovered that Wharton was a stickler for quality: "Eight days after her return to Paris, Mrs. Wharton in a becoming checked suit, with a sable scarf thrown around her shoulders was taking orders from the case of knit goods prepared by the women of her ouvroir, comparing her *passe-montagne* and *cache-nez* and *gilets* with the production of an unnamed ouvroir of great repute, much to the detriment of the unnamed one, need it be added."[85] Wharton assured Lily Norton, Sara's sister and another of Charles Eliot Norton's six children, that she could produce extremely fine work at one-third less the cost of the other workrooms.[86]

Most of the sewing went to the French Red Cross, various hospitals, and other charities. With the time left over, her skilled needlewomen filled private orders for dresses and lingerie. By early October, the press of applicants at Wharton's workroom made it impossible for her to limit her workers to those living only in the local sixth and seventh *arrondisse-ments*. She already had taken a second room in the rue l'Université apartment and by mid-October would need a third. She soon adopted a policy of limiting workers to a one-month stay so that they would be encouraged to find outside employment. Throughout her appeals she emphasized that if her skilled seamstresses were given enough private orders for lingerie and dresses, they could get out on their own and provide space for others on the waiting list.

A new department was established that allowed women to do plain sewing in their homes. To encourage private orders, Wharton opened an exhibition room for displaying the work. The mayor of the seventh *arron-dissement* visited and left a large order. Aside from the free work for the Red Cross, the women were making flannel pajamas, which were delivered every day to the Hôtel Astoria. In addition, they made flannel shirts and woolen bandages for soldiers. These goods were taken directly to the front in the automobiles of Comtesse Joachim Murat's charity "Pour le Front," with headquarters in the neighboring rue Saint-Dominique.

At this early point in the war, the *ouvroir* was also making clothes for Belgian refugee children delivered through Children of the Frontier, an organization set up by Mildred Bliss, wife of Robert Woods Bliss, consul to the American embassy. Mrs. Bliss was a formidable organizer; one well-placed observer described her as a "charming woman and the brains of the whole Embassy."[87] She and Wharton served on many of the same committees, and in spite of their powerfully independent personalities, they worked well together.

By mid-October the demand for military supplies had become so great that Wharton was forced to suspend private work temporarily. Since the arrival of refugees from Belgium and northern France, she again had an overwhelming number of requests for jobs. By the end of the month the workroom was employing seventy women. The donors' list shows that the work was supported by Mrs. Bliss and Wilson's new appointment, Ambassador William Sharp, each contributing 250 francs. Wharton herself gave 200 francs, and a number of other Americans still resident in Paris made liberal donations.

A month earlier the embassy had estimated that there were perhaps 5,000 to 6,000 of the American colony still left in Paris. Many of those who stayed were women, and their actions so impressed the citizens of the capital that even the radical socialist newspaper, *La Guerre Sociale*, which usually vented its harshest sarcasm on them, now observed, "The German shells would not have spared them more than us if the Prussians had bombarded the city, but they preferred to remain and attend our wounded."[88]

&

With all of her charity activities, Wharton was not getting much literary work done. *Scribner's Magazine* had accepted her long story "The Bunner Sisters" (written several years earlier) for publication. The editors made plans for Anna Bahlman, Wharton's childhood German tutor and now her secretary, to read the proofs in New York, if Wharton was unable to do so. The story was eventually published in the October and November 1916 issues, and Scribner's paid Wharton $2,000 for both installments.[89] She told Charles Scribner that she still intended to write the article describing Paris during the opening days of the war, and now that she was back in Paris the impressions came flooding back.[90]

Wharton asked Lapsley, who shared her friendship with the usually calm Henry James, if he didn't "think that the martial truculent Henry is by far the best we've seen?" In thinking about recording her own impressions of Paris, she inevitably wondered how Henry James, the finest perceiver of all, would see the city. "I hope to beguile him over here later, for Paris is well worth seeing; and he WOULD see it. It's all so quiet—and yet one has so completely the impression of having one's ear at the receiver."[91]

Unfortunately James would never visit Paris again, but with his typical imaginative sweep he was surveying the war as a terrible yet fascinating subject. In the early months he was full of optimism, announcing to Charles Scribner, "Those of us who shall outwear and outlast, who shall above all outlive, in the larger sense of the term, and outimagine, will be able to show for their adventure, I am convinced, a weight and quality that may be verily worth your having waited for."[92] By December he would be writing Scribner again, but this time the imaginative possibilities of war seemed well beyond artistic capacities. He at first offered the attractions of the subject: "but War even on the abominable scale on which we are being treated to it has in it this of infernally inspiring and exciting and even sustaining, that after the first horror and sickness, which are indeed unspeakable, interest rises and rises and spreads its enormous wings." But against such a huge "hovering predatory vulture" of a subject "from the poor old discomforted artist's point of view . . . such realities play the devil even with his very best imaginations and intentions—so that he has, unless he gives everything up, to contrive some compromise between the operation of his genius (call it) and that of his immediate oppression and obsession, in which all sorts of immediate and subversive sympathies and curiosities and other damnable agitations are involved."[93]

෴

Not everyone found appropriate war work on the first attempt. At forty-five, André Gide was not eligible for military service. Even before he returned to Paris at the beginning of August, however, he was thinking of ways of serving as a noncombatant. In Dieppe, when he learned of a plan to organize an information service to correspond with families of the wounded, Gide gave his address. Once in Paris, he and his fellow editors of the Nouvelle Revue Française met at the office to divide up the meager contents of the safe, and Gide set off to find Jean Schlumberger at the French Red Cross headquarters. He did not find Schlumberger, but instead encountered "extraordinary activity; ladies of all social classes, but chiefly of the highest, are noting down the offers of volunteers."[94]

Gide spent a short time at the French Red Cross headquarters, registering volunteers for stretcher duty, but he lost heart when he learned that male ambulance volunteers would not be accepted. He felt his work had been useless. After three weeks of "doing nothing but discouraging those who offer their services," he concluded, "Nothing is so silly as this work that I now know can lead to nothing. Hospitals are well organized and refuse the teams we offer them. These unemployed teams break up. Many offered their services in the hope of being fed. What are all of these people without money and without work going to do now?"[95]

After these three frustrating weeks at the Red Cross, he still maintained his sense of duty: "Yet one must let oneself be convinced that the front line is not the only place where one can be of service; the important thing is that each man should be at his post."[96] In his search for his own proper post, Gide met with another dead end when his friend Elie Allégret offered him a job in the sixteenth *arrondissement* registering and supervising boys between twelve and eighteen. The homosexual Gide delicately declined: "I told him I didn't think I was quite the right man for the job."

A more suitable job would come in aiding the refugees whom he had begun to see "walking the streets, hugging the walls, odd lucifugous creatures such as the tide uncovers when the water withdraws."[97] When thousands of refugees from Belgium and the invaded provinces of northern France streamed into Paris in August, September, and October of 1914, Maria Rysselberghe, wife of the Belgian artist Théo Rysselberghe and the "Mme Théo" of Gide's *Journals*, helped establish a relief society called the *Foyer Franco-Belge*.[98] Mme Théo already had enlisted the aid of Charles du Bos, who, as a member of the group of the *Nouvelle Revue Française*, was a friend of Gide's. Their *Revue*'s aim was to publish English literature in French. Du Bos, whose mother was English, spoke French and English with equal fluency. He had studied art history with an intention to do research on Botticelli and Van Eyck, and he had done translations, among them Wharton's *The House of Mirth*.

The refugees' problems were so immense that it was difficult to know where to begin. When du Bos and Gide offered their services, Mme Théo sent them to the *Cirque de Paris*, where hundreds of refugees were camped in stables. The huge building, formerly the site of famous boxing matches, had been transformed into a makeshift dormitory. Iron bedsteads had been delivered, but in the general confusion it was discovered that there was no bedding. Du Bos, Gide, and the other volunteers at the *Foyer Franco-Belge* worked in two teams from one-thirty until four each day finding work for those refugees who could work and housing and food for the rest. Even so, the problems of resettling the refugees simply had too many facets for a single organization to handle effectively. The French government did its best to send the refugees on beyond the capital, but many regarded Paris as the only safe place.[99]

"My sense," Wharton wrote to Gaillard Lapsley in early November, "is completely of living again in the year 1000 with the last trump imminent." She noted that people without a job to do in the great upheaval "seem nowadays like leftovers—dead flies shaken out of a summer hotel window curtain!" By now she knew that earlier predictions of a short war and a rapid French victory were wrong. Lord Kitchener had told English political leaders that the war would last at least three years. And Wharton, reflecting on the *fin de siècle* summer through which they had just passed, concluded her simile prophetically, "We shall never lodge in *that* summer hotel again."[100]

In a postscript she added that Charles du Bos was working twelve hours a day in a refugee center while his wife, Zazette, was working as a volunteer in Wharton's own shop.[101] Du Bos's association with Wharton as her translator would lead to the formation of her second charity, the American Hostels for Refugees.

ð♣

In November, Wharton, with a small group of Americans, French, and Belgians, founded the American Hostels for Refugees to work in collaboration with the *Foyer Franco-Belge*, by now overwhelmed. Her organizing committee, a sprinkling of prominent American and French names, worked closely with the *Foyer Franco-Belge* to avoid duplicating efforts. A system was soon established, wherein the *Foyer Franco-Belge* received the arriving refugees, classified them by need, and passed them along to the American Hostels for Refugees. The American Hostels committee began operations with 1,000 francs and a house equipped with forty beds loaned by Mr. and Mrs. Edward Tuck, who also established an endowment of 5,000 francs to furnish and maintain the first hostel. The Tucks were the leading American philanthropists in France. Their generous contributions and endowments were recognized in 1916 when they received the French *Prix de la Vertu* for their good works.

A second house, accommodating about a hundred, was soon given by Comtesse Berthier. Each of the large homes was equipped with a kitchen; and soon each, following the model of Wharton's successful *ouvroir*, also organized sewing workrooms. An early "circular," or prospectus, appealing for funds said the organization planned initially to provide living accommodations for 140 refugees. Since it was clear to Wharton that the French social services, already overburdened, would be able to do little for the influx of refugees, she appealed to friends in the United States and quickly succeeded in establishing auxiliary committees in Boston, New York, and Washington. These American branches raised funds and publicized Wharton's subsequent appeals for blankets, furniture, and men's clothing.

Wharton told Sara Norton that the plight of the Belgian refugees in England had so moved her and Henry James that she now felt something must be done for those wandering aimlessly through the streets of Paris. In a letter to the *Boston Transcript* she explained to potential contributors that the French were too poor and too occupied with the mobilization to do very much. Contributions from America soon followed. Wharton was genuinely shocked to learn that a generous Boston contributor had decided that he and Henry Higginson, a Boston banker and founder of the Boston Symphony Orchestra, had decided to withhold any further aid for civilian relief until the war was over. They apparently believed it would be a brief war. Wharton urged Norton, "If you have any influence with Mr. Higginson, and could see him about our Hostels, and ask him to do what he can to send us donations, and especially monthly subscriptions, it would be the very greatest kindness." When speaking of du Bos, she proclaimed his "genius for administration," an assessment that would be open to correction as events unfolded. She closed, "It is really impossible to write of other things, and I know you feel this, and are in the same state of mind, so I make no excuse."[102]

Monthly subscriptions were prized most for the continuation of the hostels, and in the next list of donations prominent among the contributors were Wharton herself for 1,000 francs, Minnie Jones for 500, as well as Wharton's friends Mrs. Bayard Cutting and Mrs. Blair Fairchild. Walter Berry subscribed for 100 francs.

For ten days in mid-November Wharton was hostess to Mary and Bernard Berenson at 53 rue de Varenne. She was busy organizing the American Hostels all day,[103] but in the evening she and Bernard discussed the germ of a short story called "Count Unterlinden." It was to be a satirical sketch about a tiresome exile who bores all of his hosts until he is finally not invited anywhere. In early-morning notes they exchanged between bedrooms within the large apartment, they debated whether the

Count should inflict his tiresome pedantry on the society of Paris or London. At eight-thirty Wharton was for London as "the snobbishness there is so much ampler and more substantial."[104] Half an hour later she saw the wisdom of Berenson's insistence that the tale be set in Paris.[105] After the Berensons had returned to Italy, Wharton wrote Mary, "Unterlinden is fading on his stalk, and as for his authoress, she looks more and more like an elderly philanthropist who wears Jaeger underclothes!! (I evolved this morning the useful axiom: 'It takes a great deal more to do good than to have fun.' From one who had Tried Both.)"[106] Mary was not deterred by Wharton's comic warnings about what becomes of philanthropists; the following year, when Italian casualties were beginning to become numerous, she set up a sewing circle to make felt slippers for wounded soldiers.[107]

By November André Gide was so busy at the *Foyer* that he began to feel his own personality being absorbed by the needs of the refugees. When a wealthy American made the grisly offer of a large sum of money if the *Foyer* could produce a child who had been mutilated by the Germans, Gide began a frustrating round of inquiries. He remembered a journalist who had written that 4,000 children had had their right hands cut off. When he went to see a volunteer at the Red Cross who had told him of a procession of children, all boys from the same village and all similarly amputated, he waited in vain for photographs of the atrocities. Jean Cocteau promised an interview with a Red Cross nurse who had cared for the boys. She never came. His friend Henri Ghéon told him about two children with amputated limbs, one fifteen and the other seventeen, who were being cared for at Orsay right then. But he never brought the promised further information. Gide was finally forced to admit "Not one of these statements could be proved."[108] Like the contemporary legends told by "a friend of a friend," the stories of atrocities and mutilation could not be confirmed. After the war the Bryce Report detailing supposed German atrocities would be refuted, creating a skeptical climate during the 1930s and early 1940s in which the atrocities of the Holocaust could be carried out.[109]

At the same time, work at the *Foyer* was providing Gide with ideas for stories. One he recorded in his journal was about the arrival of a family of refugees and their disappointed hopes. Another provided by Jean Cocteau dealt with a volunteer who grows increasingly distressed as his work, which began as altogether charitable, gradually became administrative. This second idea was uncomfortably close to the pattern experienced by Gide, du Bos, and Wharton herself. Wharton's three short stories from the war reflect a progression from the propaganda story "Coming Home" in 1915 to the satirical "The Refugees" (1917) and "Writing a War Story" (1918), by which time she had recaptured her sense of irony. By then the war was coming to an end, and the outcome was no longer in doubt.

ﻻ

With so many American charities opening in Paris, Myron T. Herrick, the lame duck ambassador, had proposed the establishment of an American Relief Clearing House to centralize information and the collection of donations. The clearing house would oversee the shipping of donated supplies from New York to Paris and assist in distributing goods throughout France and elsewhere. Members of the organizing committee, in addition to a long list of distinguished French members, included a number of American citizens resident in France. Part of the motive was what has come to be called accountability:

> The committee proposes to have its own warehouses, and will insist upon an inventory being taken of everything being dispatched from America to France. By systematizing the distributing bureaus a complete record will be kept of the donations received, and of all persons, districts and countries benefiting by the donations. The conception of a Relief Clearing House is the result of experience. Gifts of all kinds have been made so lavishly that the resources of private agencies have been overtaxed. The American Embassy, occupied with the interests of the belligerent countries, Germany, Austria-Hungary and Turkey, has found itself handicapped in keeping track of contributions which have come from America.[110]

There was also the troubling policy inconsistency of the American embassy, committed ostensibly to its government's aim of strict neutrality, receiving and distributing war relief aid. In addition, a centralized agency with strict accountability procedures would be able "to avoid the insinuations that are almost invariably made in connection with great funds raised for charitable purposes."[111]

The front page of the Paris edition of the *Herald* for December 2, 1914, contained a scattering of criticism of Woodrow Wilson and the handling of the ousting of Ambassador Herrick by Secretary of State

William Jennings Bryan. Observers agreed that to remove Republican Herrick when he was obviously doing an effective job in a sensitive post was simply a political move.

৯৯

One measure of how interrelated Wharton's charities were becoming was a two-day sale held in her apartment of fancy items from her *ouvroir*, with the receipts going to aid the newly formed American Hostels for Refugees. The sale, held on the Friday and Saturday afternoons of December 4 and 5, raised 8,700 francs. Reporting on the visit of the new ambassador, William Sharp, and the sale in general, Wharton wrote a teasing letter to Alice Warder Garrett, whom she had met a number of years earlier.[112] Her husband, John Work Garrett, was a career foreign service officer. He was in charge of seeing to the condition of German and Austro-Hungarian civilian prisoners of war. When the French government decamped Paris for Bordeaux in early September of 1914, he was the American embassy's representative. After thanking Garrett for her own "fat & fat-producing cheque," Wharton could not resist teasing the very social Alice by observing that while the ambassador was there, he had picked out one or two intimate items for her: "His first thought was to pick out a present for you, & his choice fell on our best *parure* [attire, finery] *de lingerie*, real lace & 'yours'—(He *said* it was for Mrs. Sharp—but it's a long way to Ohio!)"[113]

William Graves Sharp was a manufacturer of chemicals and was active in Democratic politics in Ohio. Sharp had served in the House of Representatives as the ranking member of the House Foreign Affairs Committee, and Wilson appointed him ambassador to France in June of 1914. His wife's illness meant that Sharp did not sail for his new post until August 25, 1914. Sharp did not speak French well; Herrick did. For the first three months of his residence in France, the two ambassadors split the duties, with Sharp not taking the reins officially until December.

The success of the sale offset the bad news of German strength that Walter Berry observed firsthand. He had returned recently from a fact-finding trip to Germany, where he had visited prisoner-of-war camps. Berry found the German people committed to the war, and he saw fresh troops everywhere. Returning through Belgium, he brought back war souvenirs from Louvain, where, Wharton claimed, "the town was burnt systematically, *after* looting." They told Mary Berenson that all of the books and incunabula from the famous old Belgian library were no doubt safe in Berlin. Berry also had picked up some "tiny silvery lozenges which [the German soldiers] threw into the burning houses to make them blow up—& as he always has it in his pocket, & has had a very bad cough ever since he returned, I never see him slip a tablet into his mouth without expecting him to go through the ceiling."[114] When Elisina Tyler met Henry James for the first time in early December in England, she found him charming but at the time wholly absorbed in Berry's stories of what he had seen in Germany.[115]

ื๛

The complex operations of the American Hostels and the need to keep contributions from the United States flowing led Wharton to a new literary genre—the periodic organizational report to contributors. The statistical report of the new charity's activity was certainly encouraging. Between October 27 and November 27 the combination of the *Foyer Franco-Belge* and the American Hostels for Refugees lodged and clothed 878 refugees, found work for 153, and served 16,287 free meals. They were setting up a third hostel and hoped to use increased funds coming from America to open still other hostels for refugees. Through strict accounting they found that they could house a refugee for 34 francs a month.[116]

By mid-December the hostels were caring for 500 refugees and had found work for more than 300. The second hostel at 18 rue Taitbout had recently opened a restaurant for 228 persons, smoking and reading rooms, a small medical clinic, and a sewing workroom. The new American ambassador had visited a few days earlier. A large clothing depot opened at 64 rue La Boétie, and there were urgent requests for men's clothing, overcoats, and shoes. On the fairly long list of monthly subscribers, Wharton herself was down for 1,000 a month. The American ambassador gave 1,000 francs, Walter Berry 200 francs, and Henry James 125 francs.

All of this organizing and fund raising for refugee organizations left Wharton little time for writing. Charles Scribner correctly surmised what her silence meant: "I don't know how far you have progressed on the serial proposed for 1916 [the big novel she tentatively titled *Literature*] or whether you have yet been able to begin work upon it. It has seemed probable that the interruption and distraction caused by this dreadful war might have made it impossible for you to manage a large and continuous work."[117] Wharton replied that Scribner had been correct: The demands of the war had destroyed any possibility of concentrated work on the novel. "For the present there is too much to do for the unfortunate creatures all about one to think of literature." She hastened to add that she planned to get back to writing her novel as soon as possible, and in the meantime she generously and fairly offered to release him from the amount contracted for the serialization. She was still hoping to send "Count Unterlinden" very soon, as she hoped the return of Anna Bahlmann from New York to Paris would relieve her of a great deal of secretarial work.[118]

    Things in New York that winter, Scribner told her, were going along about as usual. The editors of the *Literary Digest* had polled 367 American writers and editors; they announced in their November issue that 105 favored the Allies, that only 20 were for the Central Powers, but that the vast majority, 242, favored neutrality.[119]

ॐ

On December 19 Wharton appealed for funds to establish a small hospital of thirty to forty beds to be fitted up for the invalids among the 700 refugees the organizations now served.[120] The proposal for a small hospital for ill refugees would expand during the next four years into a far-flung health program that would care for not only the residents of the American Hostels but tubercular soldiers and citizens as well.

    In her Christmas letter to Lapsley, Wharton mentioned the recent visit of Percy Lubbock and dismissed her own work:

> There is no merit in digging 12 hours a day at the nearest "social" job this huge disorganization may have put in one's way. It's the only means of keeping a little oxygen in one's lungs—and I can imagine how you must feel the great weight of that deserted place.
>
>   The only consoling thought is that the beastly horror *had* to be gone through, for some mysterious cosmic reason of ripening and rotting, and the heads on whom that rotten German civilization are falling are bound to get cracked—and that, this being so, the crash has come at a moment that seems to find the other nations morally ready. I wish I could include the U.S.—but it sticks in my innards that the great peace-treaty-Hague-convention protagonist shouldn't rise in its millions to protest against the violation of the treaties she has always been clamouring for. We *are* smug just now, aren't we?

She encouraged Lapsley to visit her ("It's a time when people who are fond of each other ought to be together") with the invitation: "Do come, my dear, and let us warm both hands a little at the good fire of an old affection for each other."[121]

Her anger at the United States was expressed most openly in a letter to Beatrix Farrand, her niece. She said that Americans ought to give generously to civilian charities in France "to atone for the cowardice of their government." And in a moment of anger she anticipated Henry James's action: "The whole thing makes me so sick with shame that if I had time—& it mattered—I'd run round to the Préfecture de Police & get myself naturalized, almost anything rather than continue to be an American."[122]

On Christmas Eve the American Hostels entertained some 125 children and their mothers at the Hôtel Lutétia with presents and cake. The following day about 800 refugees were received in detachments of 200 at a sitting, and again presents were given. This Christmas celebration would become an annual event, and in the following years Wharton and her volunteers would have to protect the American ambassador and his wife, who would be almost trampled in a stampede when the doors were thrown open.

The American Hostels were now delivering 1,260 free meals a day. On the contributors' list, Henry James was down for another 50 francs.[123] Broad American support also went to charities for the wounded and to refugees in England. Mrs. O. H. P. Belmont had received several letters from her daughter, the Duchess of Marlborough, who was helping the wives and children of Belgian soldiers in London hospitals. Mrs. Belmont gave up her autumn season at her Hempstead estate to return to New York to oversee a fund suggested by her daughter.[124] And the Queen Mary fund established to aid women in England who were out of work received donations of $25,000 from W. W. Astor, $5,000 from Andrew Carnegie, and lesser but significant amounts from other members of America's wealthiest families.[125]

After the first rush of charitable donations, stateside fund-raisers insisted that organizers of American charities in France be specific in their appeals. A plaintive letter from an attorney in New York attempting to raise money for The Children of the Frontier, a charity organized and promoted by the Blisses, shows that by December of 1914 the American public was becoming saturated with begging appeals:

> Nearly everyone here is collecting for something. Mrs. Whitney
> Warren is collecting for the women and children of France and

unless we could have made our appeal in a somewhat different form
from the others, we could have done nothing at all.

In addition neither you nor Mrs. Bliss have sent me sufficient
detailed information as to what you were doing, in order to allow
me to make effective statements. I do not know how many children
you have, where you have put them, what you are doing with them,
how long you mean to keep them, exactly what it is costing you,
who is managing them, where they come from, etc.? Do give me all
this data and I will begin another campaign of advertising, much as
I hate it.[126]

The proliferation of war charities led Wharton to encourage her American contributors always to specify that their gift was for the American
Hostels for Refugees, especially when they were making a donation
through large charitable collection organizations.[127]

ɤ

During the first five months of the war, Edith Wharton established two
large civilian charities: the sewing workroom for unemployed Parisian
women and the American Hostels for Refugees. Her literary output was
understandably small while she threw her considerable energies into
administering and raising funds for the new charities. She called on her
large network of social and literary friends for help, and she was rarely
disappointed. Wharton, like almost all others, believed that the war
would be a short one and that, with its conclusion, the need for relief
work would be over. Both she and Henry James believed that unchecked
German aggression would mean "the crash of civilization." She was
disappointed in America's neutrality, but she returned to the pages of
American newspapers again and again to appeal on behalf of her charities.
At the end of 1914 the war was still regarded as an interruption, a
temporary break in the normal course of life. That life for Wharton was
one of writing novels, and she assumed that with the imminent end of
hostilities she could get back to it. In the meantime, she was determined
to do what she could for the refugees with the talents at her disposal.

2

੨ॳ

Reporter at the Front and Organizer at the Rear: 1915

War is the greatest of paradoxes: the most senseless and disheartening of human retrogressions, and the stimulant of
qualities of soul which, in every race, can seemingly find no
other means of renewal.

—Edith Wharton,
Fighting France, 53

EDITH WHARTON HAD SPENT THE AUTUMN AND THE WINTER OF 1914 ORGAN-
izing war charities and raising money for the refugees flooding Paris. She
told Mary Berenson, who had been staying with her during the creation
of the American Hostels for Refugees and who had asked how the new
organization was getting along, that the hostels took "a lot of nursing, &
reams of letter writing."[1] The writing was of a kind, however, that did not
lend itself to producing fiction. In a New Year's greeting excusing
"put[ting] off even the letters one most wanted to write" she said she
wished she could write "when evening came, [if] my brain were not too
sodden & my hand too tired to pick up a pen."[2] She confided to Charles
Scribner that while she had managed to raise $100,000 during the
previous five months, the daily demands of fund raising had left her
"absolutely pen-tied."[3] Her literary production had fallen off so sharply
that for 1914 she filed taxes on an income of only $900.[4]

  Before work with the war charities finally exhausted her, Wharton
struggled to maintain some continuity in the face of competing claims for

her time and energy. Her first biographer, R.W.B. Lewis, does not exaggerate when he says, "The range of Edith Wharton's activity in 1915 staggers the mind."[5] At the same time that she was supervising two large refugee and relief organizations, she was also writing a series of powerfully evocative magazine articles for Scribners about life in wartime Paris and at the front. She made five trips to points along the front in 1915: to the Argonne and Verdun once in February and again two weeks later in early March, to the Vosges in May, to Belgium in June, and to Alsace in August. In the spring she would open a third major charity to look after homeless Flemish children and old people sent to her by a Belgian government now largely powerless to relieve the suffering of its own civilians. Through the summer and fall of 1915 she would conceive the plan for and do much of the editorial work on *The Book of the Homeless*, a beautifully designed and printed gift book sold to make money for her war charities. Any one of those projects would have been a year's worth of work in a normal year. But 1915 was not a normal year, and it is little wonder that Wharton's output of fiction was small.

❧

As the new year got under way, Wharton continued to arrange concerts to aid out-of-work musicians. The series was the suggestion of conservative French composer Vincent d'Indy. Indy began the series by accompanying a group of solo vocalists at a concert held in Wharton's apartment on the last day of December. Wharton entered into the project with great enthusiasm. "I vaguely thought one had only to 'throw open one's doors,' as aristocratic hostesses do in fiction," she told Mary Berenson. "Oh, my! I'd rather write a three volume novel than do it again."[6]

Since part of the receipts from ticket sales went to her American Hostels, Wharton offered a tour of the hostels before the concert. What attracted some concert goers was a chance to see her apartment. The wife of one American embassy official recorded her impressions: "It [the American Hostels for Refugees] is wonderfully well done, in a way, but I don't see how they can keep it going; it costs 30,000 francs a month, and between six and seven hundred people are fed there. . . . In the afternoon to a concert at Mrs. Wharton's for the benefit of poor artists, and the Hostelry. A Mr. Capet played beautifully on the violin and Madame Croiza sang. There were about fifty people present. The apartment is very attractive."[7]

"There isn't a quartet left! Isn't it melancholy?"[8] Wharton told Alice Garrett; and, as if to illustrate her statement, the violinist Lucien Capet played without his usual quartet: His friend the cellist Marcel Casadesus had been killed on October 31. Wharton soon grew weary of struggling with the details of having the programs printed, adjusting to the moods of temperamental performers, and looking after refreshments for the afternoon musicals. After a half a dozen successful concerts, she turned over the organizing and the hosting of the fund-raising musicals to friends and urged Alice Garrett "to get up a concert for the Hostels at the Ritz, charge 10 fcs a ticket & have lots more people. I believe it would have a big success. Do!"[9]

To recover from the crush of the concerts, Wharton escaped to Chartres, where the cathedral, "in a glow of winter sun, seemed more magically beautiful & appealing than ever."[10] Returning to Paris, she made a stop at a military hospital supervised by her own physician, Dr. Isch Wall. After the intense beauty of the cathedral, the hollow faces and expressionless eyes of the wounded left her shattered for the rest of the day.[11] Yet Wharton was to describe those same faces of the young wounded as "the very essence of what I have called the look of Paris. They are calm, meditative, strangely purified and matured. It is as though their great experience had purged them of pettiness, meanness and frivolity, burning them down to the bare bones of character."[12] This ambivalence between the horrors of war and the purifying crucible of war on human character runs through all of her writing during this period.

෧ଊ

The former elegance of Paris held little attraction for Wharton. When she dined one evening with Adele Essex and Mrs. Astor in the freezing solitude of the Hotel Ritz, only four other tables were occupied. As the waiters glided spectrally around the large room, the three women huddled in their furs on one sofa in an effort to keep warm.[13] Thus, it was with a certain amount of chilliness that she observed that Walter Berry clung to his old ways, in spite of self-evident changes the war had brought: "Walter tries to pretend, by means of one professional beauty, a restaurant table, and a new cigarette case, that he is still Seeing Life in the good old Ritzian style, but all the rest of us have given up the pretense and surrendered to the d . . . and dowdy. —Anyhow, I can't quite see how the other thing fails to be rather the more macabre just now."[14]

Wharton would satirize insensitive American expatriates who continued with their social lives as if the war had never happened in her war novels *The Marne* and *A Son at the Front*. For his part, Berry resented what he saw as Wharton's preoccupation with her charities. Privately he told Berenson that he was becoming "more and more fed-up with the obsession of refugees and relief."[15]

ह▲

It was not only the public rooms of her apartment that were full during concert afternoons; her guest rooms were occupied as well. Anna Bahlmann arrived in Paris just before Christmas, and Percy Lubbock was staying at 53 rue de Varrene while doing research work in the hospitals for the Red Cross. Wharton quipped to Mary Berenson that unlike the Ritz, which was almost empty, her apartment had no more guest beds available.

Wharton's philosophy of social assistance was to make the refugees self-sufficient as soon as possible. She explained in a letter to the *Herald*, "the aim of our committee is always to enable the refugees to form a home for themselves rather than remain in the Hostels."[16] Her first broad appeal for American aid appeared in the *New York Sun* in mid-January. She explained though it "is easy to get gifts of underclothing for both sexes and dresses for women and children; . . . mens suits and overcoats have to be bought." Cash was urgently requested too, for renting and fitting up a sanitarium for those refugees whose medical and dietary needs were not serious enough to place them in hospitals but that made it impossible for them to manage on their own.[17] Charles Scribner saw the article and enclosed a check for 500 francs in his letter of inquiry about status of the projected novel *Literature*.[18]

ह▲

The newspaper appeals brought an avalanche of business and personal mail that would sap Wharton's energies over the next months. She frequently complained about the mountain of correspondence that kept her too busy during the day and too tired at night to write even to her friends.[19] In the future, she remarked playfully, it would be necessary to imagine even the dapper art connoisseur Berenson as a refugee, for in her new "categorical imperative" there could be no other reason for writing. Even the satirical sketch "Count Unterlinden languished in his corner" and other fictional subjects would flit past without coming within her reach. Experiencing what Gide described as "the dangerous intoxication that self-sacrifice brings,"[20] she told Berenson, "The worst of doing good is that it makes one forget how to do anything more interesting."[21]

As the winter wore on, she saw that her English friend Robert Norton was the only one who had been realistic about the projected length of the war instead of serving up "the old optimistic sugar plums of last August." For her "[t]he ouvroir and the oeuvres help to keep one from hanging over the abyss of the war, but not, alas, from breathing the chill of one's own private abyss." And a Dantesque Wharton, assigning Woodrow Wilson and Pope Benedict to a ring of hell reserved for ineffective leaders, commented, "It is sad that, at the world's greatest hour, two such pantaloons as Wilson and Benedict the Last (I hope) should hold the threads of destiny in their wobbling fingers." She went on with mixed playfulness and regret to say "I had a really big novel in me a year ago (excuse the gynecological metaphor), but things have killed it." And much as she would like to break away for a rest and a visit to Italy, she was worried because Berry and others told her that her automobile was sure to be confiscated as soon as she crossed the frontier. In connection with Italy's indecision about entering the war, she teased Berenson that the Italian sword must have gotten stuck in the scabbard.[22]

In January she managed to collect her impressions of Paris during the opening days of the war. After the misadventures of missed cables and her inability to recall the scene when isolated at Stocks the previous August, she finished the first of her essays on wartime France, mailing "The Look of Paris" to Scribners February 20. It was received on March 11, and after Minnie Jones read the proofs, it was published in the May issue.[23] For those who remained neutral in spirit in the United States, she expressed exasperation: "I don't understand how people can go on behaving as if we were on the same planet, when we so obviously are *not*." The war reached her own family of loyal servants when her footman, Henri, who had been running the hostel in the rue Taitbout, was mobilized early in the new year.

She reported to Mary Berenson, "I am hoping to get permission to carry supplies to two or three hospitals *dans l'est*," and she was furious when her pass was delayed because two or three titled women who had been allowed to go to the front had behaved so "riotously" that the government was chary about issuing passes to civilian women. In an earlier letter to Mary she had said that she didn't "know anything ghastlier & more idiotic than 'doing' hospitals *en touriste*, like museums!"[24] Reflecting on the curiosity of society ladies at the front, she commented, "I don't know anything that horrifies me more than the mixture of flirtation and surgery, of opoponax [perfume] and chloroform."[25]

With official passes granted, she carried medical supplies in her own car to distribute to ambulances and hospitals. Her visits to the front, officially sanctioned by the French Red Cross and the government, to units in the Argonne in late February and later to other points offered material for articles published in *Scribner's Magazine* in monthly installments during 1915 and collected the following year in her book *Fighting France: From Dunkerque to Belfort*. Wharton discovered the scope of the war in the massing of automobiles, horses, and men at every crossroads. Passing through Châlons, she saw her first "long line of 'éclopés'—the unwounded but battered, shattered, frost-bitten, deafened and half-paralyzed wreckage of the awful struggle."[26]

Her dedication to the French cause was complete. In February she wrote Judge Robert Grant, then serving on the Boston Committee of her American Hostels: "Of course you know that all of the wild rumours about 'atrocities' are *true and are understated*, and that the question of abolishing the penalty for abortion and infanticide is to be considered in the French Senate!"[27] She went on to claim that priests had indeed been assassinated and that mutilated old ladies from the invaded regions were beginning to appear in Paris hospitals. The stories would be even grimmer when the Belgians could begin to talk without fear of reprisals. She too had been skeptical at first, she assured Grant, but evidence from Belgium and the northern provinces had convinced her that the horrors were true. When Mrs. Grant later had a serious accident, Wharton claimed to have detected the influence of a "Boche" terrorist in the Grants' leafy suburb of Boston.

For anyone working so directly with the refugees, it was easy to lose objectivity. André Gide's recent visits to the American Hostels' low-priced housing project did him "no good." He felt that "too much sensuality is constantly slipping into my charity. My heart, my whole being go out unreservedly and I come away from those visits quite undone."[28]

ð

During February Wharton looked at the news from America and was heartened by the appearance of Theodore Roosevelt's book *America and the World War*, which caused a stir. Its partisan tone and its preparedness argument were denounced by the *Nation*: "In execrable taste and offensive to all fair-minded readers is his openly contemptuous abuse of the President and administration."[29] Charles Scribner, who published the book, regretted its tone and would later discourage Wharton from using an introduction by Roosevelt in her next project. In the American news-papers Roosevelt was telling curiosity seekers to stay home. He argued that the embassies and diplomats were already overworked and that "there is something cheap and vulgar to high-minded Americans in seeing their fellow countrymen going abroad to look on at the agony in a spirit of vapid and idle curiosity."[30]

As it was, they could stay home and gain as much understanding of the conditions in Paris and at the front by reading Wharton's articles then beginning to appear in *Scribner's Magazine*. In her article "The Look of Paris," she described the refugees entering Paris with "nothing left to them in the world but the memory of burning homes and massacred children and young men dragged to slavery, of infants torn from their mothers, old men trampled by drunken heels and priests slain while they prayed beside the dying."[31] Early in March Wharton cabled Scribners: "Just returned from the fighting line in Argonne. Mailing article next week."[32] She used direct, on-site observations for her war articles, each of which took her about a week to write.

Her second trip to the front, with a fresh load of supplies, was, she told Henry James, like other sequels "less high in colour than the first adventure." During the four days that she and Berry spent on the road to Verdun and back, they distributed shirts, fresh eggs, and bags of oranges. Describing herself and Berry modestly as "two neutrals carrying bundles to hospitals," she dwelt on dramatic juxtapositions offered by situations in the war. With an eye for the Tolstoyan detail amid the sweep of battle, she painted in her letter to James a graphic picture of a chilly scene from "Winter War."

> Picture this all under a white winter sky, driving great flurries of snow across the mud-&-cinder-coloured landscape, with the steel cold Meuse winding between beaten poplars—Cook standing with Her [Wharton's Mercedes automobile] in a knot of mud-colored military motors & artillery horses, soldiers coming & going, caval-rymen riding up with messages, poor bandaged creatures in rag-bag clothes leaning in doorways, & always, over & above us, the boom, boom, boom of the guns on the grey heights to the east. It was Winter War to the fullest, just in that little insignificant corner of the immense affair!—And those big, summing-up impressions meet one at every turn. I shall never forget the 15 mile run from Verdun

to that particular ambulance, across a snow-covered rolling country sweeping up to the white sky, with no one in sight but now & then a cavalry patrol with a blown cloak struggling along against the wind.—[33]

They were stuck for the night at Châlons-sur-Marne with no beds available. Finally Wharton's friend Jean Louis Vaudoyer offered his place if they could find their way in the dark to the house where he had a bedroom and if they could wake his landlady. Before parting, he gave them the password for the night, "Jena," in case they were stopped or challenged. The circumstances in Wharton's mind wavered between melodrama and farce: "I suddenly refused to believe that *any* of it was true, or happening to *me*, or that a nice boy who dines with me & sends me chocolates for Nouvel An, was whispering a *pass-word* to me." Certainly her chauffeur believed that it was happening to him, because while Wharton was successful in finding a bed for the night, he "slept in the motor, wrapped in Red Cross dressing-gowns & pillowed on gauze pads!"[34]

In a 1987 survey of war articles contributed by Scribner's authors to the magazine, James Sait argues: "Male war correspondents, and male and female writers in Europe and America kept within decorous bounds in response to editorial policy and in response to their American readers' inability to grasp the horror of a war that, until 1917, did not touch them personally. Only the work of Mrs. Wharton shows signs of being radically altered because of her first-hand experience of the War and, as we have seen, it evoked strong emotions in its readers. The fact that such an outstanding writer could respond to the war by extending her art certainly owes as much to the special relationship she had with Scribner's as it does to her living in Paris."[35]

Occasionally her propaganda work extended into official government circles, as when she asked John Garrett at the American embassy to advise a French inspector of propaganda about which American journalists could be used in support of the Allied cause.[36]

≈

Meanwhile both of her charities were having an active winter. The *ouvroir* contributed shirts, sweaters, underclothes, and socks to the Fund for Serbian Wounded. And in the four months since its establishment, the American Hostels had grown so that now the organization was caring for over 800 refugees and had found permanent employment for nearly 700 others. Following the model of her *ouvroir*, Wharton had established sewing workrooms for refugee women in three of the houses. Contract physicians dispensed free medical advice daily at each hostel, while American and French nurses visited at their homes those too ill to attend. A nursery school employing the innovative Montessori method had been started for the youngest children; the older ones were enrolled in the local schools. The clothing depot, at which Gide sometimes worked, had distributed over 20,000 garments in the first two months of 1915. The hostels continued to provide rent subsidies for large families and those who were destitute, but Wharton kept to her original aim of helping refugees find employment and a home rather than remaining dependent.

Monthly operating expenses had climbed to 30,000 francs; however, support came from diverse and sometimes official sources. Baron Guillaume, the Belgian minister to France, visited the American Hostels and was so impressed that he made an immediate personal donation of 1,000 francs to aid his country's refugees—an expression of governmental recognition that was to have important consequences for Wharton during the following months. The lengthening lists of contributors to her charities included friends from a variety of backgrounds: Bernard Berenson for 625 francs; Egerton Winthrop and Max Farrand, both down for 500 francs; Tiffany and Cartier, each for 100 francs. Among the monthly subscribers remained Wharton herself at 1,000 a month and Walter Berry at 100 francs. Even Teddy Wharton's family in Boston, with whom her relations were far from cordial, sent a contribution to her charities.[37]

The need was great in many areas of Europe. The American Commission for Relief in Belgium estimated that of the 7 million remaining in the country, 1.4 million were destitute, absolutely without means. In Serbia things were hardly any better. Nish, which usually had a population of 25,000, now had 50,000 refugees as well.

≈

On February 28 Wharton wrote Henry James a long letter describing the hospitals in Verdun, and she wrote him again on March 11, describing the conditions of the ambulances. These visits provided the background for a story that was germinating in her mind.[38] Throughout the fall of 1914 and the winter of 1915, editors at *Scribner's Magazine* kept urging Wharton to send them a short story. They were slow to recognize that her emotionally evocative article "The Look of Paris" indicated a new direction for her literary energies.

In mid-March Wharton acknowledged a donation from Sara Norton, one of her most loyal contributors, but mildly protested that the gift of 315 francs might have gone to her brother Richard's ambulance corps: "It is almost wrong of you, when you have your own urgent job to stick to, and collect funds for—but bless you all the same!" Offering a brief review of her recent missions to the Argonne and Verdun, she told Norton that she was writing up the narrative for *Scribner's Magazine*, "for the best of reasons, to make a little money!"[39] Even while wanting to add picturesque details, Wharton was cognizant of what would pass the military censor and occasionally asked her editor, Robert Bridges, to suppress the name of an ambulance mentioned in an article she had recently submitted.[40]

By now it had become impossible for her to leave for a projected rest in Italy "for the refugees and the ouvroir are still too much on my rather tired shoulders, and the most I can hope is a few days' escape like the last."[41] Directing the charities, raising funds for each of them, and writing up magazine reports of her trips to the front had left her exhausted. This pattern of working to a point of physical collapse, then going off (usually under a doctor's orders) to rest and hurrying back under a cloud of guilt became a rhythm she would repeat throughout the war.

≥≥

In March Wharton was about to take on her third major war charity, the Children of Flanders, which she described as "my prettiest and showiest and altogether most appealing charity."[42] The impetus to do something for infants and refugee children from Belgium grew out of letters she had seen describing the deplorable and dangerous conditions there, especially in the western regions of Flanders. She wrote a long letter to the *Herald* vividly describing the conditions in the ruins of Ypres, where over 200 children ranging in age from four to ten were living in cellars without clothing, food, or heat. Quoting from letters she had recently received, she offered heartrending accounts of a number of individual cases. Her public letter ended with an appeal for clothes, shoes, socks, underclothes, groceries, especially condensed milk, flour, fruit, and chocolate. A truck going to Ypres the following week would supply the children with any donations clearly labeled *Pour les Enfants d'Ypres* and sent either to Wharton or to Mme de Bormans.[43]

The response was immediate and extremely generous. Three days after her initial appeal, Wharton published a list of contributors to the

Children of Ypres fund that included a number of prominent French and American names. Wharton herself gave 100 francs, and a substantial number of others contributed food and clothing. The response was so good, in fact, that during the first week of April she was forced to publish an announcement thanking donors for the flood of supplies and asking that no more gifts be sent until some definite arrangements could be made for the children.

At the same time she was mindful of the American contributors to her hostels charity. Realizing now that her greatest success in raising funds came from presenting individual cases steeped in misery, she promised Robert Grant "as soon as I have time I shall write a little report for the U. S. Committees bringing our record up to date, and infusing into the narrative as much 'human interest' as possible." The spring, she told him, was a painful time to regard the incongruities of the war, "to see the trees budding and the punctual flower beds of the Champs-Elysées putting out their neat pink daisies, with the Monster only 80 miles away." She reassured herself that "steady drudgery is the best cure for thinking about these things."[44]

By the end of April, the report on the activities of the American Hostels for Refugees was ready. Along with moving descriptions of individual cases, it offered a crisp summary of the services provided during the first six months:

> The work accomplished by the Hostels and the Foyer Franco-Belge between October 27 last and April 25 is as follows: 5,113 refugees provided for; 142,480 free meals served; permanent employment found for 1,372 refugees; 51,918 garments distributed.
>
> Three hostels have been opened to lodge and board refugees: Hostel of the Franco-Belge, 5 rue du Colisee; American Hostel No. 1, 4 rue Pierre-Nicole; American Hostel No. 2, 18 rue Taitbout.
>
> Total expenditure to date is 161,755 francs.[45]

Because the war had extended well beyond the earlier optimistic estimates, the report asked for donations of substantial pieces of furniture (a desk with a key, wooden wardrobes, and kitchen tables) and monthly subscriptions. The headquarters of the organization would soon move from 20 rue Royale to larger quarters at 63 avenue des Champs Elysées. Several of Wharton's old friends, including Ogden Codman and Robert Grant, were serving on auxiliary committees that had been formed in Washington, Boston, and New York.

In spite of illnesses brought on by exhaustion and the demands of organizing yet another charity, Wharton was able to do some literary work. In April the editorial staff at *Scribner's Magazine* knew that a story with the title "Coming Home" was in progress, for they cited it by name in a letter to Wharton. Robert Bridges, her editor there, sent a cable urging her to finish the story—needed for the August fiction issue—before she sent any more war reports. Wharton's sharply etched descriptions from the war zone were clearly not what her editors and publisher expected from the foremost novelist in their stable. As an indication of their preference, they paid her $1,000 for each of her two stories published in 1915, but only $500 for each of the articles on the war.

Though Wharton was not deaf to Bridges's appeal that she finish the story quickly, the sight of refugees from Belgium and the occupied provinces of France wandering through the streets of Paris must have made the makeup of the August fiction issue seem trivial, if not unintentionally heartless. Nevertheless, on April 22 she sought to reassure Bridges: "I hope to send you 'Coming Home' in about ten days. It would have been finished long ago but for the rush of charitable work, which seems to increase every day."[46] That "rush" was soon to include the development of a wholly new charity to deal with hundreds of Flemish children consigned to her care.

Wharton used the pages of the *Herald* to report the success of her appeal for the children in Flanders. Her earlier letter of March 24, reproduced by the French press throughout the provinces and the colonies, had brought in 432 gifts of food and clothing, and 13,060 francs from France, England, Italy, and Algeria. Schoolchildren had taken up collections and emptied their savings banks. Through the *Appui Belge*, Wharton's group sent two railroad cars loaded with supplies and clothing and 520 francs to Comtesse van den Steen de Jehay, who was caring for the homeless Flemish children at the Hospital Elisabeth at Poperinghe.[47] Because her group still had a considerable sum in hand, Wharton proposed to the *curé* of Ypres that they set up a home near Paris for sixty Flemish orphans. The offer was accepted, and she obtained the permission of the *Curé Doyen* of Sèvres, M. L'Abbé Lejeune, to place the children, at her committee's expense, in the Ecole Brazillier at Sèvres. While at the last moment other arrangements were made in Belgium for the sixty orphans of Ypres, the plan and the arranged facilities remained in Wharton's mind.

Meanwhile there were between 700 and 800 orphaned or abandoned Flemish children still in need of care. A particularly urgent case occurred in late April when a group of 90 orphaned girls were turned out of the convent where they had been sheltered to allow its conversion to a military hospital. The Belgian government, remembering Wharton's aid to its refugees through the American Hostels, appealed to her on behalf of the children, and her committee agreed to devote to the girls the remaining funds sent as a result of her appeal for the children of Ypres.

To staff her new project Wharton turned for help to Elisina Tyler, the wife of Royall Tyler, who told Mildred Bliss when she was accepting a role in Wharton's charities: "What I would like above all things is to supervise babies. I know that very few people understand the *biberon* in this country."[48] Elisina was soon to get her chance. On April 27, with less than twenty-four hours' notice, the Belgian government put in Wharton's care one hundred children and twelve nuns. Dashing off a note to excuse her absence before rushing to the dormitory at Sèvres to receive the children scheduled to arrive at two that afternoon, an excited Elisina told Mildred Bliss, "Royall is their Honorary Secretary and I am the Lady in Charge. This is all so sudden, as they say in books. It won't look so sudden I hope in a day or two."[49] The numbers soon grew. Within a week Wharton told Lily Norton, "The evacuation of Flanders is a new problem, & I am trying to house 200 children and their Flemish nuns."[50]

In a day or two things did not "look so sudden" for Elisina. Her organizational skills began to set a pattern for the staff. Within two weeks the school and the hostel in Sèvres were humming along efficiently, and Elisina could report: "Monsieur Brunet, 'membre du Gouvernement Belge,' said that a fortnight ago there was in Belgium a great deal of opposition and mistrust about sending children to Paris, but thanks to us this reluctance had changed into the opposite, and he asked me to undertake the housing and looking after of another 180 who are to arrive tomorrow."[51] Wharton managed to arrange housing and care for the children and the old people who accompanied them, though she was suffering for much of the time with otitis (inflammation of the ear) and was counting the minutes until she could get away at the end of the first week of May for a hospital tour, this time to the Vosges.[52] Few of the children or the sisters who accompanied them spoke French, so language classes were among the first that Wharton instituted.

Wharton's huge effort to get the Children of Flanders charity under way was overshadowed in the press by news of the sinking of the *Lusitania* on May 7 and all of the subsequent stories and reactions, which ran more than a week. The total loss was 1,198 men, women, and children; of the

Fig. 2 A group of the Children of Flanders. Courtesy of the Yale
Collection of American Literature, Beinecke Library.

Fig.3 Lace school of the Children of Flanders, House at Sèvres. Courtesy
of the Yale Collection of American Literature, Beinecke Library.

218 Americans on board, 128 died. In the face of the sinking, even so balanced a senior diplomat as John Coolidge at the American embassy in Paris wrote privately in his diary, "We should break off diplomatic relations with the Central Powers, and adopt an attitude of benevolent neutrality to the allies. If the Central Powers resent this, let them make the declaration of war and cut off their noses to spite their faces; they would thus achieve that which we so earnestly desire."[53] Though Americans' attention at home and abroad was riveted on the sinking of the *Lusitania* and its possible consequences, it was clear that by the first week of May, the Children of Flanders charity was fully launched. By the first week of June it had received another 300 children.[54]

While Wharton was preoccupied with setting up homes in the Paris suburbs of Sèvres and St Ouen for the children arriving in boxcars from Flanders, she still had to parry the demands of her editors at Scribners. They continued to ask for a short story. Her cables reveal that she was more excited about an anticipated pass to visit Lorraine and the Vosges than in writing the promised story. On the last day of April her editors firmly instructed her, "Want Vosges after story."[55] Two days later, accepting the one assignment while not commenting on the other, she wired back, "All right Vosges."[56]

In the midst of establishing new charities, arranging visits to the front for the French Red Cross, writing up her impressions for *Scribner's Magazine*, and dealing with her editors' demands for short stories, Wharton still managed to remain gracious during visits from the children of friends. Laura Chanler, the older daughter of her dear friends Winthrop and Daisy Chanler, came to see her after a six-month training course as a nurse's assistant in a New York hospital. In writing a reassuring note to the girl's mother, Wharton sympathized with Laura's "joy of being able to help a little," adding "it's the only thing that lifts the horror of blackness; and that excuses one to one's self for being a subject of Wilson's!"[57] Wharton had been ill with the flu and an earache when Laura, "blooming and full of zeal," arrived. So she had only a glimpse of the girl before Laura set off for her base at Juilly, where Mrs. Harry Payne Whitney had opened a hospital for the wounded. Laura's stay was to be a short one. One morning she woke up with watery eyes and itchy skin. A doctor mistook a case of measles for eyes swollen from crying by a homesick girl and the red blotches for the result of body lice. The illness took a turn for the worse before a more accurate diagnosis was offered and a serious plan for treatment prescribed. By then Laura's enthusiasm for front-line medicine had cooled, and she was soon back in a studio apartment in New York following her avocation of art.

When Laura's sister Hester arrived in Paris a month later, Wharton immediately put her to work in a division of her own charities, but she was not optimistic that the girl would find enough to do: "There is so little choice, in all these war charities, between carrying the whole load and just puttering around and waiting to run errands." Much as she suspected, Hester returned to the United States and soon married.[58]

Immersed though she was in her charities, Wharton was not immune from personal grief. In February she had been saddened by the news that Jean du Breuil de Saint Germain had been killed in action near Arras while trying to save two of his men. She remembered sharing an adventurous automobile trip to Spain with him and Rosa Fitz-James in the spring of 1913.[59] And she reminded herself that in a sense his death was unnecessary, for he was old enough to have been exempted from service.[60]

Bessy Lodge, widow of Wharton's friend Bay Lodge, was attracted to du Breuil and mourned his loss. Wharton told Daisy Chanler confidentially how much du Breuil had meant to and how much he had done for Bessy: "[h]e was a great friend of mine, charming, intelligent, serious, and caring for worthwhile things—and he pulled her [Bessy Lodge] out of the mausoleum damps into the sunlight."[61] Stunned by her loss, Bessie was strongly drawn to Catholicism. Wharton was convinced "[i]t would be the best thing that could happen to her" if the families, the Lodges and the Frelinghuysens, would accept the conversion. But Wharton was worried that they would punish her by isolating her even more and withdrawing financial support from her and her children. Wharton asked Daisy to encourage Bessy not to take any decisive step. In a subsequent letter Wharton proved herself a shrewd psychologist: "Yes—Bessy has a noble scorn for consequences, but NOT always the nerves to face them when they come close. I have seen her in one or two crises, and she always lets herself be brow-beaten, even when she has the keenest sense of her rights, and of the insignificance of people who are bullying her. It has been, in part, the cause of her greatest unhappiness that she is never quite sure of herself about essentials, although 'intraitable' about comparatively small things."[62]

On May 12 Wharton followed through on her decision to visit the Vosges front. With Walter Berry she went to Nancy, traveled through Commercy and Gerbéviller, and continued to Ménil-sur-Belvitte, on the edge of the Vosges, which had been the scene of heavy fighting. They also stopped at the village of Crévic, where every home had been spared except that of General Hubert Lyautey, the French general who had denied Morocco to the Germans, and who in October of 1917 would be Wharton's host on her state-sponsored tour to Morocco. On May 16 and 17, in tour of the front, they went down to the front-line trenches.

During their trip through the Lorraine and the Vosges, Wharton met "the happiest being on earth: a man who has found his job."[63] She was referring to a cleric she met in Ménil-sur-Belvitte on the edge of the Vosges, whose avocation had been to turn one room of the village parsonage into a war museum cum chapel: "The candelabra on the altar are made of 'Seventy-five shells,' the Virgin's halo is composed of radiating bayonets, the walls are intricately adorned with German trophies and French relics, and on the ceiling the curé had painted a kind of zodiacal chart of the whole region, in which Ménil-sur-Belvitte's handful of houses figures as the central orb of the system, and Verdun, Nancy, Metz, and Belfort as its humble satellites." Wharton tried to soften the surreal effect by commenting "This particular man was made to do this particular thing: he is a born collector, classifier, and hero worshipper."[64]

🍃

Soon after her return from the front, she defended her shift away from fiction to her old editor, William Crary Brownell, by reviewing the circumstances that led to the change: "I promised Mr. Scribner, long ago, a little sketch called 'Count Unterlinden.' The war has become too vast and terrible for such things; but I hope it will find its opportunity when the tide turns." She outlined for him the setting and the plot summary of the story in progress: "Meanwhile I am writing, and think I can promise you within a month, a longish story called 'Coming Home,' which deals with the return of a French officer to his château in Argonne, where the Germans had been quartered for a fortnight with his family, who had been unable to get away. I think it will run to 10,000 words or perhaps more. I will cable as soon as it is finished."[65] She did cable three days later, but with bad news: "Story delayed by illness. Mailing positively this week. Length about thirteen thousand."[66]

By now she had changed the location of the occupied château from the Argonne to the Vosges, the site of her recent tour and "convalescence." To Bridges she explained the fortuitous delay: "I am sorry that 'Coming Home' was so long in justifying its title, but I had a long interval of grippe and earache, and then had to go off for a change for nearly a fortnight—all of which made a month's delay. It was not an unmixed disadvantage, however, for I traveled over all the country I describe in 'Coming Home,' and revised and completed the story from direct personal impressions."[67]

Her remark that she had "revised and completed the story" using "direct personal impressions" shows that she was deliberately drawing on the descriptive material from her war reporting in her fiction. Finally she cabled Scribners on May 29: "Story mailed."[68] They received the manuscript in mid-June, set it in type immediately, and mailed her the galleys.

≈

Wharton was very proud of getting journalistic scoops and exclusive coverage. She assured Bridges that she and Berry had been given exclusive coverage during their trip to the Lorraine and the Vosges, "We were given opportunities of seeing things that no one else has had of seeing things at the front. I was in the first line trenches, in 2 bombarded towns, etc. etc.—" then, catching herself, she added, "don't proclaim it too soon, for I don't want to be indiscreet." But she could not help adding "[war correspondent Norman] Hapgood has just come back from the same quarter having failed to get into the first line trenches."[69]

Having won the confidence of the French general staff, she soon had a permit to make a trip to the North. She dangled the exclusive before the editorial staff at the magazine: "Of course one can never tell beforehand just what one's opportunities may be; but if I have anything like the good luck I had on my last expedition I can promise you an interesting article for October."[70]

When Wharton returned from her trip to the Vosges, she found another visitor, Percy Lubbock, perched on her doorstep at 53 rue de Varenne. Lubbock had stopped off on his way to Alexandria, and the two had a few hours of conversation before his train left for Marseilles. He told her of the death of a good friend of Lapsley's, and Wharton wrote Lapsley the next day with "sympathy du plus profond de mon coeur." She too had "lost the best friend I had at the front, and now poor Robert d'Humières, whom I liked very much, and had been here a few weeks ago, has gone back and got killed too."[71] She was worried about her friend John Hugh Smith, who was with the Cold Stream Guards in a forty-kilometer line that seemed unable to hold.[72]

From June 19 to 24 Wharton and Berry took a trip north and west to the coast of Belgium. On June 21 they passed through Ypres, which she described in *Fighting France* as the town most destroyed by the Germans.[73] The next day in Poperinghe she wandered through the ruins from convent to convent looking for lace cushions of a special pattern required by her Flemish refugees for the lacemaking classes. When she finally located the right religious order, she "came to a class room with lines of empty benches facing a blue-mantled Virgin; and here, on the floor, lay rows and rows of lace cushions. On each a bit of lace had been begun—and there they had been dropped when nuns and pupils fled. They had not been left in disorder: the rows had been laid out evenly, a handkerchief thrown over each cushion. And that orderly arrest of life seemed sadder than any scene of disarray. It symbolized the senseless paralysis of a whole nation's activities. Here were a houseful of women and children, yesterday engaged in a useful task and now aimlessly astray over the earth."[74]

That night she was awakened from her sleep in the aptly named Wild Man Inn in Cassel by soldiers shooting at a Taube reconnaissance airplane. An hour or two later she was again awakened, this time by the thunder of the big siege gun at Dixmude. "Five times while I was dressing, the thunder shook my windows, and the air was filled with a noise that may be compared—if the human imagination can stand the strain—to the simultaneous closing of all the iron shop-shutters in the world. The odd part was that, as far as the Wild Man and its inhabitants were concerned, no visible effects resulted, and dressing, packing and coffee-drinking went on comfortably in the strange parentheses between the roars."[75] Later that morning, after having their photographs taken with some Zouaves on the beach at a little seaside colony near Nieuport, where the hotels were filled with troops fresh from the trenches, she and Berry traveled to La Panne, the spit of sand where the king and queen of Belgium and the remainder of their army were holding out.[76] The following morning she had an interview with Queen Elisabeth. In leaving the town the next day, she apostrophized the quiet heroism of the royal couple.[77]

During June she had a conversation with Norman Hapgood, recently returned from England, where "he seemed to have found some sentiment . . . in favor of not being too severe with Germany in the final settlement, as in the next fifty years Germany may be a useful barrier between Russian and English interests." Wharton's vision was on the immediate French predicament, not on long-range interests. She concluded, "I do not believe that there is much in it or that it is the opinion of a very important element."[78]

Her earlier appeal through the New York Times for specialized motor ambulance units to assist at the French front was answered by an anonymous American friend of France who gave 40,000 francs in July.[79] The generous donation allowed the French Red Cross to establish a "motor-unit of six small automobiles for use at the front. Four of these units are already in use, and are rendering invaluable services. They comprise a sterilizing plant, an electric dynamo, kitchen, douche, laundry, and complete outfit for installing an operating-room at the front."[80] Such an infusion of American generosity was exactly what Wharton's own charities needed.

The range of her concerns through mid-July shows how easy it was for her to exhaust her energy reserves. On the microeconomic front, for example, she deputized Lily Norton in England to buy for the ouvroirs quantities of wool for knitting by machine and by hand. Always conscious of cost, she insisted, "Of course we ought to get a slight reduction on current prices for such a quantity, & also on the ground of being a charity. (What English! I'm so tired I can hardly write.)"[81]

On the personal front she was worried about her former governess, secretary, and friend Anna Bahlmann. Anna had been operated on for cancer by Wharton's doctor, Isch Wall, and while the operation was "successful," Wharton knew that there was "no hope of an eventual cure, but of course temporary benefit—et puis ce sera à recommencer!"[82] She was clearly annoyed that Morton Fullerton, who had known Anna well during the period of their romance, neither telephoned nor asked for news of her throughout the ordeal.[83]

Wharton explained her daily schedule to Bernard Berenson. She spent the mornings writing and revising her series of war articles and the afternoons administering the charities. This schedule "relegates business letters till evening, and leaves friendly correspondence quite out in the cold."[84]

Other health care situations were also cause for concern. Elisina Tyler, who had managed to get away for a few days' rest at Semur-en-Auxois on the Coté d'Or, was furious when she learned that one of the children from Flanders would die because of what Elisina saw as inattention to hygiene by the Flemish sisters who accompanied them: "I am very sorry to hear that you don't think Martha has much chance. It is too dreadful to see children die when a little prudence, a little care would have saved their lives. In spite of the unquestionable devotion of which the good nuns are capable, their insensibility in this respect makes my blood boil. It isn't necessarily the fault of their religion. I was surrounded by a very religious atmosphere at St. Anna, but we were taught to be as clean as one could wish and every care was taken of our health and well being. These nuns have the fatalism of the contented poor, or of the despondent rich,—I can't quite say whether its the one or the other."[85]

Despite the subsidy paid by the Belgian government for the homeless children and the aged people who accompanied them, Wharton found it necessary to call again and again upon her committees and friends in the United States for financial help. She told Charles Scribner, "Since the beginning of the war I have raised nearly $100,000, all in small sums, and the correspondence necessitated by this work has been overwhelming; but no one living in Paris can do otherwise than strain every nerve to help."[86]

ಶಿ

As she looked to the second year of the war, Wharton knew that she would need still more funds. She described her next project in her autobiography: "Another effort was presently required, and this time it fell to my lot to put together 'The Book of the Homeless,' a collection of original poems, articles and drawings, contributed by literary and artistic celebrities in Europe and America. I appealed right and left for contributions, and met with only one refusal—but I will not name the eminent and successful author who went by on the other side."[87] The defector was Rudyard Kipling, who claimed in a note to Henry James that he was too busy with nonliterary work to take up his pen for Wharton's charities.

Also in A Backward Glance, writing there some eighteen years later, Wharton records graciously, if incorrectly, "the overwhelming needs of the hour doubled everyone's strength, and the book was ready on time." Actually, the strain of gathering materials for The Book of the Homeless and the subsequent pressures of marketing a book unavailable because of production delays left Wharton exhausted and publication more than two months behind schedule.[88] She edited the book during the summer and fall of 1915, hoping for, and clearly expecting, a pre-Christmas publication date. The actual publication date was January 22, 1916—missing the Christmas book-giving season. For a gift book, and an expensive gift book at that, this delay was clearly a reason for disappointment.

The idea of a gift book to support the Belgians was not new. Wharton herself had contributed to King Albert's Book, published in 1914; and The Book of France, made up of contributions by French authors translated by eminent English writers, was published in 1915. While the plan may have been in her mind for some time, it was in July of 1915 that she began sending prospective contributors a circular, or prospectus, outlining the design and the purpose of the book. Even as she did so, she wrote Bridges, her editor at Scribner's Magazine: "The only apology I can make for the delay in sending my article is the usual one of an unexpected 'rush' of refugee work here. Every American in Paris who is working at all is overworked and we all feel that everything must be set aside for this urgent job."[89]

Soon Wharton or her emissaries were asking the most reputed French, Belgian, English, and American artists and writers to contribute to the project. Alice Garrett secured a stylized watercolor sketch of an exotic Ménade with "banana peel fingers" from Léon Bakst, designer for the Ballet Russe.[90] Through her intermediary Ambroise Vollard she got from Pierre-Auguste Rénoir a charcoal portrait of his son, who had recently been wounded at the front. There was a watercolor sketch of two women by Auguste Rodin and a crayon drawing of boats on a beach by Claude Monet. A popular subject for the artists was to supply portraits of the literary contributors. Jacques-Émile Blanche supplied portraits or photographs of portraits of Thomas Hardy, George Moore, and Igor Stravinsky; Léon Bakst offered a sensitive drawing of the head of Jean Cocteau, and John Singer Sargent sent a photograph of his portrait of Henry James. Charles Dana Gibson entitled his picture of a Gibson Girl with pen in hand and eyes raised in a pensive mood "The Girl He Left Behind Him." Wharton asked Bernard Berenson to approach Herbert Trench, his neighbor in the Fiesole hills above Florence, and ask for some verses for what she described as "the literary salad I am mixing in a last passionate effort to raise money for the winter for my oeuvres!"[91] Later she would ask him to join forces with another neighbor, Carlo Placci, to ask Eleanora Duse for a "sentiment" for "her ever-faithful and adoring American public."[92] Wharton had recruited both Berensons for the cause.[93] To Mary Berenson, taking the cure for her headaches in Bath, Wharton sent thanks for soliciting contributed poems from George Santayana and from Laurence Binyon. Mary had also secured a promise of a poem from John Masefield.

After receiving promises of contributions from several French artists and authors in July, Wharton sent her ever-dependable and hardworking sister-in-law Minnie Jones (who had been staying with her during the summer) to London with copies of the prospectus and letters appealing for contributions addressed to the foremost writers and artists in England and

America. Minnie delivered her dispatches to an enthusiastic Henry James, whose part in the process was to pass on the appeals, with an accompanying letter of his own, to Thomas Hardy, William Dean Howells, John Singer Sargent, Joseph Conrad, Rudyard Kipling, and others.

James sent his "unsurpassably distinguished old Friend" a typewritten letter, apologizing for the mechanical script with metaphorical high jinks. Casting himself in the role of a literary broncobuster, cowboy James prepared for the "wealth of verbiage" Wharton's scheme was likely to require by "just catching Remington by the forelock. In fact I see I must ride him, so caught, as hard and as far as my poor old heels will help me to jab into his sides; which means, less hyperbolically, that I will pass on your earnest prayers at once to the individuals you name, and back it up with my own—and also that I will of course, with the greatest pleasure, try to knock something into shape for you myself—at the same time that I promise to forge for you such a simulacrum of my script as will successfully pass in the New York market for the copy sent to the printer."

The reference to "a simulacrum of my script" concerned a planned auction of the contributed manuscripts and drawings in New York. Even as James expressed doubt that some of the individuals she had named would contribute, he continued to ride his metaphor: "I haven't for instance much hope of Conrad, who produces by the sweat of his brow and tosses off, in considerable anguish, at the rate of about a word a month. But I will try, I will do my best. Of course my own incorrigible habits in the tossing-off way will bring me on with an inimitable dash."[94]

The same day that James was writing to Wharton—July 19—she sent a long letter to Charles Scribner describing the project and asking him to publish *The Book of the Homeless*: "Will you please read the enclosed circular and cable me if you care to undertake this publication in the autumn? Two or three books of the same kind have, as you know, been brought out successfully in England, and I believe that a similar publication with such contributions as I think I can guarantee, would have a good sale in the United States, and a fair one in England if brought out in November. So far, everyone I have asked has accepted, and I think that I shall get few refusals as my Relief Work is beginning to be known." She offered Scribner the distinguished cast of contributors who had accepted or who she was sure would accept. In a postscript suggesting a deluxe edition of one hundred copies, she asked, "What do you think of getting Berkeley Updike to get up the book? I am sure he would make a *very* special price for such a job."[95]

The project was apparently foremost in her mind because even before she had Scribner's answer she was writing him again on July 22, suggesting that Maxfield Parrish might do the cover ("a *refugee* book cover, of course!") and saying that she had asked Robert Grant "to 'centralize' the American contributions so that they need not be sent out to me." Again she suggested, this time more insistently, that Daniel Berkeley Updike be commissioned to design and print the book: "If, as I hope, you entrust the printing to Mr. Updike, I know no one better fitted than he to the editorial part of the work, the placing of the articles in the best order, of the illustrations, etc. He would enter into it with enthusiasm, I know, and the book, if done by him, would certainly have an international bibliophile value it could not otherwise offer. Would you be kind enough to cable me your decision about publishing the book, and also if I may write Mr. Updike on the subject, so that we may gain time."[96]

Her choice of Boston book designer and printer Daniel Berkeley Updike should not have surprised Scribner: She had made exactly the same request when his firm agreed to publish her first collection of short stories, *The Greater Inclination*, in 1899. Updike had been a frequent summer houseguest of the Whartons, first at their home in Newport and later at The Mount in the Berkshires. For his part Updike credited Wharton's generosity with putting his Merrymount Press on its financial feet: "To Mrs. Wharton's thoughtful act the Press owed not merely the prestige of printing her books, but also the printing of many other volumes for Scribner's—indeed we were constantly employed by the firm until it set up a press of its own. Nothing could have helped the Press more, just then, than the Scribner connection, for it showed that we were not amateurs but could hold our own with larger printing-houses; and this was all due to the friend who used her influence as generously, intelligently, and effectively then, as many times before and since, for persons or causes that she thought deserved a 'lift.'"[97]

Scribner cabled an enthusiastic acceptance of Wharton's proposal the first week of August: "Glad to publish refugee book. All profits to be paid to societies deducting actual expenditures. Forwarding Parish [sic] letter. Approve Updike if he will take full responsibility for preparation. Writing. SCRIBNER."[98]

And indeed he was writing. In a letter mailed the same day as his cable he began by confirming its message, and he generously added, "my proposal is to place the services of this house fully at your disposal to get the best results on the book, charging only for the money actually expended—I mean making no charge for the personal services of anyone here, for commission or anything of that kind; we should make no charge either for advertising in our own Magazine or catalogue."[99]

As a sales strategy he suggested charging a higher price rather than trying to reach "a tremendously large sale," but he was in full agreement with Wharton's earlier suggestion that the advertising for the book should say "'Edited by Mrs. Wharton'—that is, it might help the sale, as so many people from all over parts of America have sent me donations for my war charities."[100] They later agreed on an advertising circular to be sent to each of the Edith Wharton Committees to boom the sale of the book.

The mails were filled that summer with letters from eminent authors and artists answering Wharton's appeal for contributions. Max Beerbohm told John Singer Sargent that he would send something. Joseph Conrad told Henry James that, much as James had suspected, he had not written ten pages since the previous November "which is absurd for a writing man—but then I am rather an absurdity altogether."[101] John Masefield admitted to Berenson that he had not written in six or seven months either, but that he would try to send something. Yeats sent a note along with his brief, self-effacing "A Reason for Keeping Silent," explaining that the poem was all that he had on hand, and though he thought it appropriate, he wished it were longer.[102]

There were inevitable problems with contributors, not all of which had to do with their being away in August, as Scribner had feared. Encouraged by Wharton to send something "ringing," for example, Robert Grant passed along a partisan essay that Scribner suggested "would make an excellent editorial but contributions of that kind would not justify us in asking a very high price for the book or making it a beautiful one."[103] Wharton wrote to Grant immediately: "I can't tell you with what a contraction of the heart we Americans over here read of Newport balls and tennis tournaments and of President Wilson's meditations," and asked him to write a poem and withdraw the caustic article he had submitted.[104]

ᘏ

With preparations for the gift book well under way, Wharton took a break from her editorial work to tour the front in Alsace with Walter Berry. This would be her fifth tour of the French front in seven months. She took along Henry James's recent pamphlet on the Norton-Harjes Ambulance Corps for reading material.[105] Their tour began August 13, in a village near Rheims where "one of the new Red Cross sanitary motor units was to be seen 'in action.'"[106] On August 14 and 15 they traveled over the Alsace. On August 16 they went up into the mountains, finally finishing their trip on mules in the middle of a downpour. After being in sight of the German artillery, she and her group retired to safer terrain where the incongruity of enduring nature set against man's destruction struck her forcefully: "We retreated hurriedly and unpacked our luncheon-basket on the more sheltered side of the ridge. As we sat there in the grass, swept by a great mountain breeze full of the scent of thyme and myrtle, while the flutter of birds, the hum of insects, the still and busy life of the hills went on all about us in the sunshine, the pressure of the encircling line of death grew more intolerably real. It is not in the mud and jokes and every-day activities of the trenches that one feels the damnable insanity of war; it is where it lurks like a mythical monster in scenes to which the mind has always turned for rest."[107]

She returned "exhausted from mountaineering in the Vosges"[108] and was determined to go off to Brittany in about ten days for a rest. Wharton was still toying with the idea of making a trip to Italy, perhaps by train, in October or November.

ॐ

As the contributions to her gift book began to come in, Wharton could see that certain offerings might be embarrassingly out of character with the rest of the book. Having already straightened out the matter of Grant's editorial, she suggested that Scribner forward to her anything he received from John Jay Chapman: "He is so eccentric that what he writes may not be in harmony with my plan, and as I have known him all my life, I can find some excuse for leaving it out without involving you in any way."[109]

She was clearly disappointed in the defections of Kipling, Pierre Loti, and, from America, Maxfield Parrish. And there were problems of editorial taste, as when with the André Suarès text she "marked in brackets two or three passages which we thought too Lesbian for publication."[110] Suarès describes young women whose lovers and bridegrooms have gone to war:

> Here comes the night. The maidens of the West come out across
> the meadows, and the young women of the land come to meet them.
> Two singing choirs, they mingle in the flowered grass, and in the
> smell of the black wheat that is like the smell of honey and vanilla.

Forward they go to meet each other, maids and they that once
were maids—nests of kisses, and those that willingly would be so.
They long to dance, but lovers and bridegrooms are far away: all
have gone out to the stern work of war. No more can the women
tread the red wine of joy in the dance; they have no mind to dance
with one another, and so they sing instead.[111]

On the last day of August Wharton apologized to Scribner for her
tardiness in writing her articles about the war: "The pressure of work here
is so great that I am often too tired to detach my mind from it and do any
decent writing."[112] In a letter a month later, she promised him a series of
short stories on subjects suggested by the war.[113] Scribners continued to
pay her well for the stories she did complete: She received $1,000 for her
recently completed ghost story "Kerfol."[114] That she wrote so few stories
on the war is a pretty clear indication that what energy she had was going
into reportage.

The immediate incident took some time to be transmuted into the
stuff of fiction, as another Scribner author found. Henry van Dyke,
Murray Professor of English Literature at Princeton and since 1913
ambassador to the Netherlands, wrote Bridges that he too had difficulty
getting a handle on the rich war material available: "I spent all day
yesterday at the Belgian refugee camp at Nunspat, where there are eight
or ten thousand of the 'uprooted ones.' I got material for a splendid story
which I shall never have time to write."[115]

A thornier problem arose between editor Wharton and the publisher Scribner when she proposed that Teddy Roosevelt write the introduction to The Book of the Homeless. Scribner had agreed but later, stung
by the justifiable criticism of the tone of Roosevelt's recent America and
the World War, he became dubious. When he had not received the
promised piece after a month, Scribner admitted, "I have not stirred him
up because there is an opinion shared in by Mr. Updike that an introduction from Roosevelt might give the book a somewhat controversial
character; he is so much disliked in some quarters and has hit the
Administration so hard." He went on to suggest that "an introduction
from Mr. Choate would be free of any criticism."[116] But Wharton stuck
to her guns and replied sharply, though diplomatically sidestepping the
fact that Scribner as well as Updike objected to Roosevelt's introduction,
"I do not agree with Mr. Updike that an introduction by Mr. Roosevelt
will affect the popularity of the book, especially such an introduction as

he has written."[117] The last shot had not been fired. To a later letter, Scribner added a testy postscript: "I regret Col. Roosevelt's reference to 'our national shortcomings' which will irritate the friends of the administration. But what can I do at this last hour. And you think it all right."[118] She apparently did, for the introduction appeared as Roosevelt wrote it.

A less contentious matter was Wharton's own preface to the book. Scribner had quite rightly noted that a preface would give her the opportunity to "tell how the book originated and for what purpose it was made and possibly give some brief account of the charities it is to help. Without something of that kind the book does not explain itself."[119] The reluctant editor did write the preface, objecting, however, when Updike proposed setting it in italic type. Of her effort Wharton wrote Minnie Jones, "I hope my idiotic preface didn't arrive too late; I never sweated out anything with such anguish."[120] Reviewers certainly did not find it "idiotic." The New York Times commented, "Mrs. Wharton's preface strikes the keynote of the book in its direct, simple, and graphic style, its personality, and its singleness of heart. Notwithstanding the few lines of statistics sandwiched between its sections, it is, as almost is every contribution, a piece of real literature."[121]

With her work on The Book of the Homeless and a heavy burden of letter writing, Wharton had been pushing herself hard since her August trip to the front. In a letter expressing sympathy to Sara Norton, whose uncle had just committed suicide, she added "I understand his doing it—even without any uncurable disease," and, wistfully, "one would be so glad, just now, to follow him!!" She complained that her correspondence was unusually onerous because some of her workers were ill and others away for their August vacation. Sara Norton had been the go-between with Paul Elmer More, who promised to write an article for The Book of the Homeless. She told Norton about the state of other contributions:

> With regard to Mr. Howells, the question was settled long before you wrote. He sent a ringing little poem to Mr. James, and when he wrote to recall it, Mr. James flatly refused, to my eternal gratitude. The poem is just what I wanted—and curiously enough, it is very much like the one which Mr. Hardy has written for me.
>
> Mr. Santayana has sent a lovely bit of verse—also written "on purpose." It is wonderful how kind every one has been. I think the auction sale of the mss. and drawings after the publication ought to bring in a great deal. I have a really perfect sentence or

two from General Joffre, who has written for no one else, an
introduction from Mr. Roosevelt, and probably I am to have a word
or two from the Queen of the Belgians, whom I saw when I was at
La Panne, and who is much interested in the "Children of Flandres
Rescue Committee."

Though she was staying with Wharton, Minnie was working so
hard at the American Hostels' registry office that they saw each other
only for meals. One day Wharton took Minnie to see a battlefield, an
outing that made the reason for her work clear. Wharton was concerned
about Anna Bahlman, still recovering from a cancer operation, and
about White, her butler, who was also ill. "But it is such a bedevilled
world this year that everything seems to heap itself up on one, as if the
microbe were in the air."[122]

Wharton must have read with interest a small item in the *Herald* of
September 12 announcing that Mrs. Alfred G. Vanderbilt was negotiating to buy Erskine Park, the Berkshire estate of George Westinghouse,
which bordered The Mount, her own former estate in Lenox.[123] Memories
of America and a quieter time must have been tempting because on every
return to wartime life in Paris she found herself "at once engulfed—as
usual! It's the penalty of every little flight from Paris."[124] But she was off
to London at the end of the week to see Henry James, who had been ill.

≈

Wharton now began to lean increasingly on Elizabeth Sherman Cameron.
Lizzie Cameron was the estranged wife of James Donald Cameron, the
former senator from Pennsylvania. She had been forty when her husband,
convinced that he could not win reelection, left Washington. After the
marriage of her only daughter, Martha, in 1909, Lizzie gave up her house
in Washington.[125] She was emotionally attached to her only child even
though she knew it was time for the young woman to live on her own.
Lizzie was at the pivotal dinner at Voisin's restaurant in Paris in 1910,
where Henry Adams tricked Bernard Berenson, who had a poor opinion
of Wharton, into spending an evening with a veiled and charming
stranger. As a result of this easier meeting, Berenson and Wharton became
close friends. In the prewar years Lizzie Cameron lived in a three-story
apartment in the old Avenue du Bois de Boulogne (now the Avenue
Foch). She had conducted a salon, attended by Henry Adams, Henry
James, Bernard Berenson, and Auguste Rodin.[126] In 1915 she was fifty-

eight, roughly Wharton's contemporary, and was a good friend of Henry Adams. When not in Paris, Lizzie frequently visited Stapleton, the eighteenth-century manor house that her daughter and son-in-law owned in Dorset, in the heart of Thomas Hardy country.[127]

Lizzie was so moved by Elisina Tyler's description of the refugees at her first luncheon with Wharton and Tyler that she immediately made a contribution of enough money to buy twenty pairs of American boots for the children.[128] Wharton offered her a job with the refugees and soon found herself relying increasingly on Lizzie as well as Elisina.

In late September Wharton wrote a postcard to Lapsley in French, so as not to alarm the censor, telling him that she would arrive at Buckland's Hotel in London the following Sunday evening and would be staying a week. She hoped that he could round up Lubbock and that the old crowd could assemble at Howard Sturgis's Queen's Acre. Originally she was to have been joined on the English trip by André Gide, but Gide, despite the attractions of seeing Henry James and Arnold Bennett, was not looking forward to it. He was saved at the last moment by French bureaucracy: "Fortunately I encounter insurmountable difficulties at the prefecture. Before getting my passport I have to go to the Invalides to regularize my military status or at least to prove that it is regular; then to the local police station with two witnesses and my photograph; then to the British Embassy; then to the Ministry of Foreign Affairs. . . . And, since there was not enough time for all these formalities, I suddenly found myself extraordinarily relieved to give up the project altogether. If I got some pleasure from the idea of going away, my pleasure at the idea of staying was certainly much greater, and I enjoy this late afternoon, here, like someone who has just had a narrow escape." He added, "Yet it would have amused me to travel with her. But this was not the moment."[129]

Wharton spent the opening ten days of October in England, first with Henry James in London and then with Lubbock and Lapsley at Queen's Acre. James was "very preoccupied," "not very well," and preferred to be alone.[130] She cut short her visit in London. When she reached Windsor, she had the misfortune to find her excitable host Howard Sturgis even more distressed than usual over the disappearance in battle of his friend Wilfred Sheridan.

She kept in touch with her charities, asking Elisina, "How are things going with the Flanderesses?" and expressing some optimism about her health: "I think that I am getting rested in spite of the ear-ache, and shall be of more use when I get back."[131] Increasingly conscious of just how heavily she was coming to lean on Elisina to attend to the administrative details of the various war charities, Wharton was always modest in her letters to the Tylers about the quality of her own work.

&

Once back in Paris, Wharton gave a luncheon where one guest found the hostess "very charming, and her apartment is charming."[132] She was tidying up details for the publication of The Book of the Homeless and for the manuscript auction. She wrote to Theodore Roosevelt, asking him to copy out his introduction by hand so that the manuscript might be sold to "the Tru-fool who wants your handwriting; we even hope to find two or three & pit them against each other." She was disappointed that she could not persuade Roosevelt to come to Europe to see the front, as she was sure that his description of the French cause would shake America out of its neutrality. In the meantime she had begun to extend her dislike of neutrals and the spirit of pacifism well beyond Wilson: "I do agree with you that the Wilson apologists are partly, & largely, responsible for our shame. I think it was the saddest moment of my life when I realized that my country wanted him to be what he is; & shook in its shoes for fear he wouldn't understand how thoroughly they were 'behind' him & meant to stay there."[133] She promised "to allegorize it in a short story—my only weapon" and told Roosevelt how even her timid footman, Henri, had suddenly found courage when he learned that he was to be mobilized.

During the last week of October Wharton made appeals on successive days in the pages of the Herald. First she announced that the American Hostels had funds sufficient only for carrying on their work for two more months, and the next day she appealed for boots for the children in the hostels. She confided to Minnie Jones, "The appeal is blatantly personal, but that seems to be the only way to get money, et j'ai su me faire un front qui ne rougit jamais."[134] She had learned not to blush when asking for money and was not afraid to use sentimental appeals to get it.

She explained her long silence to Sara Norton as "a sudden complete surrender to fatigue, coming after the intense worry of Anna's operation, a rather serious illness of White's, and the extra hard work necessitated by the absence, in July and August, of all my chief helpers." Despite crawling away for three weeks of rest in Brittany and Normandy, she found herself unable to attend to the big bundle of unanswered letters she took with her. "It is always like that: one can keep going as long as one is rushed, but when one finally has a chance to rest one can do absolutely nothing." Other areas of recent experience were no more encouraging. She reported to Norton that in London she had found their mutual friend Henry James depressed: "I think the sadness of every one about him is beginning to tell on him. England seemed to me much sadder than France: such discouragement with the government, and then such dreadful losses at the last offensive. However, neither here nor there is there the least doubt as to the final outcome. Only the German horror is becoming an even blacker nightmare." Wharton had made plans for Anna to go to America to a niece in the West, where her rheumatism would not be aggravated by the damp French winters. In Paris she was worried about seeing her charities through the winter and added to Norton, whom she knew shared her views, that she wished for sentiments other than sympathy from America. After a year of war she was exhausted: "I am very proud when I look back at the last year and find that I have collected altogether over $100,000 for my two refugee charities, workroom and my Red Cross sanitary motors. But, oh, I'm tired."[135]

One relief was that all of the materials for *The Book of the Homeless* had been shipped and were in the hands of Scribners and Updike. The original circular that went out in mid-July to potential contributors stated, "The Book of the Homeless is to be published simultaneously in New York and London, in October 1915." Perhaps sensing that this would have been an overly ambitious publication schedule, even had all of the contributions been in hand, Wharton suggested in her first letter to Scribner a November publication date. From his end, Scribner could see that the project was likely to be much more complicated than she anticipated and that delays would be inevitable. In his reply to her initial letter he made it clear that she must not be impatient, that there would be delays, the most immediate ones probably on the part of her contributors: "My fear is that you have underestimated the time necessary for the preparation of the book; at this time of the year [late July and August] so many people are away and it does not seem to me possible that the articles can be written and assembled by the end of this month." He added prophetically that he thought the book would do just as well were it to come out in January.[136] In a letter to Grant, the man who was to "centralize" contributions in America, Scribner sensibly commented: "It seems to me that Mrs. Wharton has not allowed enough time. All you can do is get the articles in as soon as possible. The book cannot be printed until the last article is received and somebody will surely be late."[137] Later he commented to Grant, "It is a more difficult matter to get such a book into shape than she perhaps realizes, but we shall pull through in some way." And after noting that Daniel Berkeley Updike—at Mrs. Wharton's specific request—would attend to the makeup of the book, Scribner added in a hurt tone, "For some reason, possibly because she wants to save us the trouble, Mrs. Wharton does not seem disposed to put the responsibility upon this house."[138]

By late August, Scribner could write Wharton that he had just concluded a satisfactory meeting with Updike. Despite the fact that they still did not have the contributions in hand, he offered a cautiously optimistic timetable: "It is pretty clear that the book cannot be ready in October but I hope it will be possible to bring it out by November, if nothing fails us."[139] But things did fail them, including late contributions and tardy translations from Paris. Scribner was conscientious in passing things along in what for him was frequently a troublesome Paris—New York—Boston triangle: "It does make me impatient to send everything to Boston and not be able to crowd the work, as we could do in our own factory or if done under our direction, but I shall live up to the understanding with Mr. Updike and try to help him all I can without hurrying him unduly."[140] By the middle of October he could report that he had sent everything to Boston except the dreaded introduction from Roosevelt and the preface Wharton was to contribute.

For her part, Wharton did not trust the steamer mails after the *Arabic*, a White Star liner headed westward, went down on August 19, 1915. Out of Liverpool with 425 passengers on board, the ship was sunk fifty-five miles south of Ireland by a German submarine. Also carried to the bottom were several of Wharton's appeals to American contributors. As she said, "It adds new terrors to letter writing (when one is as tired as I have been lately) to know that one's letters are more than likely not to arrive."[141] After the loss of the *Arabic* Wharton sent manuscripts in the company of a ship's passenger whenever possible, apparently feeling that a personal courier ensured a safer arrival.

Through November Updike and Scribner were making decisions about the size of the book and the kind of paper to print the limited number deluxe editions on. Wharton, always casting long transatlantic glances over their shoulders, sent cabled questions about the number of each edition or the type of paper. As late as November 26, Scribner was writing her, "This morning I have a dummy of the book showing its size, type-page and reproductions of two of the illustrations and it is certainly handsome." But this piece of good news was followed by the inevitable caution, "My chief anxiety now is that it shall be ready before Christmas; that is still dependent upon Mr. Updike and I am sure he is trying his hardest."[142]

૨**

Meanwhile, help in managing the charities was soon to arrive in the form of Lizzie Cameron. Wharton had invited her to lunch in early November so "we could talk a little about refugees—if you still want a dull job."[143] Within two weeks Wharton pressed Lizzie to attend a meeting of the general committee of the American Hostels, where Wharton reviewed their progress during the previous year and laid out plans for the winter.[144] Part of those plans involved a long rest for Wharton in the south of France, which would eventually leave Lizzie in charge of dealing with her mail and many of the details of administering the charities. Already Lizzie ran the green-and-white grocery depot of the American Hostels in the rue Pierre-Charron, where she handed out certificates that allowed refugees to purchase food at a savings of 50 percent.[145]

Once into the charity work, Lizzie described the force of the administrative team of Elisina and Wharton: "She is Italian, a direct contradiction to all of one's traditional ideas of an Italian woman. A steam-roller is easy compared to her. Clear-headed, executive, practical, she drives us all before her. You can imagine what a team she makes with Edith when they are together."[146]

Wharton was busy before she left for vacation in the third week of November. On November 16 she attended a meeting at the American Chamber of Commerce to establish a charity to assist maimed soldiers;[147] there Walter Berry was elected to represent the American colony in a federation of foreign groups resident in Paris. Two days later Wharton placed a letter in the *Herald* opening a coal fund to assist some 3,000 refugees from the invaded regions. Despite the fact that coal was soon to be $30 a ton, when it could be obtained, Wharton already had half the funds needed and had a chance to buy large quantities of coal at very favorable prices.[148]

Occasionally there was good news. The company La Mutuelle de Seine et Seine-et-Oise had turned over a large building in the rue Boissy-d'Anglas to the American Hostels to use for its clothing depot. Mrs. Scott remained in charge of the depot.[149] (Earlier Mr. Pardoe, an art dealer, had turned over his shop to the American Hostels to use as a clothing depot.) And Americans in Paris had answered Wharton's appeal for 15,000 francs to buy coal for the winter for the hostels with such generosity that more than 20,000 francs were collected in the first week.[150] Sally Fairchild, sister of Wharton's Paris worker Blair Fairchild, had had a very successful rummage sale in the United States,[151] and when the receipts reached Paris, Wharton remarked that "in this golden down-pour . . . I can truly say that after having begged, bullied, grovelled and nagged for money for over a year it is positively intoxicating to have it drop into one's lap unannounced." In her first hour of fantasy she had spent the unexpected largesse on a Red Cross radiography ambulance and on a mountain of warm jerseys and flannel shirts, but she finally decided to put the whole amount in an interest-bearing account and dole it out a franc at a time. If her decision was hardheaded, her gratitude led her back to the world of fantasy: "When I think of all I shall be able to do for them I long to take a bite of Alice's cake, & grow arms long enough to reach across and hug you."[152]

☙

As late as Thanksgiving, Scribner was optimistic about the progress of *The Book of the Homeless*. He had sent the original manuscripts and drawings to be sold at the auction and the proofs of the book to Minnie Jones—Wharton's deputized proofreader in New York.

Gradually Lizzie Cameron took over the opening and forwarding of Wharton's mail and the important job of placing contributors' lists in the *Herald*.[153] From Avignon in late November Wharton, on her way to Costebelle, directed Cameron to send on her personal letters and a selection of the others ("i.e., anything except notes & donations & *bills*!") every two days by registered mail.[154] A few days later she directed Lizzie to have an American photographer named Ellis take photographs of the lace-making classes and of the line of refugees that formed each morning outside the hostels office at 63 Champs-Elysées. Minnie had been clamoring for photographs with human appeal.

Despite Wharton's attention to details of the Paris operation, the change of scene was beginning to have its effect. She was starting to relax and enjoy her vacation: "It is heavenly here, & I marvel at the thought that I used to be *bored* on the Riviera! I didn't realize how tired I was until I began to rest. It is delicious just to dawdle about in the sun, & smell the eucalyptus & pines, & arrange bushels of flowers bought for 50 centimes under a yellow awning in a market smelling of tunny-fish & olives—."[155] The next day she wrote Elisina saying that she was "eating, knitting, and 'resting' arduously. It is a difficult exercise and the first few days nearly killed me; but now I have got back to the rapture of story writing & when I can do that nothing else matters a fig!"[156]

From November 22 to 26 André Gide accompanied Wharton (unlike the aborted trip to England in October) on an automobile trip to Hyères. They lunched at a restaurant on the quais of nearby Toulon, which Wharton found as picturesque as Naples. At Costebelle he met Wharton's friend, the socially and artistically conservative novelist Paul Bourget. During that meeting, with Wharton out of earshot, Bourget insisted on knowing whether the character in Gide's *Immoraliste* was "a practicing pederast." When Gide replied that he was probably an unconscious homosexual, Bourget launched into classifications of perversions before an astonished Gide. Once composed, Gide idly asked if Bourget classed homosexuals under a particular perversion. Bourget was in the midst of a spirited reply when Wharton rejoined them. "I was sorry," said Gide, "that he turned the conversation into another channel; it would have amused me to have Mrs. Wharton's opinion, if she had one."[157] Shortly after Gide left Wharton, she and Bourget had discussed Gide's *Strait Is the Gate*, which Bourget admired very much.[158]

Though she visited the Bourgets' villa, she found the location too damp and shady to accept their invitation to stay there. Gide was still with her, and Robert Norton, the cultured English friend who worked during the war for the British Admiralty, was expected on December 4. The conditions for her rest were perfect, almost: "It's all perfect, except that I can't sleep; which is a bore when one is rest-curing."[159] She complained regularly about the mixed blessing of the deluge of letters, ten that day, which often brought splendid donations but which always meant extra work. One recent letter brought 124,000 francs, enough to outfit two complete motor convoys.

By the first of December Wharton had started two short stories and was counting the days to see if there was any chance of finishing them before she had to go back. In all of her letters she credits Lizzie for her escape: "If it weren't for you I shouldn't have been able to begin them even,"[160] and "What should I have done if you hadn't been angel enough to take this load of work off me."[161] The fund drives for the refugees were going well, and Wharton leaned on Lizzie to check on the illnesses of her servants and even to get a clock in her Paris apartment fixed.

Wharton's rest was shattered on December 4 when a telegram from Theodora Bosanquet, his secretary, announced that Henry James had had a stroke. Luckily Wharton was visiting the Bourgets with Robert Norton when the news came, "So I was able to talk of him to people who understood."[162] "It is a dreadful shock to me, for while I knew he had heart disease & might die at any moment I had never foreseen the possibility of this far worse thing. . . . In any case, it has taken all the sun & warmth out of this peaceful place, & all possibility of rest out of my mind. It is as if I had been plunged leagues & leagues deeper into the desert I was in before!"[163]

Four days after James's stroke she received word of a second attack. Though Elisina reassured her that things were going very well in Paris and urged her to stay another two weeks, Wharton returned on December 17. There she discovered a crisis at the *Foyer Franco-Belge* and the American Hostels: Elisina had had to have a very serious talk with du Bos about the necessity of reducing the number and the generosity of his handouts to the refugees.[164] He was soon to lose the confidence of his fellow workers and the administrative committee.

ﾂ

These days of anguish were capped by the disappointment in the delay of the publication of *The Book of the Homeless* until after the first of the new year, missing the Christmas book-buying season—clearly a major setback for a gift book. One of the first letters she received on her return to Paris, from Charles Scribner, brought the bad news: "Unfortunately Mr. Updike finds it quite impossible to have it ready before Christmas. This is a distinct disappointment and makes it difficult to know how to manage exploitation, but it cannot be helped and we must try to make the best of it."[165]

Wharton was bitterly disappointed by the delay. She responded: "It was a great blow to hear that The Book of the Homeless was not, after all, to appear till after Christmas. I had worked so hard to get the contents together, and I counted so much on the Christmas sale, that I was much depressed when your letter came."[166]

If the three weeks leading up to Christmas had been a disaster, the week after the holiday offered no relief. In a note thanking Lizzie Cameron for a Christmas gift of a glass bowl, Wharton suddenly shifted moods and added with a sarcastic fatalism, "Yesterday I heard the pleasing news that the gov't has taken the whole of the Petit St Thomas building & that I must 'evacuate' before Jan. 1st. It is a bad blow because I don't know where on earth to find another apartment in this quarter for a big ouvroir & vestiaire—& I'm so tired & poorly already that I haven't the courage to bear the hurt."[167]

The year 1915, which had began with fund-raising concerts and an essay on "the Look of Paris" for *Scribner's Magazine*, ended with the bureacratic muddle of having to relocate her women's sewing room. In broader matters Wharton had enjoyed the sanction and cooperation of the French Red Cross and the French military during her five trips to sites along the front. These trips allowed her to collect impressions for a series of articles published almost monthly in *Scribner's Magazine*, which kept her name before the American reading public even though she had turned away almost entirely from writing fiction. To satisfy her editors' demands, she produced a war story, "Coming Home," using the setting from her visit to the Vosges in April and May of 1915. Charles Scribner called it "by far the best war story which has yet appeared,"[168] and when it was reprinted the following year in the collection *Xingu and Other Stories*, the reviewer for the *New York Times* singled it out as "the most notable in the book."[169]

But the insistent demands of her charities limited Wharton's output of fiction. When the Belgian government sent her several hundred orphaned and abandoned Flemish children and scores more aged, infirm people during the spring of 1915, she responded by organizing the Children of Flanders Rescue Committee to care for her new charges. She was fortunate to find a new administrator in Elisina Tyler, who became Wharton's right hand in the relief organizations and her closest friend for the rest of her life.

Housing, feeding, and educating hundreds of children and aged people took money—large amounts of money. So during the summer and the autumn, Wharton asked for contributions to and oversaw the editing and production of *The Book of the Homeless*, the most elaborate and beautiful gift book produced during the war. Artists, musicians, and writers in England, France, Belgium, Italy, and the United States recognized Edith Wharton's name and the force of her appeals for her charities. Mrs. Wharton asked and the artistic world responded generously: Sarah Bernhardt, Jean Cocteau, Joseph Conrad, and Thomas Hardy sent work. Wharton deputized her friends Henry James and Bernard Berenson on behalf of *The Book of the Homeless* and contributions came in from William Dean Howells, John Galsworthy, George Santayana, Igor Stravinsky, William Butler Yeats, Max Beerbohm, Claude Monet, Pierre-Auguste Rénoir, Auguste Rodin, and John Singer Sargent. The beauty of the final book almost entirely overcame her frustrations over production and publication delays.

3

෪

HONORS AND LOSSES: 1916

THE YEAR 1916 DID NOT BEGIN AUSPICIOUSLY FOR EDITH WHARTON'S WAR
work. In late December of 1915, the French Ministry of Public Education
requisitioned the building where her sewing workroom was located,
displacing its ninety women. Wharton closed the workroom for a length-
ened Christmas vacation and took her fight to the French bureaucracy.
She spent the week between Christmas and New Year's Day in the offices
of the ministry, trying first to arrange a delay and then to secure a new
building. Finally the government, "realizing they have made a 'gaffe,'
have ordered me an 'amende honourable' by hiring & putting at my
disposal 'pour la durée de la guerre' a whole floor in a big building of the
Boulevard St. Germain, in wh[ich] I hope to be installed at the end of
next week."[1] Relieved but exhausted, Wharton spent New Year's Day at
the Children of Flanders refugee center in St Ouen and at the Bureau de
la Santé.[2]

Other delayed projects were finally moving forward. When Charles
Scribner saw the proof pages of *The Book of the Homeless* during the first
week of January 1916, he proclaimed it "a very fine example of bookmak-
ing." Yet even on the publication day, January 22, 1916, he had only 500
copies to sell. A month into the new year he could make some early
predictions about sales, and they were heartening: "We have been hand-
icapped by not having the copies to supply but all our wants are now met
in that respect. The book is well worth the money and in New York and
where the work can be made well known the sale will be very satisfactory.
It is difficult however to excite interest in other centres except by personal
effort; circulars and even newspaper support seem to count for so little.

Mrs. Cadwalader Jones's work in New York has been worth all the newspapers put together."[3]

Indeed, Minnie Jones, who had performed in so many capacities on behalf of The Book of the Homeless project, now turned herself into a very effective one-woman publicity department. The enterprising Minnie moved the location of the auction to the American Art Galleries at 6 West 23rd Street and arranged for a preview reading from the works two days before the sale to spark interest.

Under the supervision of professional auctioneer Thomas E. Kirby, the sale began promptly at three o'clock on the afternoon of January 25. Scribner reported on the event: "I attended with my daughter and at first was quite alarmed, as the number present was not large and I feared a failure. But the right people were there; the bidding was brisk and animated; there was abundant appreciation of the pictures and articles and throughout it all an evident intention to support your work, which was really inspiring."[4] Scribner was himself inspired enough to pay $575 for the autograph manuscript from General Joffre, $400 for a Monet landscape, and another $100 for a pen-and-ink drawing of a Gibson Girl.[5]

Another big winner was the autographed and annotated typescript (the promised "simulacrum") of Henry James's "The Long Wards," whose price of $500 made Wharton especially happy. When she learned to her amazement that the copy of her own little poem had brought $350, she wrote to Minnie Jones in playful astonishment, "As for the kind gentleman who gave that 'faramineux' price for my doggerel, wouldn't he like to marry me and have me with it? Who on earth is he? I'm willing, anyhow!"[6]

The idea that a match might be made for her reappears in her private correspondence. When Wharton learned some months later that a young woman who worked in the hostels' clothing depot was engaged to be married, she again flirted—this time in a letter to Lizzie Cameron in Paris—with the possibility of finding someone for herself: "Your news about Mlle Baïy thrills me more than my Legion of Honour can possibly thrill you!! What a tribute to woman's inexhaustible charm. And why won't you take me on at the shop, & see if you can't find a match for me next? It really rouses dormant hopes!—"[7]

The sponsoring New York committee pronounced the auction of The Book of the Homeless manuscripts and drawings a great success. After deducting expenses (the auctioneer's services and those of his assistant were donated), the committee reported that "$6,829.57 was sent out to

France."[8] In March of 1916 a vacationing Wharton alerted Royall Tyler, acting as treasurer of the Children of Flanders Rescue Committee and also an officer of the American Hostels, that the sum of "41,204.90 fcs [is] to be *equally divided* between Hostels and Flanders. . . . The big sum is the result of the sale of the mss. and belongs of course equally to the two charities."[9]

By late April Scribner could report that 2,000 copies of the $5 edition, half of the $25 edition, and all of the $50 edition had been sold, and that these sales came to nearly $9,000. He lamented the high cost of producing the book, "which has been very great amounting to $7,500. Our [Scribner's] own expenses of various kinds are estimated at less than $1000."[10] The following week he sent her an advance (against sales) for 5,950 francs, the equivalent of $1,000 at the current exchange rate. Wharton was quite happy about the $7,000 that Minnie's auction of the drawings and manuscripts from *The Book of the Homeless* brought in, but as she quite accurately noted, "It was certainly a bad blow to have the book so long delayed."[11]

೭ೞ

At the beginning of 1916 Wharton's secretarial arrangements were unsatisfactory and would remain so for several weeks. Anna Bahlmann, recuperating from recent surgery, had left things in a state of confusion. Wharton had trouble finding even the addresses of the chairmen of her American committees. Her new secretary, Dolly Herbert, was hardly an improvement. "Miss Herbert is a broken reed as a secretary," Wharton told Minnie. "She is ill half the time, & has not yet learned stenography, so I am not much better off, except that she must not get things so inextricably muddled. It seems impossible to find anyone here, except Elisina, who is efficient, & I can't load her with my whole job besides her own!"[12]

Throughout January Wharton continued to have trouble with her new secretary: "The wretched Herbert is still ill, and I am 'aux abois' [in a fix, on my last legs]. Today I am setting out on the hopeless hunt for a new secretary." She offered the job to Theodora Bosanquet, Henry James's secretary, listing as three difficult conditions the hardships of life in wartime Paris, the necessity to speak and write French easily, "and having to do queer odds & ends of things for me—a muddle of charity, shopping & literature."[13] When Bosanquet turned down the job to stay with the ill James, Wharton understood completely.

By the end of the first week of January, an exasperated Wharton cried out, "The fact is, I am on the brink of a complete break-down. My rest at Costebelle was shattered by the terrible shock about Henry, & I came back here to a 'surcroît de besogne' [excess of work] & a mountain of letters wh[ich] I have not been able to deal with."[14]

Among the distracting duties was the arranging of the donors list of those responding to her recent appeal in the *New York Times*. The whole process was confusing: Some donors (such as Olivia Cutting, who sent Wharton 5,000 francs) preferred to give anonymously, and Wharton was always careful to see that their wishes were followed. At the other end of the scale were donors who wanted their gifts to be recognized publicly, sometimes over and over again. When a Miss Robinson Smith and the War Relief Committee in New York gave a convoy of motor ambulances equipped with radiographic equipment, Wharton was at pains to satisfy their voracious appetite for recognition. She took the ambassador to see the convoy, made sure Emile Berr of the *Figaro* was on hand, and sent a copy of Berr's article to Minnie, hoping that the article would satisfy Miss Smith and her committee. Wharton complained that this type of bother was symptomatic of Americans' inattention to the war: "Then the demand of Miss Robinson Smith for official recognition by the War Office gave me a good deal of trouble & involved great fatigue. People in America don't seem to understand that at the most critical period of a terrible war it is hard to get the attention of the War Office for any matter outside the real business of the nation."[15]

Wharton's next fund-raising idea was, predictably, an elaborate one. Sergei Dhiagilev, the Ballet Russe impresario, was a friend of the Blanches and Alice Garrett. Through these connections, Wharton was able to secure his promise that the Russian ballet would perform a benefit matinee at New York's Metropolitan Opera House with the receipts split equally between a Russian war charity and her charities. The big hitch was securing the approval of Otto Kahn, chairman of the board of the Metropolitan Opera, whose patronage extended to the ballet company. Wharton's solution was to enlist some of New York's best society ladies: "The thing, of course, is for some of the opera ladies who had hitherto cold-shouldered Mr. Kahn to 'jolly' him enough to obtain his consent to this benefit, and then make it as fashionable as possible."[16]

In addition to stage-directing social relations in New York, Wharton wrote to Elsie de Wolfe, the actress turned interior decorator, and asked Minnie to see her as well. De Wolfe's long lesbian liaison with Elizabeth

Marbury, manager of theater rights, made the approach a ticklish one for the disapproving sisters-in-law.

Paris was generally tolerant of American lesbian couples. For example, the openly lesbian Natalie Clifford Barney, of whom Wharton disapproved, entertained Bernard Berenson and Walter Berry at her temple to love in the garden of her house on the rue Jacob. (Ernest Samuels, Berenson's biographer, argues that the middle-aged art connoisseur fell in love with Barney.) Berry and Berenson also regularly visited Marbury and de Wolfe at their home, the Villa Trianon in Versailles.

The idea of a benefit performance by the Russian ballet was tossed back and forth for several weeks. In mid-April Wharton wrote to Minnie, "I have just received your cable asking me to send you an 'appeal' to be read at the Russian ballet on the 29th. This brings me the good news that Mr. Kahn has yielded, in spite of a very 'snippy' and patronizing note I got from Elsie de Wolfe a few weeks ago. Those two women [de Wolfe and Marbury] are really not fit to traffic with, and I always feel degraded when I go against my prejudices and treat them as if they were."[17]

Kahn made it clear that the benefit's promoters would have to guarantee the Metropolitan's directors $6,000 before the performance could go forward.[18] The New York committee was nervous about the sum, but Minnie argued that Nijinsky could pull in an audience to cover it.[19] Finally, however, plans for the benefit matinee performance fell through.[20] In June Minnie would suffer a breakdown, which Wharton blamed on stress caused by the preparations for the benefit.[21]

Even small artistic projects caused problems. The photographs requested by Minnie of refugees in small groups and in appealing individual shots to boost the contributions were a nuisance for Wharton. While she clearly knew that snapshots of refugee children would capture the hearts (and dollars) of donors, the photographs produced by American and by French photographers were not of the right groups. Wharton had to balance Minnie's requests for poignant photographs of refugees (which she dutifully pursued at the French Office of Illustrations) with the demands of a large order from hospitals for her *ouvroir*. Just then her sewing women were making 1,500 pillow cases for the clearing house. Wharton was too overworked herself to arrange the groups and position the photographer, though she understood the visual rhetoric and knew what would be effective.

Wharton was learning to say no in other matters as well. After so many months of appealing for work for her seamstresses, she began to see that some small orders were not worth the effort. Now that the *ouvroir* had been operating for a year and a half, she felt able to refuse sewing orders for $20 or less. Larger orders would be welcomed and filled quickly, but the details of small orders and daily supervision were becoming a strain: "I feel I shall have to go away in February for a week or two, and this will relieve me of one fussy thing, & she [the workshop manager] can do it perfectly."[22]

❧

Wharton was soon back in the pages of the *New York Times*, thanking generous readers whose contributions allowed her and her workers to "care for the great throng of homeless people and little children whom the war has cast here among strangers. It is thanks to American generosity that the 'American Hostels' have been able to keep their doors open for over a year, and the 'Children of Flanders' to live in health and comfort for nearly ten months; but the war goes on, and so must our war charities." Therefore, she renewed her appeal for funds for the charities, asking "your readers to help us by buying 'The Book of the Homeless' which will not only give them a full account of the charities they are aiding, but will also show how richly the world of art and letters, both in Europe and America, has poured out its gifts to further our work."[23]

In personal letters to Lapsley and other close friends at this time, Wharton adopted the self-dramatizing voice of one who could only write "[i]n defiance of the Stern Daughter of the Voice of God, who is waiting to dictate business letters to me." She was disappointed that Lapsley had scratched a planned trip to see her: "I do so yearn for my friends these days—& now, especially, the longing to be with one of our little Qu'acre group is acute," acute because the declining health of Henry James reduced the number of her "inner circle."

Though she tried not to meddle in Minnie's decisions, Wharton did object to her putting Clement March, whom she had known in Lenox, Massachusetts,[24] on the New York committee for the Hostels. She told Minnie that March was "very eccentric and dangerous in his way of speaking of people, and quite unscrupulous in his statements." Two months earlier March had written Wharton a letter denouncing a prominent New Yorker as a German spy. As a further proof of March's instability: "He and Teddy [her former husband] are bosom friends now, and they have the two most poisonous tongues I know."[25] To show March's wide mood swings, the same day she posted her objection to his sitting on the New York committee to Minnie, Wharton received a contribution of 4,000 francs from him, with a note asking what she had done about the spy. Wharton told him to take his charges to the French embassy in Washington if he had proof, but only if he had proof.

Making deliberate executive decisions, she decided to take the Baltimore committee out of the hands of the firm of professional fund raisers: "I would rather have no committee in Baltimore than one so inert that it may do us harm if any enquiries are addressed to it."[26] And she showed her exasperation with people in the United States who wanted war souvenirs and photographs of refugee children: "Mrs. Poindexter has just asked if White [Wharton's butler] has brought her a Prussian helmet! I can't understand how anyone living here can fail to realize how over-worked everyone is. It is SUCH letters that kill! Do excuse the cross outburst, but while I am struggling against a flood of letters, notes like that seem the last straw."[27]

Others in Paris were also tiring under the strain of philanthropic work. "I no longer have any justification at the Foyer and don't like it there," Gide complained. "For more than a year charity kept it alive and throbbing; now it is becoming a philanthropic undertaking in which I have neither intellectual or emotional interest."[28] Yet there was a strong pull to remain in harness despite "striving to free myself from the Foyer, to cease being interested in it."[29]

There were always problems with the accounting in Wharton's war charities. Wharton was dealing with two bankers: the Equitable Trust Company in New York and the Paris office of Munroe and Company. She wanted the banks to divide the contributions between those intended for the American Hostels and those destined for the Children of Flanders.[30] When the money from *The Book of the Homeless* auction, for instance, was passed along to charities' treasurer Royall Tyler, Wharton commented rather uncharitably, "My poor sister-in-law does muddle things. The 41,204.90 fcs deposited by her with 'se décompose ainsi': 41,028.80 fcs to be EQUALLY DIVIDED between Hostels and Flanders. 176.10 fcs donation to Children of Flanders."[31] The accounting procedures for the relief agencies were complex, as Lizzie Cameron would soon learn when she became Wharton's secretary in Paris. All checks for the hostels and Children of Flanders went to Royall Tyler. Checks for the *ouvroir* and for unspecified charities, however, were to be deposited in a bank account by Lizzie. Wharton instructed her in the complicated financial proce-dures: "We keep all the money in one account, but the Tylers like to know how much of the sum in hand was actually destined for the housing fund, & it would be better to correct this little mistake."[32]

While Minnie may have been muddled frequently, she was also too good-hearted for Wharton to remain angry with her for long. She had thoughtfully sent personal New Year's cards to every one of the Paris workers.[33] By late January Wharton adopted a sensibly direct approach of numbering the points in the business portions of her letters to Minnie, in the fashion of memoranda. She asked Minnie to follow her example and put their letters on a businesslike footing: "Your letters are so full of detail that I am always afraid, in the mad haste of my life here, that I may overlook some of your questions. Would you mind, in future, writing on a separate sheet of paper all the business questions and numbering them as I have done?"[34] Even so, Wharton would later complain to Lizzie Cameron, "Minnie's letters are appalling. She does splendid work but she does not spare me a thought."[35]

❧

Early in February Wharton went to "the front with Etienne de Beaumont on Tuesday for two days' rest, was in two bad motor accidents, one in my motor & a second in his, & crawled home yesterday by train! I am now trying Paris as a rest-cure." She concluded sarcastically, "Isn't it pleasant to be an American citizen???"[36]

She immediately wrote a letter to the *New York Times* giving an update of the American Hostels, which were caring for 3,000 refugees and had found employment for 4,000 others. To bolster her appeal for funds, she cited specific incidents: a family of ten living in a room ten feet square; a formerly well-to-do family of five forced to pay $10 a month for the single room where they sleep, cook, and bathe; a woman who had just given birth forced to sleep on two chairs in the absence of an available bed. The immediate need was to rent and fit up a fifty-five room house for the refugees. "Those we are trying to rescue are not only in the deepest misery themselves, but are a source of disease and demoralization to others; and the one way to lift them back to health and decency is to give them lodgings fit to live in." Wharton knew that suffering extended to the those who had never before known poverty, too. She had, after all, projected herself empathetically into the character of Lily Bart and other heroines whose stylish clothing often hid emotional and physical suffering. Throughout these appeals Wharton was especially concerned with refugees "of the better class, whose less apparent misery is so often more cruel and more difficult to relieve."[37]

As the war wore on Wharton turned increasingly to her contacts in the American embassy and the French government to find help with difficult individual cases. Twice in February, for example, she asked the American diplomat John Garrett to inquire of his counterpart at the American embassy in Berlin about displaced persons. (Garrett had been an official observer of the prisoner-of-war camps in Germany, so his contacts with German officials were extensive.) The first case was that of Odette Lesne in the occupied north of France. Knowing the number of personal appeals the embassy must receive, Wharton added for emphasis that if the reunion could take place, "I believe the child's mother will be saved from going blind."[38] Later in the month she wrote on behalf of a Mademoiselle Depreaux, an accountant at her *ouvroir*, whose fiancé had been taken prisoner during the German attack on Frise on January 28.[39]

In addition, she asked Garrett to arrange a meeting with Etienne Hevelaque, Inspecteur Général de l'Instruction Publique, who had been charged with reorganizing the press office at rue François Ier and wanted advice on the various American journalists in Paris. "At any rate," she suggested, "it might be a good thing to call him up when you can & ask him to come see you at the Chancery." Since Garrett worked at the Chancery of the American ambassador, it is clear that she was involving herself in official French propaganda.[40]

The Garretts were contributors to her charities as well, having made a donation of 5,000 francs to the housing fund for the American Hostels for Refugees.[41] On a more personal matter, Wharton asked John Garrett to witness a codicil to her will.[42]

She told Lizzie Cameron that one of their donated Red Cross motor convoys had been cited for good work in the orders of the day. The money to fund it had come from the Vacation War Relief, which led her comment hopefully: "So things are decidedly worthwhile, aren't they?"[43]

To Gaillard Lapsley, Wharton had written in January that the Henry James they revered and loved was already a physical shell when she had visited him the previous autumn:

> Certainly, we 'had him first', didn't we, in the sense of having the finest, rarest & fullest of him whenever he was with us? And so, now, after suffering dreadfully at the thought of being so far away, & of not even having had a real goodbye from him before leaving England, I have reached a mood of acceptance, & quite realize the uselessness of going to England, even if I were allowed to see him—I

don't suppose he suffers as much as one's imagination suffers for him; & I feel that the poor dear being who is carried every day to the drawing-room window to look at the boats on the river is just a shadowy substitute he has left with us for a little while—to take in kind enquirers!

Our Henry was gone when I was in London in October.[44]

Through November and December Wharton corresponded with Theodora Bosanquet, Henry James's secretary, who gave her reports on the state of James's declining health on an almost daily basis. When the end came on February 28, 1916, Bosanquet telegraphed Wharton immediately. Wharton expressed relief that the ordeal was over and the end came quietly for "one of the wisest & noblest men that ever lived."[45] Responding to Alice Garrett's message of sympathy, Wharton wrote:

Thank you so much for your little word. Yes, the "great good thing" of my life is gone, & I feel alone as never before.

But there was never an instant's shadow on our friendship, never any disillusionment or diminishing (how *could* there be, with such riches as his?), & so I've got it *all* to live on & think over & treasure.

No, I never believed or hoped that he would "recover", & I am glad he is dead. He had a short moment of consciousness two or three weeks ago, & sent me a message I may have told you—& that brings him so close that I feel his loss infinitely less than if he had died earlier. But I knew that no real recovery was possible, & dreaded above everything a prolonged state of half-life.[46]

In the middle of March, Wharton sought refuge at the Costebelle Hôtel in Hyères, leaving the day-to-day operation of the hostels in the capable hands of Elisina and Royall Tyler and the secretarial duties to Lizzie Cameron. She wrote Lizzie a postcard with a view of the open market in Toulon: "Here I am, in peace & warmth & silence." She looked forward to a few days in the open air, saying on another note sent the same day: "My thanks for giving me this blessed holiday."[47] As she had the previous autumn, she asked Lizzie to open all of her mail in Paris and make a résumé of each of the personal letters and the important business letters. She did not feel up to reading the long letters that even her most generous patrons sent. (Lewis Ledyard had burdened her with an eight-page letter the previous week.) The weather continued cloudy but warm. She noted, "I am just beginning to realize how dead tired I am, nerves & head & all, & I am trembling at the vision of the deluge of letters that will descend on me in a day or two."[48]

Two days later she could report from "the blessed quietness of this place . . . [m]eanwhile I've started a novel, & am as happy as a Queen!" The novel, called *Summer*, was to be a companion piece to *Ethan Frome*. Though Wharton promised to get to work on the report of her charities the following week, she was even then making plans to travel down to the Berensons' home in three weeks and spend a couple of weeks with them.[49] She was pleased with donations to the recently announced housing fund, but she could not believe that the appeal had already appeared in the American papers. As she was doing with Minnie, Wharton soon began enumerating the points in her letters to Lizzie. Though the weather was discouraging, she could say that the military communiqués were not.

To Elisina, her chief administrator in Paris, she couched her gratitude in Jamesian hyperbole: "It is wonderfully kind of you to undertake to carry all this great load for me, but I feel now that my letter was a mere outcry of fatigue, and that I could never consent to leave such a burden on your shoulders unless we find, in time, the Not Impossible She to share it with you. No doubt when I have pulled myself together and got my novel fairly started, I shall be able to keep it going and still do a little work for the oeuvres—alas, I have for so long done only a little that I don't know how I could reduce the fraction further."[50]

⁂

While in the south of France, Wharton was awarded the French Legion of Honor. The citation read:

> Article 1 —Madame Wharton, an American citizen and woman of letters, has been nominated as a Knight of the National Order of the Legion of Honor. (Since the beginning of the war she has won broad sympathy for the French cause through her speech, her articles and other publications; and she has been widely recognized for her charities and her devotion to humanitarian relief.)[51]

One of the first to contact her with congratulations was Lizzie, to whom Wharton replied: "Thank you for your 'félicitations' on my Legion of

Honour. I am very glad to have it, but I don't think my coyness will suffer, for women never wear it do they? I never saw a woman with a red ribbon, did you? Hereafter I shall be on the lookout."[52]

Wharton promised that she would not hide her red ribbon, as the Legion of Honor decoration was familiarly referred to, under a bushel. She joked that if the decoration the notoriously heavy Elizabeth Marbury received (for seeing that plays by French playwrights were produced in London and New York) was proportionately a "broad ribbon," then on Wharton it would be visible only under a microscope.[53]

Acknowledgments and congratulations on the Legion of Honor pleased her. Egerton Winthrop cabled, "Congratulations with all my heart."[54] The fifty-eight workers at the *Ouvroir de Madame Wharton* in Paris signed a special proclamation expressing their pride in their patroness. Max and Beatrix Farrand sent her a fruitcake to celebrate the honor. Wharton answered André Gide's letter by saying that she was proud because from now until the end of the war the ribbon would be given only to combatants.[55]

Years later when Wharton and Nicky Mariano, Berenson's assistant, were in Rome together, Mariano borrowed Wharton's coat on a chilly day to attend the autumn opening session of the Italian Academy. She was astonished at the commotion that surrounded her entrance in the assembly hall of the Farnesina and the speed with which she was ushered to a front-row seat. Only later did she realize that everyone in the concert hall recognized the small red ribbon attached to the lapel of Wharton's coat as the highest French decoration.[56]

૨⋅

From her retreat in the south of France, Wharton instructed Lizzie Cameron in the daily operations of the charities: Upon receiving a donation, a "menu" was attached to the envelope immediately listing the amount, the address of the donor, and whether an acknowledgment had been sent. Wharton was pleased to add, "Money is coming in very satisfactorily now." And she seemed acclimated: "It rains here every day, but I've grown used to it!"[57]

Soon, however, the rain had stopped and the countryside was abloom with flowers. Wharton thanked Lizzie for her telegram. "How nice of you to take such an interest in a base deserter like me!" While her plans were still to meet the Berensons at Ventimiglia on the fifteenth and spend ten days with them,[58] twin blows soon would make the trip less appealing.

On April 6 her old friend Egerton Winthrop died at the age of seventy-seven, leaving her "perfectly heart-broken." She wrote Lizzie, "I had a cable from him the day before yesterday, & yesterday his son cabled me that he was dead!" It was, as she said, "a ghastly day." The receipt of the Legion of Honor was especially poignant because it was so close to the deaths of two of her greatest friends—James and Winthrop. Next to the loss of Henry James, that of Winthrop hit her hardest. "No one will ever know what a friend Egerton Winthrop was to me for 30 years." She confessed, "No loss could leave me so utterly alone."[59] To Minnie she wrote that Winthrop "was the best and the tenderest friend I ever had, and the one to whom I gave the least in exchange for all he gave me." She was pleased, however, that she had told him about the award before his death. She had hesitated for three days, and then cabled him, receiving a warm reply. "I am very glad to have received the Legion of Honour because it IS an honour now, and especially so as the gov't is not supposed to give any until after the war to civilian strangers; but it has brought me already about 150 letters, to be answered without a secretary."[60]

Walter Berry is generally credited with helping to form Wharton's mind. More attention, however, should be paid to the rigors Egerton Winthrop put her through. In A Backward Glance she noted that Winthrop shaped her reading habits:

> When we were alone I saw only the lover of books and pictures, the accomplished linguist and eager reader, whose ever-youthful curi-osities first taught my mind to analyze and my eyes to see. It was too late for me to acquire the mental discipline I had missed in the schoolroom, but my new friend directed and systemized my reading, and filled some of the worst gaps in my education. Through him I first came to know the great French novelists and the French historians and literary critics of the day; but his chief gift was to introduce me to the wonder-world of nineteenth century science. He it was who gave me Wallace's 'Darwin and Darwinism', and 'The Origin of Species', and made known to me Huxley, Herbert Spencer, Romanes, Haeckel, Westermarck, and the various popular expo-nents of the great evolutionary movement.

Winthrop, a descendent of John Winthrop, governor of the Massa-chusetts Bay Colony, was a prominent New Yorker, serving on several bank boards.[61] Wharton maintained that many thought him dry and misunderstood the man: "He was one of the rare people who seemed to live all for the world, & who really lived only for the high standards of duty and friendship."[62] Here are the suggestions that Winthrop had given Wharton many years earlier on reading a book about Darwinism:

Darwinism, etc. Suggestions

Read slowly, marking important parts in the margins with pencil. Re-read marked parts after finishing a chapter, and *all* back marked parts before beginning a new chapter.

If a passage is not understood after two readings, mark an X in the margin, and wait till book is finished before trying again.

Try to think over, at night, what has been read that day.

Learn *each definition* of as many scientific words & terms as possible and write them in the book, as indicated. Most people's idea of what a word means is "à peu près"!

Also write in it the most important things that strike you. When the book is half full you wouldn't change it for the best book written!

Learn a few definitions, like that of evolution for instance "by heart,"—while your hair is being done!

If you haven't a good dictionary at your elbow, let me know and I'll send you one.

In the book, put definitions of words on one page and terms and quotations on the other.

Don't forget that this sort of thing will make you able to do everything better—from grasping the absolute to playing with— [Gherardesea]![63]

Wharton's response to the news of Winthrop's death was to invite Lizzie Cameron to join her for the Italian sojourn. "I haven't the courage to go alone, for my visit must be a short one, but if you'll come and join me about the 19th at Beauvallon or Mentone, we might pop over the frontier & spend a week at I Tatti."[64] As they contemplated this joint trip, Wharton's old tutor and secretary Anna Bahlmann died, and Wharton, devastated, lost her appetite for travel. On receiving her note of sympathy, she told Lizzie, "I am completely crushed by this last blow. It is an unhoped-for blessing that my poor little Anna should have died so quickly & painlessly, & I can't regret her death, but—I do so grieve for her having been away from me." And she concluded her letter, "I am coming back on Tuesday next. I've no heart for anything. Egerton's loss is irreparable."[65] To complete her grief, she had recently learned that her friend Robert Minturn was dying of a brain hemorrhage.[66]

Her moments of grief were shared with literary matters. When Wharton was not writing herself, she was thinking about the effects of the war as a subject for the coming generation of novelists. She wrote to Robert Grant, "Thank you so much, also, cher confrère, for what you say of 'Coming Home'. One wonders what the novelists will do, in the next years, with all the super- abundance of incredible romance that is coming out of this world upheaval? After the first cheap harvest, some great slow fruit will no doubt ripen."[67]

The steady drudgery and personal losses, however, had taken their toll on her health. By the end of the second week of April she was at the Golf Hôtel, Beauvallon sur Mer, in the south of France ("This place is delicious—all forest and sand and the bluest of bays, with St. Tropez just opposite"), where she had been sent by her doctor to rest. Wharton was still planning an "appeal" for the annual report, much as an advertising account executive might mount the fall advertising campaign. She wrote Elisina Tyler that the report she was writing was exactly "the contrary of what I approve in that line, but I always get money by the 'tremolo' note, so I try to dwell on it as much as possible." She had learned that "all our American 'clientele' clamours for 'cases' and so I thought I ought to serve up some." And with an editor's eye for layout and saving space, she advised, "As we give the total of expenses on the first page I don't think there is much use in publishing details at the end of the report; no one ever reads them."[68]

She wrote a note to Lizzie Cameron from the hotel, insisting that Lizzie's refusal to take a break from administering the charities in Paris and to travel to Italy with her was a simple matter of obstinacy. She scolded Lizzie with diplomatic affection: "I feel all the more cross with you because it would have been such a good pretext for me to prolong my sinful loafing, & because I know what my 'courrier' must have contributed to your fatigue!" Saying that Cameron's own "stern example calls me back to duty," she instructed her, "Don't tell *anyone* please (of course Elisina knows & the servants & my ouvroir) or I shall be submerged as soon as I get there." Wharton planned to go to Italy alone and return to Paris sometime in May. She asked Lizzie to join her for the return trip and motor back with her: "You must take a little holiday at Easter—, & I don't see why not this one." In the final paragraph she argues, "Wire me anyhow when you get this, & don't think me a bore with my many invitations. I only feel that I should like to have a little of my idleness with you. You know even Elisina took three weeks in February!"[69]

Lizzie remained in Paris, but had an azalea waiting for her grateful boss who was still "abrutie" (driven silly) on her return: "What a joy, & how it consoles me for the flowers I have had to turn my back on."[70] Now it was Lizzie's turn to go off, and off she went to Chamonix.

Wharton was away from Paris for six days in early June. On her return she found fifty-three letters and thus she could say with all sincerity to Lizzie, "You did help me, no end, with the letters, for your reading them enabled Dolly Herbert to make me a typed summary of each one, & that took half the horror from the perusal." More than anything she could not stand the strain of answering the avalanche of correspondence. She was already planning her escape: "I am going to fly to Fontainebleau for the summer before long, for I can't stand it."[71] Wharton's schedule for the early summer was to visit Arromanches for three days and then go on to visit her friend Madame de Béarn at her chateau at Fleury on July 1 before going on to Fontainebleau on July 15.[72] The Comtesse de Béarn had donated the building at 63 avenue des Champs-Elysées, which became the headquarters of the American Hostels.

In the meantime, she again called on John Garrett to exercise his diplomatic charms, this time to get $100 to a relative of her housekeeper, Gross, in the German-controlled city of Mulhouse. Wharton had reason to be grateful to the Garrett family—she had just received 9,000 francs from the Baltimore chapter of her charities, a chapter now headed by Garrett's mother.[73]

But a sudden change in Wharton's health left travel plans unsettled. She wrote to Lizzie Cameron at the end of the first week of July that the doctor had told her that her heart was "off the track" and had ordered her to go to the mountains. She asked Lizzie about accommodations in Chamonix, where Lizzie was staying. And since Wharton never traveled alone, there was the usual list of special needs. One of her servants needed to be lodged in a nearby pension and, since the maid was very anemic, one with good food. Wharton herself required a bedroom with a bath and a room for her personal maid as close by as possible. At this point she was expecting to leave on July 13 without her automobile, unless Lizzie recommended bringing it, "as walking is what I most need, & sitting out of doors."[74]

However, as she was planning this rest in the mountains, disaster struck again; this time her housemaid suffered a hemorrhage. "I couldn't in any case have gone far off now, until her case has been dealt with," Wharton explained to Lizzie, "even if I had been up to the journey." As to her own health, Wharton learned that she was suffering from a bad case of anemia and an irregular heartbeat. With the household complications and her own weakened condition, she had to abandon her plans for Chamonix and settle for a brief visit with Madame de Béarn in Fleury and then go on to recuperate at the Hôtel Savoy in Fontainebleau. In spite of the change of plans, she thought that she would see Lizzie on her way through Paris.[75]

She missed Lizzie then, however, because, loving quiet as she did, Wharton "had parcelled out every minute in order to escape on Friday afternoon & not spend two nights in Town.— The good air & the quiet here [Fontainebleau] are doing me so much good that I try to resist the temptation of lingering in Paris." She tried to entice Lizzie to come out to Fontainebleau, where the nights were cool even after hot days.[76] Her offer of a fortnight's rest in the forest was made without the request that Lizzie return to administrative work with the charities: "But I have several active understudies now, & really don't need help."[77] Even when Lizzie offered to return to the charities in early August, Wharton told her, "Please loaf in Paris till Sept. 1st, for I think that everything is working well till then. After that we shall welcome you back with open arms."[78]

The two women had always worked very well together. They shared the same social class, unhappy marital histories, and many friends, including Henry James, Bernard Berenson, and Henry Adams. When Lizzie needed a new maid, Wharton recommended an excellent woman who had been released from one of the hostels' *Maisons de Repos* because of personality differences with the local administrator.[79] Later, when Lizzie contemplated replacing her furs, Wharton told Lizzie about a Mlle Valentine, who supplied Wharton's furs at a very reasonable cost.[80]

Near the end of July, Wharton reported to John Garrett's mother on the new convalescent homes for women and children who needed special care:

> To receive ill women and children from the invaded provinces we
> have hired a large well-built house in a small park, splendidly
> situated at Groslay, near Montmorency. There is a large productive

kitchen garden, and the house, which faces full south, is large enough to contain seventy patients. It is in such good order that the expense of fitting it up will be very slight and we hope to have it running by the middle of August. A tuberculosis specialist will visit it once a week, his assistant will come every other day and there will be a complete staff of trained nurses.

In addition to this house we have hired a large villa directly on the sea at Arromanches, in Normandy, where we propose to send about twenty children with tuberculosis of the bone or other complaints requiring sea-air. This will be an offshoot of the house at Groslay, and the two houses will be known as 'Maisons Américaines de Convalescence'.[81]

By the end of the month Wharton was telling Lizzie, "I have sent word to Elisina that you are ready to begin on Monday the 4th. She will communicate with you; but I fancy she means to ask you to go back to the shop [the clothing depot]." With her own chauffeur off on vacation, Wharton was especially conscious of the automobile news of her friends: Both the Bourgets and Matilda Gay had had recent motor accidents.[82]

She wrote to Minnie the last week of August, "I should like to go home for a while, but I am afraid the trip would tire me too much, and besides it would interrupt my writing, and I should regret that. By the way, will you undertake to revise the proof of a long short story (about the length of Ethan Frome) which I hope to have finished some time in November. I do not yet know in what magazine it will appear, but of course I will tell you in time. It would be a great kindness if you would do this for me, and save the endless delay caused by sending proofs backward and forward at the present time."[83] The story was to turn into the novella *Summer*, which with its New England setting and tale of seduction and incest Wharton was to term her "hot Ethan."

With her during the last week of August at the Hôtel Savoy in Fontainebleau was Judge Robert Grant from Boston. She was able to make arrangements for him to tour the front, though she asserted that with more advance notice she could have arranged for him "to go on a less tourist-like trip—in fact, I could have arranged to take you with me to the front." In the meantime, she had a favor to ask, as Grant was an officer of her Boston committee. She offered him a letter of introduction to a Lieutenant Pechkoff, who had lost an arm at Carency. Pechkoff would be touring the United States, and she wanted him to meet Grant and Roosevelt. The lieutenant's American lecture series would "rouse interest in the moral issues of the war." Simply put, "It would be good propaganda to do it."[84] In December she would write letters of introduction to Nicholas Murray Butler, president of Columbia University, and to Max Farrand at Yale on behalf of Jacques Copeau, who would tour the United States as a representative of the French government to lecture on French literature.[85]

On August 28 she wrote Lizzie Cameron, "I'm going back for good this afternoon." She had to forgo her trip to Salso with Madame de Béarn, where she was to have met the Berensons. Dashing back and forth to Paris had worn her out, so she decided to just stay in Paris.[86]

Her resolution to stay there was short-lived. The first week of September she was back at the Hôtel Savoy in Fontainebleau "nursing a beastly grippe."[87] She thanked John Garrett for sending the money through the American embassy in Berlin to a relative of Gross's in the Alsace and asked him once again to use his diplomatic channels to get news of little Odette Lesne.[88] Garrett responded that he had "annoyed everyone I saw in Germany who I thought might be able to help in the matter of Odette Lesne and I finally got the definite promise that as a special favor to me (I was being 'specially favored') they would let her go although there was no such thing as a 'prochain convoi', and absolutely no one, men or women or children, is now being allowed to leave the invaded districts. But promises are one thing and their fulfillment another and it would not do for you or the little girl's mother to place much hope in them."[89]

By mid-September Wharton was excusing tardy replies to letters on the grounds that "I am deep in my novel and have grown very lazy about letter-writing."[90] During Grant's recent visit, Wharton read him the opening chapters of *Summer*. She had drafted two-thirds of the book and hoped to finish it with another month of uninterrupted work. The writing "takes every drop of grey matter that isn't used for greasing the philanthropic machinery";[91] and she admitted, "It is such a relief to get away from refugees and hospitals."[92]

Two weeks later she told Gide that her novel was "not only started but close to being finished." She had completed six chapters and said that she was about to start down the mountain. "I have never written with such joy or, perhaps, it is more appropriate to say, with less anguish." Since Gide had once said that he wished he had had the opportunity to translate

Ethan Frome, she challenged him: "The new novel is set in the same location and is about the same length. What do you say?"[93] She would keep after Gide about the translation for the next several weeks, but nothing would come of it.

‏‎ 🙣

More than any other civilian or military disease, tuberculosis was the killer in France. Before the war, one death in ten was attributed to the disease. That proportion shot up with the close confinement of refugees in tenements and soldiers in damp, rat-infested trenches. Unless France could develop tuberculosis sanatoriums to treat the disease, Wharton reasoned that her other efforts would be wasted. She realized that tackling tuberculosis would mean a whole new fund drive, but, as she had told Minnie in March, "it seems to me to be a case where we ought to be able to get help from the Rockefeller Fund."[94] She had written to her former Lenox neighbor Ellen Barlow, a New Yorker who was slightly acquainted with John D. Rockefeller, Jr.[95] Mrs. Barlow passed along Wharton's two-page letter to Rockefeller and urged him to get the foundation involved.[96] While the Rockefeller Foundation was exploring the health situation in France, a number of prominent French and American citizens, including Wharton, founded a large new charity with official French sanction entitled *Tuberculeux de la Guerre.*

During a meeting on July 3 with the counselor of the War Relief Commission of the Rockefeller Foundation to explain the need for tuberculosis relief in France, Wharton emphasized the extent of the emergency and the need for large-scale appeals in America to raise funds. When the counselor wanted guarantees that the French government would continue the work after the war, she patiently pointed out that there was no way to bind future leaders and ministries.[97]

Although Wharton was unaware of the fact, there was unpleasantness connected with her petition to the Rockefeller Foundation for a large infusion of cash into the tuberculosis sanatoriums. During the summer the foundation commissioned Wallace Sabine, professor of physics and dean of science at Harvard University, then in France as an exchange professor at the Sorbonne, to evaluate the tuberculosis situation in France. Wharton's standing with the foundation was not helped when Sabine wired, "Would again urge against alliance with, taking advice of, or trusting in any way Mrs. Wharton's Committee. Mrs. Wharton has bitterly assailed and antagonized the government and the best of the medical profession. If follow her lead, will reduce to a very minimum the service of the Foundation."[98]

Not aware of the back-channel criticism of her relations with the French government, Wharton launched extensive American fund-raising campaigns for the *Tuberculeux de la Guerre*. She deviled Minnie with proposals about exhibiting and selling the German war proclamations and the German military medals that she had sent to America to raise money for her new pet cause. On her own, Minnie exhibited the German war posters and proclamations and a number of German medals at Bar Harbor, making 3,000 francs to aid the tuberculosis campaign.[99]

Wharton was impressed by the haul and suggested that Minnie have photographs made of both sides of the *Lusitania* medal,[100] which, since its suppression in Germany, had become very valuable.[101] One German proclamation taken from the walls of a house in Louvain by Walter Berry during his trip in November of 1914 read "This house is not to be burnt *without orders*." But Minnie said that American buyers were skeptical. "I will find out how I can get 'proof of authenticity' of the proclamations," thundered Wharton, "but as they are very hard to get they are certainly not forged yet! Several of those I sent you came direct from the source—but I can't give particulars."[102] She would later acknowledge only that the proclamations Minnie had been given to sell had come from the same source as those collected for Princeton University: "It is impossible to say where, as the whole thing has to be done privately."[103]

Other fund-raising projects for *Tuberculeux de la Guerre* were also under way. She asked Berenson, then planning a trip to the United States, to send her something for a benefit auction for the newly formed tuberculosis committee. Wharton herself had donated a lacquer screen and secured a Persian bowl from Royall Tyler. In addition, the auction committee had promises of a fine Rodin drawing, a Louis XIV clock, and several other splendid art objects. From Berenson she demanded only "*one* priceless object," but quickly specified, "priceless doesn't mean something you can't sell at any price. On the contrary."[104] When his trip to America was canceled, she did not know how to hide her joy that he would not be going. She thanked him for the £20 contributed to the art auction but added, "I thought you'd just tuck a Sienese masterpiece under your arm and bring it to Paris." In a summary of her activity she told him that her charities now had fourteen houses and that her *ouvroir* had so many orders that she had been forced to open another. Nevertheless, she foresaw that "the new Tuberculosis Sanatorium job is going to be the biggest of all."[105] To his offer of a manuscript, she responded that she did not expect the auction to attract bibliophiles, but she was not particular, "Any kind of pot or pan would do the job better—."[106]

ও৯

Soon personal disasters struck two of her most loyal workers. In August Lizzie Cameron learned that her daughter, Martha, whom she idolized, had contracted paratyphoid in Egypt, where her husband, Ronald Lindsay, was serving in an important English diplomatic post. For weeks Martha lay dangerously ill in a Cairo hospital. Dazed with worry, Lizzie gave up her job of organizing the flood of mail that Wharton received. She left Paris for Stepleton, the Lindsays' home in England, where she decided to wait for them. They finally arrived in mid-December after twenty-three days at sea. Through the bitterly cold winter, husband and mother nursed the failing Martha. The grim, sunless winter gave way to a tragic spring for Lizzie. Henry Adams, her close friend, died in his sleep on March 27. When Martha mercifully died on April 28, a distraught Lizzie accused the doctors of murder. Inconsolable, she stayed on at Stepleton.

The second tragedy also brought maternal grief. After Elisina had left her publisher-husband Grant Richards for Royall Tyler in 1910, Richards made custody of their children impossible for Elisina and visiting rights difficult. When, in a vengeful mood, Richards blocked her attempts to visit their son Gerard at Eton and even threatened to withdraw the boy from school for economy's sake, Elisina's devoted friend Mildred Bliss quietly paid the boy's school fees through a lawyer in London.

In early September Elisina was concluding two weeks of rest at a château in Genay, a village two hours south of Paris. Meanwhile, fifteen-year-old Gerard Richards had joined friends at the beach in Cornwall for a school vacation. On a Sunday afternoon, as the boys were playing among the dunes and tunnels on the beach, a wall of sand collapsed, trapping Gerard and smothering him before he could be rescued. News of the tragic accident reverberated within Wharton's world. Eric MacLagan telegraphed Mildred Bliss, asking her to break the news (already appearing in the English newspapers) to Elisina. On Monday Royall wired Mildred Bliss, who had put her car at the disposal of the Tylers, that they would arrive in Paris that evening. In the meantime, using his considerable powers as the *chargé d'affaires* of the American ambassador's office, Robert Bliss cleared away all bureaucratic and security obstacles to Elisina's immediate departure for England.[107]

Wharton in Fontainebleau learned of the accident almost immediately and in a postscript to Minnie was sympathetic: "Elisina Tyler's eldest boy—Gerald [sic] Richards—whom she adored, has just been killed by a stupid accident, the falling-in of a tunnel of sand in which he was playing on the beach in Cornwall. It will go very hard with her, for he was a dear boy, so wise and so intelligent. The poor thing has just wired me the news, and is trying to get to England; but it is doubtful if the boats are going."[108]

Crossing the Channel was nothing compared to the difficulties Elisina would encounter with her former husband. After almost a week of making the funeral arrangements and sparring with Grant Richards, Elisina reported to Mildred Bliss: "I have spent 3 agonizing days of storms and uncertainties. Now at last I can tell you—and tell you first—that I have seen Gioia and Charlie [her other children by Richards] this morning, and that Wainwright [the London lawyer who paid the children's school fees with Bliss's money] has managed to wrench a promise from G. R. that I may see the children at regular intervals in the future. Some good has come out of this great sorrow."[109]

Wharton's mind was going forward with her plans for a cure at Salso. She told Berenson: "I haven't given up my rooms at Salso yet . . . on the chance that poor Elisina may have a reaction, and feel she can't go to the country and contemplate her woe. But the poor thing is so tired that this is only the faintest ghost of a hope. I fancy Tyler will insist on her resting for a month at least, and then it will be too late for Salso."[110] In the end the plan for a Salso cure and a trip to I Tatti had to be given up. Elisina was away for two weeks and on her return went into seclusion for several days.[111]

Wharton described herself as a "perfect savage (in the French sense)"[112] since the death of Gerard Richards and the absence of Elisina had forced her to set aside the writing of *Summer* and return to Paris to oversee the charities. Still, she was not insensitive to Elisina's grief. She addressed her as "the tenth wonder,"[113] and her notes and letters to Elisina reveal a genuine concern for the woman and her family. Though she could be blunt in her criticisms, at one point cautioning Elisina not to say that she avoided sanatoriums because she had once had a touch of tuberculosis, Wharton was always attentive to the Tylers. Likewise, the letters between

Elisina and Royall reveal a tender caring for Wharton, even when her highhandedness sometimes exasperated Elisina.

~

Through the fall the *Tuberculeux de la Guerre* charity made progress. "We are getting on splendidly, and the Inspector of the Service de Santé, who visited one trying-out hospital last week was so pleased that the Ministry of War has offered us a large piece of ground near Paris, and will facilitate our building baraquements, etc."[114]

However, among her committees in the United States, substantial confusion grew over Wharton's broad tuberculosis campaign with its differing organizations and differing patient groups. So that Grant could give the Boston committee some idea of what their money had accomplished, Wharton enclosed "a little 'key' to my various works, as my sister-in-law writes me that people are beginning to grow 'muddled' by my many charities!—No wonder.—I hope this will throw some light on them."[115]

Most immediate among her charities were children from the Flanders group and tubercular women and children from the hostels who needed treatment at the convalescent homes established at Groslay and Arromanches. These were offshoots of the American Hostels and clearly part of Wharton's charities. Still, her current publicity campaign for *Tuberculeux de la Guerre*, the large organization connected to the French military, left her contributors in the United States understandably confused.

To Wharton, in the middle of day-to-day operations of both groups, the distinction was clear. She was only one of several vice presidents of the *Tuberculeux de la Guerre*. (Walter Berry was treasurer of the organization.) And while she lent her name to this large organization "to 'draw' the public," she insisted to Minnie, "It is absolutely necessary that the tuberculosis campaign should be quite independent from my appeals for the Hostels and the Enfants des Flandres. It is not 'my' charity in any sense, except that I am interested in it, and working hard for it; I am not the President, or even the only vice-president." She was understandably concerned that other members of the executive board would be surprised to hear it spoken of as "her charity."[116] Beyond that, she had to distinguish the large charity from yet another one sponsored by the Interior Ministry, which helped tubercular soldiers fresh from the trenches for three months. The *Tuberculeux de la Guerre* sanctioned by the Health Ministry, on the other hand, kept the soldiers until they were cured and taught them a trade.[117]

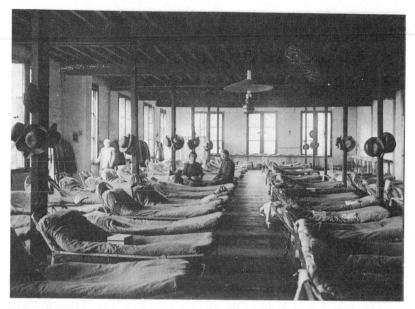

Fig. 4 A dormitory of the Children of Flanders Rescue Committee, House at St Ouen

Wharton was able to secure some photographs of the Children of Flanders hospitals, and to promote the larger tuberculosis charity she sent a photograph of a tubercular soldier, which she asked Minnie to have lithographically reproduced for large posters. There was further confusion when Minnie sent contributions through the wrong bank and was lectured by Wharton again on the need for keeping the deposits straight.[118]

Uncertainties about the various tuberculosis organizations were not the only dispiriting muddle. Political wrangles ("fatal to digestion and friendship"[119]) within the *Foyer Franco-Belge* poisoned the daily round of meetings. It had been apparent for some time that Charles du Bos was no longer capable of discharging his administrative duties. "The climate of office politics," Gide reported, "was not helped any when stormy committee sessions revealed Charles du Bos had been lavish in the grants he handed out to refugees."[120]

Wharton asked du Bos to resign quietly, but his pride required a public separation. "I have not said anything about it until now," Wharton wrote Lizzie Cameron, "as I had begged him simply to take a rest of a few months, as all have done; but he prefers to have his resignation announced, so I want to give the Housing Committee my reasons for accepting it."[121] Finally an exhausted du Bos was relieved of all power to make financial grants at the *Foyer Franco-Belge*, where he had been one of the earliest volunteers. Gide, on hearing the news, offered to resume work there for three weeks to help out.[122] The *Foyer* committee was soon dissolved, turning over 25,000 francs to the American Hostels to carry on the work. The reorganization was accomplished during November, with the American Hostels emerging on a much firmer basis. The streamlined organization, with a monthly budget of $5,000, now looked after 4,000 refugees and ill people on a permanent basis.[123]

≥▲

On the evening of November 9 Wharton's housekeeper, Catherine Gross, found her mistress unconscious on the floor.[124] The collapse, brought on by an attack of ptomaine poisoning,[125] coincided with another much larger disappointing national event—the reelection of President Woodrow Wilson. When the returns from the American presidential election began to come in from the western states, and it became clear that Wilson would be reelected by twenty-three electoral votes, Walter Berry fumed, "G_d d__n it all to H___, four more caterpillar years as they might have said in Egypt in plague time."[126] And Elizabeth Cameron wrote to her nephew Sherman Miles, a graduate of West Point: "America is rotten with Peace at any price and an incurable frivolity and lack of comprehension of serious questions. Woodrow Wilson has succeeded in making us the most despised and best hated nation in the world."[127] At the American Embassy only the ambassador, William Sharp, was jubilant. Of the staff, John Gardner Coolidge observed, "We are deeply depressed"; and Helen Coolidge was clearly disgusted with the American voters: "Peace at any price is really the only thing they care for. It is sickening."[128]

From her sickbed Wharton wrote to Grant in Boston, thanking him for his articles in the *Boston Transcript*, "which suffused Mrs. Tyler and me with blushes of pride." She promised to try to get signed books from Pierre Loti and Anatole France for the Edith Wharton War Charities booth at the Boston War Bazaar. Of her own efforts she said, "I will send a ms. of mine if I can rake one up, but I generally destroy them."[129]

She was recovered enough the following weekend to plan a luncheon with Berenson and Jacques-Émile Blanche and Jean Cocteau. The luncheon, planned for twelve-thirty, would offer an opportunity for "a good quiet talk" before she would have to excuse herself to attend a committee meeting at 3 P.M.[130] Throughout the final weeks of November she kept up a busy social schedule.[131] On the first day of December she wrote a letter of appeal to readers of the *New York Times* asking them "to remember at Christmas my destitute 735 children of Flanders and my 160 old people and nuns." With only $2,000 in the bank, she needed another $10,000; "otherwise we must close our five houses and our lace schools."[132]

When she came down with another bout of the grippe, she preferred to think it was the result of a visit to her *ouvroir*, "which was simply wriggling with microbes," rather than believe that her day of motoring with Berenson had exposed her to the bug.[133] Meanwhile she thanked Minnie for "stumping the country in my behalf."[134] Even during the second week of December she was not fully recovered from what she told Grant was the worst attack of grippe she had ever experienced. She had read his patriotic pamphlet, "Their Spirit," and had told him that "we are working for our own people in helping France and England now." The novel *Summer*, portions of which she had read to him in draft, was finished and would soon appear in *McClure's Magazine*. She added disingenuously, "I was so sorry the Scribners had no room for it. I always feel lonely when I get away from them."[135]

δ♠

Her appeals in America for the tuberculosis sanatoriums had borne rich fruit. Two wealthy contributors, Lewis Cass Ledyard and Payne Whitney, had given her enough money to build a demonstration sanatorium with 200 beds. She encouraged individuals to subscribe for the annual upkeep of a bed ($600 to pay for a bed and $400 for annual upkeep), and she urged towns and universities to underwrite an entire ward. Serving on the New York committee were Nicholas Murray Butler, president of Columbia University, Myron Herrick, former ambassador to France, and her old friend Theodore Roosevelt.[136]

She followed up with an optimistic report that they would soon have three sanatoriums with 500 beds. The facilities were to be run on the latest American model with the operation overseen by American and French experts. She noted, "The greatest service that America can render France at present is to show how to take care of her tuberculous sufferers." Vassar College had pledged a ward with seven beds, and she urged other colleges and universities to follow this example.[137] In later letters she underscored the superiority of the American fresh-air cure by quoting a letter from a nurse who had visited a French tuberculosis hospital and seen "'sixty or seventy consumptives in one room, windows and doors closed, a small smoky stove, insufficient clothing, rotting wooden beds, filthy bedding, dirty dishes, dirtier men nurses—and I asked the doctor who was showing me around what they most needed. Well, he thought a large sputum cup was most needed!'"[138]

᛫

As Christmas neared Wharton made and canceled plans. One of her happiest Christmas surprises was an azalea plant from the Garretts. She told them, "But when you two put your heads together to plan a surprise for a friend nothing is unattainable, & you make people feel as if they were living in a fairy-tale!"[139] She began arrangements for a Christmas luncheon with the Tylers, which was to include young Mr. William Tyler.[140] The lunch had to be canceled because "in the p.m. I do two Xmas trees, one at Groslay & one at the Tuberculeux!"[141] Seven years later when she was asked by *The Delineator* magazine to describe her most memorable Christmas, she chose the 1916 holiday spent among an invading army of refugee children.

In previous years the hostels had entertained adult refugees, but this year with a supply of parcels of popcorn, fancy pinafores, and chewing gum sent from a "Happy Home in Oklahoma" or given by a "Bright Little American Girl," they decided to give the children a Christmas tree complete with gifts. People in the office were instructed to give out a limited number of tickets to the smallest and most pathetic children. Helen Coolidge said that 500 were invited and that 1,000 came, "with the result that the presents and good cheer could not quite go around."[142]

Mr. and Mrs. Sharp from the American embassy, many major benefactors to Wharton's charities, and several other French and American dignitaries arrived. Alice Garrett and Helen Coolidge were ready to pour out "barrels of toys and brioches."[143] When the guests were seated, " . . . the doors were opened to the children. In they swarmed, small and poor, but not pathetic—not that day! Every face expressed a pent-up Christmas greed that made them look like little cannibals. And we had not known that there were so many refugee children in Paris, or even in the whole of France." After the supply of toys was depleted, hostels officials stripped the tree itself and handed out lanterns, tinsel, even candle ends. Still the demanding children came. One young child who received the angel from the top of the tree barely escaped with his life.

The adults formed a barricade around the ambassador, his wife, and the other honored guests and got them out safely. Then they returned to the ravaged room and double-barred the doors against the clamor of children demanding their booty. The hostels' workers sat among the ruins of the room, and Wharton concluded, "If not a pretty sight, it was an instructive one, . . . for we felt that once a year, and even on the brink of ruin, human nature needs Christmas tinsel more than coals and blankets."[144]

In her Christmas letter to D'Arcy Paul, a friend of the Garretts, in Baltimore she noted "the holy day was devoted chiefly by our little group of friends to inflicting Christmas joys on a boundless horde of unwashed & undisciplined refugeelets." Paul was starting a committee in Baltimore, and Wharton instructed him not to read the account of the refugee children's invasion at their first meeting. She assured Paul that she had relieved Mr. Herwell Griswold, head of her previous committee in Baltimore, of "the burden of the masterly inactivity which has hitherto crushed them to earth." She closed her letter, "I've got to write to a cinema impresario who wants to annex my whole 'fictional out-put' for the movies—so goodbye, or rather au revoir! (The coasting scene in Ethan ought to bring me in the value of a trip to Africa in March—so come along!)"[145]

≈

So, the year that had begun with a bureaucratic error that forced Wharton to relocate her sewing room ended with a horde of refugee children overrunning the hostels' Christmas party. Throughout 1916 she contin-ued to raise money for all of the Edith Wharton War Charities and added a huge new tuberculosis organization. The successful auction of the manuscripts and drawings from *The Book of the Homeless* softened her disappointment over the delay in the anthology's publication, but the overall project brought in less money than she had hoped. In all, 1916 was a year of muted professional triumphs and numbing personal losses. The Legion of Honor award was overshadowed by the deaths of Henry James and Egerton Winthrop, soon followed by those of Anna Bahlmann and Robert Minturn. Wharton ended the year worn out. The cycles of work, exhaustion, and rest were occurring more frequently. She found that as the war continued into years, rather than weeks or months, money was harder to raise. Furthermore, two of her best workers, Lizzie Cameron and Elisina Tyler, were consumed with grief over the tragic deaths of their children. The year's greatest relief lay in her return to her art. She produced the novella *Summer* with its setting of a New England summer so far in imagination (and in fact) from the trenches of Belgium and France. She longed to concentrate on fiction writing and in the following year would begin to turn over her charities to the American Red Cross as the United States entered the war.

4

୬

AT WAR WITH THE AMERICAN RED CROSS: 1917

EDITH WHARTON ENTERED THE THIRD YEAR OF THE WAR, 1917, EXHAUSTED. Part of her fatigue was due to hurried preparations for a recent auction of art objects, which netted over 300,000 francs for the tuberculosis hospitals. Excusing several weeks of silence, she explained to Sara Norton, "They have rushed by in such a torrent of dull work that I have lost all sense of time, and only know that long ago I used to have friends, and time to write to them."[1] When Minnie Jones wrote about the death of Frederick Whitridge, husband of Wharton's friend Lucy Arnold Whitridge, Wharton, toughened by the loss of several friends the previous year, responded vaguely that she frequently heard of the deaths of American friends only weeks later.

Early in January she received George Santayana's *Egotism in German Philosophy*,[2] a gift from John Jay Chapman, which, she told Berenson, left her as unsatisfied as a stage banquet made of *papier-mâché*.[3] She complained that though books from the United States always seemed to arrive safely, she had no luck in sending parcels the other way across the Atlantic. During January she began using the French government's secure diplomatic pouch to send photographs to her most generous benefactors, Lewis Cass Ledyard and Church Osborne, in New York.[4]

Before the French diplomatic valise left, she enclosed a packet of materials for Minnie, including books to forward to special friends. This passing along of materials may in part have been a strategy to reduce the number of letters she had to write. "I am simply so over-worked, all day and every day," she told Sara Norton in her belated New Year's greeting, "that I can't do more than wave this feeble pen at you."[5]

Soon she began including her manuscripts in the diplomatic pouch as well. The first was an article, "The New Frenchwoman," requested by Mr. Bok of the *Ladies Home Journal*. Again she asked Minnie to correct the proofs. She also included the last serial installment of *Summer*.[6] When *McClure's* sent Minnie the proofs of *Summer* to correct without sending along the original manuscript to read against them, Wharton concluded, "The modern American magazine proceedings are past finding out."[7] The editorial work and the proofreading she was asking Minnie to do from her New York base freed Wharton from the postproduction drudgery while allowing her to subsidize Minnie in a way that did not demean her. Wharton was pleased, for example, that Minnie used the $400 she sent ("It's the first fruits of 'Summer'")[8] to purchase a gala dress. When the novella had especially good reviews and strong sales in England during the fall, Wharton pressed Minnie to accept payment for her editorial duties because "my literary affairs are prosperous."[9]

The uncertainty about manuscripts and proofs was nothing compared to the confusion caused by Minnie's bulk deposits for the various charities. "You must remember that the funds of these two charities [the hostels and the Children of Flanders] are absolutely separate," Wharton lectured her, "and that it is only in America that the two are being regarded as in any way related to each other."[10] The reserve for the Children of Flanders had dipped to less than $2,000 before Minnie made a successful appeal in the United States and fattened the bank accounts. As they headed into the new year, Wharton felt financially secure about both charities.

She sent New Year's greetings to Minnie's son-in-law and daughter, Max and Beatrix Farrand, but could not resist a jab at Max: "Much as I love him, it is painful to have to read him in that vile sheet, 'The New Republic'."[11] At the time Heywood Broun was writing antiwar and antipreparedness commentary in the recently founded *New Republic*, and Wharton was clearly opposed to the magazine's liberal, noninterventionist editorial position. She added, "I do not like to see a good French name like his associated with such 'boche' neutrality."[12]

Though the art connoisseur was solidly booked for lunches, teas, and dinners throughout his Paris stay,[13] she asked Berenson to come and dine with her because Charles du Bos had secured his doctor's permission by special favor to leave a sickbed to dine out if Berenson were a guest.[14] Bernard and Mary Berenson left Paris in mid-January. Wharton thanked them for the thoughtfulness of the thank-you notes they left: "No wonder my poor little wizened self becomes a big jolly SELF in such an atmosphere as you create; it was curled up and *ratatiné* last night with the sense of your going, and now it is putting out buds and blossoms like the Paris horse-chestnuts in the autumn!"[15] She was already making plans to see them again in a few months and counting "on the distanter but no less real vision of our Grand Tour when the world is travellable again."[16] Sharing something of their own ambivalent attitude toward the very rich, she commented that she was writing to Mr. Kahn, quoting flatteringly from his own brochure, hoping that he would "succumb" to one or more of her charities. And she could not resist passing along a rumor relayed by her workroom manager, who had a relative in the French diplomatic corps. The wildly optimistic rumor, to the effect that if the Allies could hold out for two more months Germany would be begging for peace, based on "friend-of-a-friend" testimony, was one that Wharton usually would ignore. It was a measure of her fatigue and low spirits that she embraced it now.

At the end of the month she was up to her ears in the politics of the tuberculosis project. She reported to Minnie on the arrival of Dr. Biggs from the Rockefeller Commission.[17] She invited him to lunch and, by way of a demonstration of their efforts to combat the disease, took him in her car to visit the hostels' convalescent home in Groslay.[18]

In describing to Berenson the cultural limitations of Dr. Biggs and the lawyer accompanying him, Wharton anticipated problems that would surface six months later when the American Red Cross arrived in France in large numbers: "Neither one of them speaks a word of French, or has, apparently the least glimmer of a notion of French conditions, French attitudes, French history, or any of the million things that go to make up the 'problem.'—I am more and more dazed by the strange limitations of the American great man."[19]

The ability to speak French was an important criterion for Wharton when it came to accepting American volunteer war workers. When Minnie offered to send American helpers, Wharton assured her, "Anyone who speaks French well, and is willing to work, is very welcome."[20] Minnie was frequently pressed into service to interview candidates in New York and assess their ability in French as well as their other qualifications. In March, for example, Wharton asked Minnie to meet with a Presbyterian nurse in New York to see if she spoke acceptable French and seemed suitable for hospital work in France.[21] Wharton's own French was more than adequate. Despite Bourget's facetious remark that she spoke Louis Quatorze French, the French critic Roger Asselineau says: "It is a pity . . . that we have no record of her voice and cannot judge by ourselves. But we can be sure of the quality of her written French, for the letters she wrote in this language are absolutely perfect—faultless."[22] A command of French was not her only criterion for accepting helpers. Wharton told a mother whose daughter wanted to do volunteer work in France that the young woman might be acceptable "if she is willing to work seriously and steadily for a considerable number of hours each day."[23]

≈

On the last day of January the German ambassador in Washington announced that Germany would resume unrestricted submarine warfare on all ships, including those of neutrals, entering or leaving the British Isles. While the German government knew that the action would make the American government unhappy, Berlin did not anticipate the extent of American displeasure. The Wilson administration responded by break- ing off diplomatic relations and moving swiftly (though not swiftly enough for Wharton) toward a declaration of war against Germany. When news of the diplomatic break came, a cautious Wharton noted: "I say nothing about the emotions of last week. But it *is* good to be able to hold one's head up—at least temporarily."[24]

In "hyperborean" Paris, "where the thermometer has been racing the downward drop of the coal supply, and beating it," the chill began to revive and rival Wharton's memories of grim New York winters: "For the last ten days we've been having the kind of weather I left New York to escape from; blinding sky, grinding cold, searching dust—how well I know the look of the frozen ashbins along the curbstone."[25]

The situation in the countryside was little better. In her retirement home some forty miles from Paris, where she had reported on the Battle of the Marne, the American writer Mildred Aldrich ran out of coal the second week of January. Her friends Alice Toklas and Gertrude Stein were temporarily in Paris preparing "Aunt Pauline," their Ford car, for duty with the American Fund for French Wounded in the south of France. Aldrich stayed in her bed "until nine, hoping it will get warm—it doesn't." Despite blazing wood fires in the large drafty fireplace, she could not get the salon where she worked during the short January days above eight degrees Centigrade (forty-six degrees Fahrenheit).[26]

Wartime conditions in Paris in winter meant coal shortages and a 50 percent reduction in the use of electricity. The cold during February remained "appalling," Wharton told Minnie, "and the difficulty of getting fuel, owing to the transportation crisis and to ice in the Seine makes the situation of the refugees terribly sad."[27] All of the warm clothes in the box Minnie had sent in January had been distributed immediately. One donor wanted her clothes given to just one girl, and Wharton had chosen a sixteen-year-old worker in her *ouvroir* who had five younger brothers and sisters and an ill mother to care for. The cold made Wharton even more sympathetic with the fighting men in the trenches and the prisoners in the camps. She left her frigid apartment to attend a meeting of the French Academy, the first since the war began, but found it a chilly and not very illuminating experience. Despite the urge to stay under the covers, she lunched with Maurice Barrès and resumed seeing Léon Bélugou, now that he had broken free of his latest mistress.

The arrival of Berenson's debunking essay on Leonardo da Vinci in *The Study and Criticism of Italian Art* warmed her heart considerably. When Wharton received a prepublication copy of the book from New York with an enclosed printed card from the publisher blandly offering "the author's Comps," she told Berenson that the book would not be truly hers until he had added something in his own handwriting.[28] She wrote him enthusiastically, confessing her own distaste for *The Last Supper*: "Ever since I first saw it (at 17) I've wanted to bash that picture's face & now, now, at last, the most authorized fist in the world has done the job for me!" [29]

≈

The central committee of the American Hostels decided to open a third convalescent house at Groslay for tubercular boys and young men. Wharton's plan was to turn over her tuberculosis houses, used for the care of civilian refugees, to the larger organization *Tuberculeux de la Guerre* after the war. During a successful lunch with Dr. Biggs of the Rockefeller Commission, she persuaded him to become a member of the Honorary Medical Committee of *Tuberculeux de la Guerre*.

Because it was so cold, she took to reading in bed late into the night. In a letter to Berenson she opened with a passage from the correspondence of Barbey that she had come across at three in the morning. She had revised Wilson's "too proud to fight" motto to "too cold to sleep."[30] She complained that though millionaires might be keeping warm at the Ritz, she was "too hard frozen" to get at the books in her "Grand Saloon." In her late night reading she revisited the German *Chansons de Geste*, which she had not read since she was fourteen. Indeed, the only thing that warmed her at all was her gloating over Berenson's dispatching of Leonardo da Vinci.

In her next letter to Berenson she responded enthusiastically to his suggestion that he ought to offer himself for work in Paris. Qualifying her remarks in a style reminiscent of Henry James, she promised him, "I'll try to get you a job here—some sort of Embassy job—I mean the semblance of one—if you'll only come!"[31] She tried to make life in frigid Paris seem appetizing by recounting her recent talks with Maclagan and Bélugou. To help secure his placement in Paris she wrote an official letter, commenting on his language proficiency and offering him a job herself on *Les Tuberculeux de la Guerre* stationery with a copy to the undersecretary of the Ministry of Health.[32] In a private note accompanying the official letter, she said, "I do hope the consulate will facilitate your coming. We all need you dreadfully here."[33]

By the end of the month, however, Berenson was explaining why a move to Paris was impossible for him at that time. To soften her disappointment, he included a check for £50 for her charities, which she promptly designated for her refugee hospital. Wharton understood his reservations: "Yes, I see why you can't come, and it all seems part of the general wrongness of the universe, dearest B.B.!" She began to speak of plans to break away from her work in Paris for a trip to Italy in April. In the meantime, she was continuing "to pursue [her] lonely prowls through literature," at present "zigzagging through Goethe." She closed her letter with a witty aside that previously she would have shared with James but now transferred to Berenson. Earlier in the week when her dentist had "polished" her, "he said with a sigh of appreciation, when it was over: 'You *have* got a magnificent masticating surface!'—If Red Riding Hood had thought of that the Wolf might have been too flattered to eat her!—"[34]

She still acted independently and sometimes rashly about her own health. At the end of February she came down with a bad case of the grippe, which, when she went out against her doctor's orders, soon developed into pneumonia. She had to take to her bed for a week without any activity and was ill for two more weeks. When she had recovered, her secretary came down with the same grippe, which was epidemic in Paris.[35] This combination of illnesses naturally put her behind in her letter writing. She was again using the French diplomatic valise as the surest way of sending documents, and in New York Minnie apparently had no trouble retrieving those items intended for her. For larger shipments, such as boxes of lingerie and fancy sewing from her *ouvroir* for a New York charity bazaar, she asked Walter Berry to use the American Chamber of Commerce connections, as American Express had proven unsatisfactorily slow.[36]

During Wharton's illness the Humphry Wards passed through Paris and visited the front. Wharton, "shut up for a nasty stuffy melancholy fortnight, with full leisure to follow Mr. Wilson's strange contortions," was too ill to see them.[37] Her secretary began all of her business letters at this time by saying that Madame Wharton was suffering with the grippe. By now Minnie had acceded to Wharton's request that she hire a secretary for herself and the New York end of the charity business. Wharton was touched when Minnie's new secretary sent a donation of $10 for the charities from her own pay. When a Philadelphia niece of Minnie's sent a donation, Wharton applied it to the hostels' convalescent homes that she had established to combat tuberculosis and anemia among women and children and operated at a cost of about a dollar per day per patient. She sent the architect Charles Knight to examine the home of a Mme Cillois in Fontainebleau, where she was thinking of establishing a new home.[38] Throughout March she was examining and turning down properties to establish tuberculosis sanatoriums.

≈

On the literary front, during February and March Minnie was still proofreading *Summer*. Wharton sent her notes for corrections on a separate sheet and had told Joseph Sears, vice president at Appleton's, that Minnie would revise the proofs of the book as well.[39] In mid-March she thanked Minnie "for all the trouble you are continuing to take about the revision of 'Summer'. I have not had time to revise the second instalment of McClure's, but will try to send it to you next week. If it comes too late it can't be helped. Hereafter I will try to send them regularly."[40]

Wharton had recovered enough during the second week of March to fume against "Wilson's asphyxiating exhalations." She compared this period, between the break of February 3 in diplomatic relations with Germany and the declaration of war on April 6, to "the middle days of a long foggy ocean voyage, when time seems to go backward."[41] Other Americans in Paris were equally angry. Helen Coolidge recorded in her diary on March 19: "Three more Americans boats sunk, and I am glad of it, for at last that may bring a declaration of war. I am exhausted trying to explain our attitude to people and trying to be loyal when I am really sick at heart."[42] Mildred Aldrich told Stein and Toklas, "I'd like to see Wilson impeached, and it seems to me it would be far less disgraceful than for the country to stand by such a back boneless wonder. What is the disgrace of one man compared to the humiliation of a nation?"[43]

Wharton had been reading Ernest Renan, the prolific French philosopher and historian whose rich prose style, she said, would have served him better had he lived in "sugar card days." She had enjoyed his book on St. Paul sufficiently, however, to turn to the New Testament. There she was especially affected by parts of Acts and Paul's epistles. After commenting to Berenson, "there are good bits, undoubtedly," she caught herself and added with heavy irony, "How kind of me."[44] She was still planning a trip to Italy in April. She ruled out train travel, though, and asked whether there would be enough gasoline available for a private car in Italy for her to complete the trip.

Recovering slowly from her own attack of pneumonia, Wharton searched for outing flannel for sheets for her tubercular patients. Minnie sent some herself and soon located more through a British American war relief agency. In a letter of March 23, Wharton asked her to send an enclosed important business letter to Edgar Herman. The letter contained a request that Herman find a new trust company to handle her estate.[45]

On the last day of the month she sent Minnie a handwritten note. She had largely recovered from the pneumonia but felt overworked with Elisina and two of her other helpers away for a fortnight of rest. This time Wharton had made the mistake of enclosing duplicate receipts—one in francs, the other in dollars—for Minnie; these duplicates, clearly Wharton's fault this time, caused fiscal confusion in the charity accounts. Despite her fatigue, which led to this accounting error, she was "leaving for the new front tomorrow with Walter, to see some of the horrors, which are beyond imagining, they say."[46]

The first day of April 1917, Wharton and Walter Berry were touring the previously occupied area of the Valois in the valley of the Oise River some two hours north of Paris, which had been devastated in the German retreat. They returned the night of April 3, and Wharton reported "the country we went through is so ravaged that one cannot even get a piece of bread at Noyon or any of the other towns that are undestroyed; the Germans have taken literally everything."[47] For Berenson she described her trip to the north: "I must tell you, though, that last week I went for two days and a half to the devastated region. Walter went with me. How

I wish you'd been with us! I was sent to Chauny, Noyon, Ham, Lassiguy, Roye, Cuts, Carlepont, and a long etc. of wrecked villages, and on my return my account was cabled to the N.Y. Sun.

"The horrors are unimaginable. Just one long senseless slaughter of the country. Luckily they were so busy hacking fruit-trees and blowing up isolated farm houses that the damage to the roads was not half what it might have been if they had concentrated on that. Most of what we saw was just mad Gorilla-work."[48]

≈

On the first day of April 1917, Woodrow Wilson and his administration were putting before Congress the resolution to declare war on Germany. All along it had been widely supposed that Wilson had been implacably neutral. Certainly that was how Wharton and other Americans with Allied sympathies felt. Recent interpretations of Wilson's policies, however, suggest a less uncompromising position: "But for the nation to go to war a catalyst was necessary, and it proved none other than President Wilson, whom everyone had presumed to be as neutral as it was possible to be. Wilson, it now is clear, was unneutral from the beginning. He waited for sentiment to change so that forces and factors positioned themselves in such a way that a careful Chief Executive could reasonably make a move."[49]

On the evening of April 2 Wilson drove through a light spring rain up the hill to the Capitol, where he asked a joint session of Congress for approval to add American forces to a war that would make the world safe for democracy. The resolution passed the Senate on April 4 and the House two days later. The resolution of war was delivered to Wilson shortly after one o'clock on April 6, Good Friday. He signed it immediately.[50]

The same day that the official American position was catching up to the popular sentiment, Wharton described the fatigue brought on by her grinding days in Paris: "The daily mail I receive is so big, and the daily mass of business to be transacted is so immense that I am too hurried and tired to do it. . . . My day's work for the last month has lasted from 8:30 till dinner, with never more than an hour off except hurried meals; and I am utterly tired out."[51] She made it clear that it was no longer possible for her to write personally to all of the donors, especially the ones who made their donations through the New York end of the operation. To lighten some of the burden, she enclosed with her letter to Minnie another letter for the *New York Times* containing a message of gratitude to her American contributors. She added that in the future the chairmen of the American committees would write the letters acknowledging donations and closed with an expression of general encouragement: "Now that America has taken her place with nations fighting for the right, I feel sure that they will be more than ready to see me through to the end."[52]

In other newspaper activity since her recent return from the recaptured northern provinces, she had written up her impressions of her trip for the *Sun*. Refugees from the villages near Campiègne and Noyon were already streaming into Paris, and Wharton was glad that the American charities, especially her hostels, were in place to help them. As she told John Garrett's mother, whose Baltimore committee had recently sent blankets and bed quilts, the hostels had furnished lodging for about 200 of "the destitute women and children who are pouring back from the ravaged country evacuated by the Germans." As if her own charities were not burden enough, the Assistance Publique of Paris had asked her to found and run at their expense a hospital of about seventy-five beds for children with hip disease. She had arranged to do so at Arromanches in Normandy, where there was already a hospital for eighty children from the hostels. In closing the letter to Mrs. Garrett, Wharton eagerly accepted the plan suggested by the children in a Baltimore school to "adopt" children in the Flemish charity. At the moment she was down to only $400 with 800 children to care for, and the charity needed $1,500 a month.[53]

All of her travel and refugee activities had left her too exhausted to write the *Cosmopolitan* piece she had contracted to do. She explained to Minnie: "I did not ask you to do anything about my Cosmopolitan ms because there was nothing to do. I had to ask to have the publication postponed as I am too tired to write, and Mr. Sisson kindly said I might take my own time. I merely sent him the first chapters as a 'sample brick'. You may be sure that I will always let you know if there is anything of that kind to be attended to. Don't work too hard and don't worry about me." While admitting that all of the work had left her drained, she added "It's made me young again to be an 'Ally' at last!"[54]

She declared Easter Sunday a day off and took the opportunity to describe for Berenson the huge task she saw ahead of her. To bolster her with his presence, she renewed her earlier request, "Why on earth don't you ask for a job in our Embassy here. They are sure to be wanting polyglots now." With Elisina Tyler away for nearly a month and on her own return facing a deluge of refugees from "the Land of Death," Wharton declared a little smugly, "The rest of the refugee oeuvres are just fluff."[55]

When Elisina returned from three weeks in the sunshine, she found Wharton "quite reassured by my presence, and I could not help being moved and *sobered* by her dependence on my poor judgment."[56] On a personal front, a vindictive Grant Richards was again refusing to let Elisina see her children, and she discussed taking action in the courts to secure permission to visit them.

ൟ

On a typical day, May 11, 1917, Wharton's mail brought her seventeen letters to be answered.[57] A few months later she noted: "The endless deluge of letters with which I have to struggle fatigues me more than anything else; and that is growing worse since our entrance into the war."[58] Finally the workload became almost unbearable, and she appealed to Minnie in exasperation: "Please let people understand that I am really not well and cannot be much written to about trifl[ing] things or have stray people sent me with letters."[59] Clearly, keeping up with the correspondence, even with the help of a secretary, was exhausting.

Wharton announced her campaign for tuberculosis aid publicly in a long letter to the *New York Times*. She noted that France was experiencing a drop in population due to the low birth rate and the rapid spread of tuberculosis. Ninety-five percent of repatriated prisoners of war returned with the disease. Complicating the treatment were old-fashioned French attitudes about personal hygiene: Even the workers in her *ouvroir* rarely sought dental care and were afraid of ventilating the room in which they worked. She asked, "How many Americans understand this? How many are aware that in most French convent schools the children are never given a bath, and that bathing the whole body is considered indecent and immoral." To combat these habits she wanted to establish demonstration sanatoriums and hospitals where patients would bathe regularly and sleep with the windows open to the fresh air.[60]

America's entrance into the war in April of 1917 promised Wharton relief for two reasons. First, she no longer had to be embarrassed about her country's neutrality. Shortly after the declaration of war, she wrote to Sara Norton, "Let us embrace on the glorious fact that we can now hold up our heads with the civilized nations of the world."[61] Second, through May and June of 1917 she anticipated that she would soon be relieved of raising funds for her charities and of managing them. She told Minnie, "I greatly hope the Rockefeller Commission may take over my tuberculosis organization which is really going to be too great a burden for me now that our entering into the war has deprived me of some of my best workers."[62] One of those "best workers" was Royall Tyler, who had transferred to the American embassy. Thus, as Wharton explained to Sara Norton, America's entry into the war had paradoxically increased her workload: "I have a great deal more work on my hands since our declaration of war which took from me two of our best workers, and has left me to cope with a task really beyond my strength."[63]

After April 1917, the American Red Cross (ARC) became the officially designated charity of the United States government and the specified relief agency of the American Expeditionary Force (AEF).[64] In May the ARC announced a call for volunteers and in June launched a $100 million fund drive. For the many small, privately funded American charities in France now losing both their workers and their contributors, a shift of responsibilities to one large, government-sanctioned organization was, therefore, doubly necessary.

The six months from April through September saw a dramatic transformation in the nature of American philanthropy. Before April 1917, control of civilian war charities rested primarily with the socially and economically privileged classes.[65] There were committees for Edith Wharton War Charities, for example, in Bar Harbor, Maine; Boston; New York City; Montclair, New Jersey; Baltimore; and Washington, D.C. After America's entry into the war, however, philanthropy and civilian war relief increasingly took on the look of a corporate organization dominated by large-scale efficiencies.

ঽঌ

A brief history of the American Red Cross's early development and war relief policies reveals that the organization was undergoing sweeping changes. Before 1917, the ARC had always been led by determined women. The first was its founder, Clara Barton, who had camped in Washington doorways and outer offices from 1877 until 1882, when President Chester A. Arthur belatedly signed the Geneva Treaty. The American National Red Cross was officially incorporated in the District of Columbia in 1882 but had to wait until 1900 for a federal charter.

In 1904 the eighty-two-year-old Barton was turned out of office amid charges of fiscal mismanagement by a determined newcomer, Mabel T. Boardman. The two women could not have been more different. Barton came from a small town in central Massachusetts; Boardman was the daughter of a prominent Cleveland family with far-reaching social connections.[66] The candid Barton said of herself, "I was never what the world would call 'even good looking.'" Boardman and her stylish gowns, on the other hand, were the subject of contemporary magazine articles. She became one of the leaders of Washington society. As the official Red Cross history notes: "Miss Boardman represented wealth, social position and the spirit of Noblesse Oblige of her class. . . . Firmly convinced as a result of her family heritage that Red Cross leadership should be in the hands of people who command the support of the wealthy members of the community through their own prominence and social prestige, she wanted above all else to interest more persons in her own circle in the Red Cross and its activities."[67]

The conflict between the founder of the American Red Cross and her successor had long-lasting and unpleasant repercussions. For all of her active life, Mabel Boardman sought to expunge the memory of Clara Barton and her service to the Red Cross. When the national headquarters building was dedicated in 1916, for instance, Boardman threatened President Wilson that if he went forward with plans to place a memorial plaque or even an inscription to Barton in the new building, she would release "evidence concerning the misappropriation of relief funds intrusted to the old organization."[68] Consequently, there was no memorial to the founder of the American Red Cross. Even after Boardman relinquished control of the organization to others, she continued to refer to Barton as "a skeleton in the closet upon which the doors have been closed."[69]

ॐ

During the opening months of the First World War, the ARC was caught in a dilemma. On the one hand, its charter stipulated that in wartime it had to maintain strict neutrality in aiding combatants. On the other hand, vast numbers of sufferers in this war were obviously noncombatants, as Herbert Hoover's Commission for the Relief of Belgium amply demonstrated. In the first two months the Red Cross raised $325,000; by the end of 1914 it had collected a little more than $1 million for European war relief. The funds were directed almost entirely to relief of the military. Of aid to civilians, a Red Cross monograph stated: "The charter had failed to provide for noncombatant relief in case of war and it would be inconsistent with the American policy of neutrality."[70] In late 1915 Mabel Boardman tried to raise $1 million for an endowment to place the ARC on the same firm financial footing as the Rockefeller Foundation or the Carnegie Foundation. She also launched an effort to gather all of the American war relief charities under the Red Cross,[71] but this first effort to centralize the private American charities in France was not successful.

While the American Red Cross did not enter the field of civilian war relief, thousands of Americans did. By the time the United States declared war on April 6, 1917, there were more than 130 private American relief societies and agencies collecting supplies and funds in the United States and distributing them to noncombatants and refugees in Europe.[72] Some of them, like the American Relief Clearing House, received assistance from the Red Cross. Many others did not.

President Wilson, recognizing the potential for a duplication of effort, issued, on the same day as the declaration of war, a statement calling on Americans to coordinate their contributions to foreign charities through the American Red Cross. Once the Wilson administration was committed to the war, it quickly sought to put the ARC on a solid footing, even if such a step meant that the first casualties were Boardman and the idea of a national charity organization supported by the aristocratic classes.

At a meeting in Washington on April 21, Secretary of War Newton Baker told assembled members of the banking, industrial, and business communities to come up with a plan for restructuring the Red Cross. They suggested appointing a War Council made up entirely of men from their own ranks who would launch a national campaign to raise $25,000,000 or perhaps $50,000,000. On May 10 Wilson announced the formation of a War Council; Boardman was out and Henry P. Davison, vice president of the J. P. Morgan Company, was in.[73]

Davison was no stranger to the financial and industrial world. At thirty-two he had been elected the youngest bank president in the United States. Now fifty, Davison promised Wilson that he would get the best corporate leaders in the country to serve in key organizational posts of the Red Cross. Within days he had secured the volunteered services of the presidents of Anaconda Copper and the American Tobacco Company, the vice presidents of American Steel Foundries and the Guaranty Trust Company, former ambassadors to Italy and France, a former secretary of the Interior, and been loaned top executives from AT&T and American Express.[74] Many of the commissioners were "dollar-a-year" volunteers who left careers in American business, mostly banking, to become administrative officials of the ARC in France.[75]

When the War Council asked General Pershing what it could do most immediately to help the war effort, Pershing replied: "For God's sake, buck up the French."[76] To that end Davison and the council immediately pledged $1 million to the French Red Cross to be used in any way it saw fit.

In the meantime the efforts of Wharton and Elisina Tyler were being acknowledged officially. The president of the French Republic conferred the gold medal "pour dévouement" on both women. The recognition of Elisina as vice president of the American Hostels for Refugees and the Children of Flanders was especially gratifying to Wharton.[77] She wrote to John Garrett's mother in Baltimore: "You have been so kind about my work since the beginning of the war that I think it may interest you to know that the President of the Republic has given to Mrs. Royall Tyler, the Vice-President of the American Hostels and of the Children of Flanders Rescue Committee, the Gold Medal for 'Dévouement' which has been given only to two or three women."[78]

Even in these early days of American involvement, Wharton's anticipation of the coming of the ARC was edged with some caution. In a note acknowledging a contribution, she observed, "I hope the American Red Cross will come to our aid by next Autumn though I doubt if they are organized before that in such a way as to deal with French war charities, since they must naturally take up our own army organization first."[79] Wharton was privately telling her correspondents that "there seems no prospect now that the war will end for another year."[80]

Looking forward to the arrival of the ARC, some of the private American charities in France sought to coordinate their efforts. Wharton wrote to the American Ambulance describing the motor pool of her three charities (only three trucks to serve the nineteen houses in Paris and outlying regions) and asking for their help in carrying patients and supplies. "It seems to me at this stage of the war," she wrote the head of the American Ambulance, "such organizations as ours can do infinitely greater service by combining their work wherever it is possible to do so."[81] Such cooperation among the private American charities in Paris was not unusual: Nina Duryea, who had run a series of American-funded hospitals in France and Belgium since 1915, sponsored a charity that was already supplying the hostels' *vestiaire* with a monthly *bon* (gift) of clothing sufficient to outfit 150 people.[82]

Back in the United States Davison, as chairman of the ARC War Council, was about to launch the largest charity fund-raising drive the world had ever seen. While the members of the War Council were debating whether to set the goal at $25 million or the far more ambitious $50 million mark, Davison stepped forward and said that for its first drive the American Red Cross would set a goal of $100 million.

General Pershing and the officials from the ARC sailed on the *Baltic* in late May. Wharton had friends among Pershing's staff. Winthrop Chanler, Daisy's husband, had been recommended to Pershing by General William Wright. Once selected, Chanler traveled with Pershing as a private adviser and stayed in Paris until after the Armistice.[83] And once in Paris, Pershing dined with Lizzie Cameron. One of his former geometry students, the American novelist Dorothy Canfield Fisher, was among his first dinner guests when he established a Paris base in a borrowed townhouse just a few steps down the rue de Varenne from Wharton's apartment.

When the United States entered the war, the American army ranked seventeenth in size among the world's armies. It had an aging officer corps and little experience of modern warfare. Because the German high command saw no immediate threat in the ill-trained and hastily dispatched American soldiers, its strategy did not include any plan to neutralize the American military presence. American troop strength rose slowly because men had to be drafted and trained and also because of the scarcity of American or other ships to transport the soldiers to France. At the end of September 1917, American Expeditionary Force troops in France numbered 61,531. The following year during the German offensive of March through May, the British quickly provided the much-needed shipping, and hundreds of thousands of American soldiers and several million tons of supplies were rushed over.

The *New York Herald* for June 15 announced both the arrival of General Pershing and the eighteen-man Red Cross commission, whose recommendations would "guide the authorities in the United States in distributing the fund of $100,000,000 which is being raised."[84]

Pershing wrote personally to Wharton soon after his arrival, expressing admiration for her work:

> It would be impossible for me to express in a brief note the very high appreciation of your American friends in the army of your splendid service for the relief of destitute men, women and children of France and Belgium.
>
>   Your work stands out pre-eminently in the long list of devoted efforts that our people have voluntarily given to France. The Red

Cross is now undertaking to co-ordinate these endeavors and I shall consider its mission a brilliant success if it even approximates your splendid achievement.

May I not include my personal greetings when I say that you have earned the lasting gratitude of the people whom you have served and have made Americans very proud of the record of their fellow-country-woman.[85]

In her reply, Wharton graciously noted, "A great part of its [her war work in France] success is to be ascribed to my devoted and indefatigable helpers, to whom a proportionately large share of your praise is due, and who will be much gratified as I have been by your letter."[86] She had both Pershing's letter and her reply translated and distributed to the French members of the American Hostels committee and the major employees of the hostels to show them that their work was being officially recognized by the American commander.

❧

Wharton passed the first ten days of July with Madame de Béarn at her Château de Fleury-en-Bière. From there she went to the Hôtel Savoy in Fontainebleau, where she had booked the same suite she had the previous summer. Prior to going to Fleury she went on a six-day motor holiday, part of which was spent inspecting two of their tuberculosis sanatoriums in Burgundy. She saw the Fourth of July parade in Paris, where the American troops, still called Sammies based on Uncle Sam, not Yanks, presented the colors to General Pershing at his residence. After a full morning of ceremonies, the American Chamber of Commerce, now headed by Walter Berry, gave its annual banquet. Berry made a speech in his excellent French, demanding the return of Alsace-Lorraine. Wharton attended the reception at the American embassy, where General Pershing was presented to more than a thousand of his countrymen who resided now in Paris.[87]

In mid-July Wharton returned to Fleury. By now the weight of administrative duties was telling on Elisina. From Aix-les-Bains, where she had been sent for her health, she described her cure, which included reading two cantos of Dante every morning and enjoying the air of the town. She told Mildred Bliss, "This time I intend to stay here till I feel quite recovered, as I wished I could have done at Beauvallon."[88]

During the summer of 1917 a page in the history of philanthropy was about to turn; and in the transition from a *noblesse oblige* model to a corporate model, Wharton was to find herself in the middle of the struggle. The ARC commissioners in France, after surveying the variety of American charities, concluded, not surprisingly, that it would be best if many of the small private American relief societies and charities would turn over the management of their separate, scattered societies to a central agency. The agency they had in mind was the American Red Cross.

At first Wharton was compliant. On July 25, with Walter Berry at her side, she entertained two commissioners from the ARC. The commissioners asked for a statement of the monthly operating expenses for all of her charities and what it would take to keep them running through the winter. Bowing to the inevitable mergers, Wharton wrote to James Perkins of the ARC, "It is evident that, as a result of the recent successful appeal of the American Red Cross in the United States, individual charities here cannot hope for the same support from home for some time to come. . . . It seems to me that the simplest way is to state our exact needs, based on previous experience, leaving it to the Red Cross to judge how far these different charities deserve its support."[89]

The sewing *ouvroir* with 50 women was nearly self-sufficient. The Children of Flanders charity, which cared for 720 children and 210 adults, needed 10,000 francs a month in addition to the subsidy from the Belgian government. The American Hostels, offering various forms of support for 3,000 to 4,000 refugees, required 40,000 francs a month; and the Convalescent Homes at Groslay and Arromanches with 185 beds also needed about 40,000 francs a month.[90]

Most other private American charities were only too glad to fall into line with the ARC's takeover plans. The American Relief Clearing House, the American Hospital, and the American Ambulance—all large, all well established, and all privately administered and supported until July of 1917—turned over their facilities and staffs during the summer and the autumn to the Red Cross.

The mergers went smoothly for the most part. Some organizations, however, were not so willingly annexed. Nina Duryea insisted that the *Herald* print a retraction of an article stating erroneously that her charity was being voluntarily annexed by the Red Cross. Isabel Lathrop, who ran the largest privately funded American agency in France—the American Fund for French Wounded, in which Gertrude Stein and Alice B. Toklas worked—made sure that all publicity in the United States regarding her agency stressed that it had no official connection with the ARC.

Ruth Gaines, a contemporary observer of the takeover scene who took the side of the ARC, nonetheless offered this sympathetic portrait of the resisting organizations:

> The other societies had their chapters, their clubs, their clientele at home, their affiliations with the French Government abroad. Their founders had been pioneers during our neutrality, giving, many of them, of their private resources, as an expression of their passionate attachment to the cause of France. Most of their leaders were women of influence and initiative. Otherwise, in the midst of the difficulties that confronted them, their organizations never would have been born. They had succeeded, and by their success held what the American Red Cross had yet to win, the confidence of the French Government. They felt, with justice, that they had much to offer the Red Cross in the way of resources and experience. All this they did offer, but they were unwilling to give up their identity.[91]

When disgruntled and slighted American relief workers in France wrote to their committees and supporters at home, the American Red Cross suddenly found itself with an image problem on both sides of the Atlantic. In a letter to the *Herald,* Samuel Smiley proved less cheerful than his name would imply: "After nearly three years a sort of giant octopus, in the shape of the American Red Cross, enters the field and threatens to monopolize the business of dispensing human charity."[92] And when the Red Cross, with apparently limitless funds to spend, froze out the smaller charities by driving up the rents for office and warehouse space in Paris, the novelist Gertrude Atherton accused it of "acting as all the great arrogant trusts have acted since they began to crush the ambitions and prospects of the individual and without the foresight to see that they will eventually defeat their ends in the hatred they will incur."[93]

The American Red Cross worked furiously in Paris during July and August to repair its image. Major Grayson Murphy, the ARC commissioner in France, acknowledged, "There [was] some doubt as to the relations which exist between the American Red Cross and other American organizations operating in the same field."[94] But he quickly reassured the other charities that the ARC wanted only what was best for France and that it had no intention of interfering with their work.

While the official statement was "hands off" independent American relief organizations, the subtext was more ominous. First, the ARC had effectively adopted the goals of the smaller organizations. The sociologist William Gamson points out in his survey of more than a hundred organizational challenges and takeovers that if a challenge group wants to succeed, it may begin by assuming the goals of the target organization.[95]

In the same news statement in which Murphy denied any intention of taking over the smaller agencies, he immediately added, "It is obvious, however, that the large funds which have been entrusted to the officers of the Red Cross for administration must be disbursed in the most efficient manner possible and in accordance with the true spirit of the trust. Under these circumstances, much as the officers of the Red Cross might like to assist other American societies, they can conscientiously do so only in those cases where . . . those other societies fit into the general plans of the Red Cross. . . ."[96]

During late July Wharton negotiated with the Red Cross commissioners to have them take over the American Hostels. Even as she and Elisina observed the political wrangling between the ARC and the Rockefeller Foundation, Wharton resisted any suggestion of Elisina's that they continue the large charity. "Even if the conditions were entirely changed in America," she told Elisina, "I don't feel up to starting another big campaign for funds this autumn. Therefore we are somewhat in the position of the man of whom his wife was asked by the clergyman if he was 'resigned' when he died, and who said: 'I guess he had to be.'" Citing her great fatigue, Wharton wanted "to give our whole 'plant'" to the American Red Cross.[97]

Minnie's letter expressing concern about her sister-in-law's health met with a stoic response from Wharton: "I had pneumonia accidentally, as it were, because I was over-tired and run down, and we couldn't keep the apartment warm; and once it was over it was over." She said that responding to the "endless deluge of letters," now averaging more than twenty a day, tired her out more than anything else. She remained concerned about the uncertainty over what the ARC meant to do for the private war charities. One consoling event was the arrival of Max Farrand's brother, Dr. Livingston Farrand, to head the Rockefeller Foundation's tuberculosis effort. Wharton, after several shared lunches and dinners, found Dr. Farrand "perfectly charming" and asked Minnie, "How many more Farrands are there?—I should like one for myself!"[98]

Wharton's skepticism about the aims and methods of the Red Cross grew during the summer of 1917. In early August she wrote a correspondent in New York:

Here we are passing through a state of great anxiety concerning the future of all of our charities. The Red Cross seems to be planning such extensive undertakings of its own that there is a general impression that they will do little for the already-existing American War-Charities, in spite of the eloquent letter of approbation we have received from General Pershing. As the immense sums raised by the Red Cross in America have, for the time at any rate, stopped our sources of income, we are all wondering how we are to keep our charities going, and I am especially anxious about the Hostels as the organization is such a large one and is responsible for the welfare of so many people. It seems hardly fair of the Red Cross to have made such a colossal appeal in America unless it was prepared to make up to individual charities for the loss of assistance which has inevitably resulted.[99]

One way of enlisting the aid and cooperation of women from private relief organizations was to form the Women's War Relief Corps in early August. The new corps was open to "all American women whose husbands are citizens or subjects of Allied nations."[100] Somewhat prematurely, the corps listed Edith Wharton and Isabel Lathrop (of the American Fund for French Wounded) on its board of directors.[101] A week later the corps revised its statement of purpose: "The committee has been formed merely to centralize the war relief work that is being done by Americans, and it is not the intention of the committee to reorganize any of the work that has been in existence during the war, but to learn through which channels help is most needed and to give help in that direction." At first American women were asked only "to register their works, stating the direction in which their ability lies."[102]

By late August Wharton had come to the conclusion that she would have to turn over the running of her tuberculosis sanatoriums for soldiers to the Red Cross, but, as she explained to a benefactor who had bankrolled many of her charities, she was determined to retain her civilian convalescent homes:

[W]ith respect to the houses at Groslay and Arromanches, the situation is different. As you know, they are rest-houses and convalescent homes rather than actual hospitals, and the service they have rendered in helping back to health the refugee women and children cared for by the American Hostels has been incalculable.

To hand over these houses to the Red Cross would be to absorb in one gigantic organization a small formation of a special kind, which owed its success in great measure to the fact that Mrs. Royall Tyler and I are both exceptionally familiar with French ideas and social conditions, and that we have had three years of work among the refugees. Necessarily, these qualifications are exactly those which the Red Cross workers lack.[103]

Her reasons for keeping these rest houses highlights the differences between private American charities in France and the newly arrived American Red Cross. The rest houses had been established to care for the tubercular women and children among the refugees being helped by the American Hostels. The people who ran the private charities had three years of experience and a sensitivity to French customs that the newcomers could not match. The final break came when the ARC showed through its clumsy handling of personnel situations that it did not care about national or personal sensitivities, only about imposing American control and ensuring efficiency.

In the meantime Wharton met Elisina's questions and doubts with a sharp remark: "I sometimes wonder whether any organization of the kind, which has been entrusted to French hands, will ever come up to your very enlightened standard, which seeks to combine Anglo-Saxon ideas of administration with allowances for French idiosyncracies." The only solution to Elisina's objections would be to cut her up into small pieces and put her at the head of every part of the operation. Fearing a collapse of Elisina's health similar to the one she had experienced the previous winter, Wharton asked her to consider turning over the entire Hostels organization to the American Red Cross: "It seems to me doubtful if the continuation of the Hostels is a vital necessity; I am sure a good many people are encrusted on us who might be fending for themselves, or depending on other charities. Anyway, now that the Red Cross has tackled the whole refugee and repatriate problem, why not hand them over the Hostels bodily if they think them necessary?

"My own collaboration having consisted mainly in money raising, I could be of little practical use in 'running' the work, even if I were less thoroughly tired than I am. Wouldn't it perhaps be wisest to let them, after all, take over the whole group, Groslay included?"[104]

In the meantime, the power of money and the official sanction of the American Red Cross as the philanthropic arm of the American

Expeditionary Force were sweeping away obstacles blocking most take-overs. Mildred Bliss, after a visit from the Red Cross commissioners, turned over her American Distributing Service, active since the beginning of the war, with all of its supplies and automobiles. By late August Wharton was "convinced that the Red Cross will soon be in complete control of relief work in France."[105]

The first week of September she was resting in Fontainebleau and describing for Berenson her plans for the trip to Morocco. She mentioned the consolidation of her charities with the American Red Cross.[106] She told Robert Grant, "My impression is that by that time [her return at the end of October] the Red Cross will more or less have taken over the American Hostels, but not the children of Flanders or the Convalescent Houses for refugees, which I mean to hang on to for as long as I can."[107] She wrote to the head of the ARC asking that the officer in charge of one of its divisions make a tour of the American Hostels to see "certainly the most comprehensive American charity in Paris."[108]

In retrospect, not everyone condemned the aggressive actions of the ARC. One contemporary observer said, "Our American Red Cross in France, accused by some of aggressiveness, practicality and all the pushing faults of our young democracy, has nevertheless the innate shyness of its youth and its singleness of purpose."[109]

Those "pushing faults" became apparent when the ARC published a broad public policy statement. After citing the changed conditions that accompanied America's entry into the war, the authors outlined the new policy:

—that money raised by the ARC would go only to agencies under its control,

—that the ARC would take over the shipping and distribution of relief supplies, "both on the ocean and inland,"

—that the American Army "has chosen, and the people of the United States have been requested to consider the American Red Cross as the central organization through which relief work should be carried on by Americans in this war," and

—that the ARC would "classify, standardize and requisition relief supplies which are needed here."

The agreement was signed by Edith Wharton and Walter Berry, along with seventeen other prominent residents of Paris who served as the heads

of private American relief efforts. According to the newspaper announcement, the signers "recommend to their friends and fellow workers at home
the acceptance of the views and the adoption of the scheme proposed."[110]
The ARC did not say that private relief agencies could no longer operate,
just that they had to find other methods for shipping and distributing
supplies if they chose not to cooperate. That, of course, meant the end of
most private American charities and relief societies.

The shipping issue was complicated not only by the lack of American
merchant marine vessels and sailors and the overwhelming need to get
American Expeditionary Force troops to France, but by the uncoordinated
acquisition policies of the different divisions of the War Department as well,
where "Secretary Baker let the bureau chiefs run loose, and they ordered
everything in sight, without any idea of how large the AEF would be, or
how much shipping would be available to take matériel to France."[111]

Wharton was greatly relieved during the first week of September
when the American Red Cross took over the diffuse and hugely expensive
Tuberculeux de la Guerre. But she quickly drew the line when the ARC
proposed to name the recently converted château at Yerres "the Edith
Wharton Sanatorium" in acknowledgment of her contributions.[112] She
would soon use this tribute as a bargaining threat against what she saw as
the ARC's insensitive treatment of tubercular patients.

෨

Wharton had been invited by General Hubert Lyautey, the *résident général*
of Morocco, to attend an annual industrial exhibition in the capital of
Rabat. In 1912 the general had rescued the sultan during a national
insurrection. In gratitude, the sultan allowed General Lyautey to establish
a French protectorate in the major portion of Morocco. Wharton had met
the general and his wife in Paris. Now she and Walter Berry used this
opportunity of an official invitation to attend a fair displaying industrial
and craft products in Rabat, and they were greatly impressed.[113] As she
said in her autobiography, one purpose of these annual fairs was to impress
allies and enemies alike that the war did not curtail France's activities in
her North African colonies.[114]

Before leaving for Morocco, she summed up, in a letter to one of her
donors, the arrangements for her charities: "The Red Cross has also, by
an exceptional favor, agreed to assume all of the running expenses of 'The
American Hostels' while leaving the present management unchanged,
thus relieving me of a great financial burden; but I am keeping my two

other war charities, the 'Children of Flanders', entrusted to me directly by the Belgian Government, and which, therefore, I cannot hand over, as well as our 'American Convalescent Homes' for refugee women and children."[115] On September 15, 1917, the day she departed for Morocco, she wrote a memorandum of understanding to the ARC.[116] Obviously she wanted to have a clear agreement with the Red Cross that the convalescent homes were to remain independent and that her personnel at the American Hostels were to remain in place.

She instructed Elisina to convene the General Committee of the American Hostels and to "*prendre un vote au sujet de l'offre de la Croix Rouge Américaine.*"[117] This apparent formality left Elisina with the work of pushing through the official transfer to the American Red Cross. When, two months later, the French members of the committee were outraged at the treatment of the hostels staff by ARC managers, poor Elisina was the one who looked as if she had pushed through the vote.

Also before leaving, Wharton took the extraordinary step of cabling Payne Whitney and Lewis Cass Ledyard, asking them to transfer their original donation from the *Tuberculeux de la Guerre* (now operated by the American Red Cross) to her convalescent homes. In reply she received a confirmation of a large gift of almost $10,000 from Ledyard, which allowed her to "feel free now to go to Morocco with a light heart."[118] She would eventually persuade Whitney and Ledyard to transfer 150,000 francs, or roughly $30,000, from their original contribution to the *Tuberculeux de la Guerre* to her convalescent homes.[119] Another sizable contribution came from Mildred Bliss. The monthly operating expenses for the convalescent homes was 40,000 francs, and while Wharton understood that the Red Cross might give something, she knew that she would have to raise the major portion through private subscriptions. She would soon ask Ledyard "whether you think it would be possible to get from fifteen or sixteen people in New York a promise of a monthly subscription from $100 to $500 for Groslay for the year 1918?"[120] Of course Minnie would be trying to raise money, but Wharton felt Ledyard "could reach a different centre."

The two convalescent homes were at Groslay, some twenty miles from Paris, and at Arromanches in Normandy. They cared for 135 refugee women and children drawn from the families assisted by the American Hostels. In addition, there were 50 children with tuberculosis of the bone sent by the city of Paris, which paid a subsidy of 2.50 francs a day per patient.[121]

Wharton continued to be alert to the broader politics of journalism and the manipulation of public opinion. In a reverse of the Clement March fiasco of a year earlier, she informed the General Staff of the AEF that a disreputable French journalist was in the United States spreading malicious rumors about the English effort in the war. His meddling could be dangerous. "Any inquiry among serious journalists in Paris will show you that M. Le Roux's opinion is of no account here, but I am convinced that he is doing much harm at present among Americans in Paris and perhaps also in America."[122]

ᨠ

Wharton left Paris on September 15 in high spirits: "It's going to be a wonderful adventure."[123] By September 26 she was writing Minnie from Rabat, "a fairy world, where a motor from the 'Résidence' stands always at the door to carry us to new wonders, & where every expedition takes one straight into Harun-al-Raschid land." She and Berry had landed at Tangier the previous week and were met by an officer of the general's staff. After two days in Tangier, they set off for Rabat. The trip of some 150 miles over a trail only recently opened to automobiles "necessitates a strong backbone like mine." During her time in Rabat she was taken to the exhibitions and the fair by the general and his wife. Realizing that she was at a trade show, she told Minnie, "Certain things, notably the rugs & some of the embroidered curtains, would sell splendidly in America, I am sure." Despite the heat and the glimpses of rough Moroccan hotels, she closed, "Oh, the relief of having a real holiday!"[124]

She wrote to Berenson from Fez, where she was picturesquely settled: "The motor stops before a white palace front, & we enter another court full of more flowers, with orange groves bordered by rushing streams, fountains splashing into tiled tanks, yellow jasmines, pomegranate trees hung with ripe fruit, & beyond a great shady room with a bowing caïd in the step, & an inner court of green & blue & white tiles, with more fountains—for Fez is all fountains!" She teased him with hints of the ceremony of the Sacrifice of the Sheep and seeing the sultan's concubines "in clothes such as Bakst never dreamed of." She began a description of Meknès but remembered that Berry would see him soon in Paris and tell all.[125]

Despite exotic locations and royal treatment, the war was never far from her thoughts. From Casablanca she wrote congratulating an American mother, "You must be having thrilling times, with both the boys in the war already."[126] Earlier she had asked Max Farrand if he were "exercising all [his] Plattsburg muscles."[127] Of her nephew Newbold Rhinelander, who had recently left the American Ambulance Corps to enlist in the Army Air Corps, she would tell his parents, "I am so glad you have given him this opportunity of seeing this great moment of history, & lending a hand in the cause." But she immediately added, "I have been wondering why some of my able-bodied young cousins were not here taking a share in the struggle."[128]

By October 25 she was back on French soil, but she was not looking forward to the hard traveling it would take to reach Paris from Tangier. Despite the hardships she could say, "But it was really worth it all, and I'm so glad I took this chance, which will never come again of seeing that land of fairy tales in fairy-tale fashion." She repeated for Minnie many of the same details in Berenson's letter. They had visited Meknès, which Christians had been allowed to visit only for the last two years. They stayed four days in Fez, they went to the foot of the Atlas Mountains, then they returned to Rabat, Berry departed for Paris and Wharton headed south again, this time accompanied by Marquis de Légorique and his wife and Legouzac, the greatest authority on the Atlas tribes. The general asked them to accompany her. They spent four days in Marrakech, where she was invited to visit the harem of the local pasha. As in her war reporting, she could claim a scoop: "The Pasha, at General Lyautey's request also allowed me to see the tomb of the Saadian Sultans (16th century) which no Europeans are allowed to see, and of which the existence was unknown until a few months ago, when General Lyautey was taken there. It is by far the most beautiful thing in Morocco, but, alas, no good photos have been taken yet."[129]

On her return to Paris in October, Wharton collected Berenson and set off on a tour of the devastated regions of northern France. When they came to a village where workers were clearing a well destroyed by the retreating Germans, Berenson, struck with the effects of the war at firsthand, immediately offered to pay for an electric pump.[130] Wharton assigned Walter Berry and Royall Tyler the task of finding Berenson a war-related government appointment.

Berenson had come to Paris to examine a supposed "Leonardo" for his employers, the Duveen Brothers. The visit included an explosive meeting with the Duveens over Berenson's sharing his expertise (for a handsome price) with other art dealers. Some people thought that Berenson moved to Paris because his openly pro-Allied position made him a target for his pro-German neighbors in northern Italy. He said that he felt it his duty as an American citizen to offer his services to his country.

Berenson's first interview was thwarted by a dalliance of which, in other circumstances, he might himself have been guilty:

> I recall going to Paris in 1917 when we entered the war, eager to do my bit. An influential friend recommended me to the head of a department lodged in splendour on the first floor of the Crillon. I was vouchsafed an appointment, was shown to a chair in the ante-room and asked to wait. A quarter of an hour passed, and another and another and another. I was sitting, as it happened, close to the magnificent carved and gilt but not over-massive door that led to the great man. I could hear a murmur of talk, interrupted by merry laughter, the flatter laughter of a male voice and the higher, more silvery laughter of a woman. I began to think I recognized this charming laugh and lo! at the end of an hour out came one of the prettiest and most frivolous of American Parisians, a little creature too silly to seem alarming, but eager to make society capital of what she heard. Well; I was ushered in but was too furious at having been kept waiting for so long and for such a reason. The interview was frosty. When I told my friend of this result of his effort to put me in touch with the high-placed, he laughed and assured me that waiting around was the lot of the subordinate in all business whether public or private.[131]

Negotiations over just what kind of job Berenson would find suitable dragged on for weeks. Like Herman Melville's exasperating character Bartleby, he said he was not particular. Finally, in December, Tyler offered him a position as a "secret and unofficial advisor, with regard to things Italian and German too, if I can manage both, to our general staff."[132] Berenson described his duties to Mary as "to see and hear and report." He asked her to make summaries from the Italian press so that he could follow the activities and remarks of the pro-Americans and the anti-Americans. Through Tyler's influence, he ended up as a liaison between the intelligence services of the British and the American expeditionary forces. This sinecure did not take him far away from his main profession since "the British Intelligence headquarters was located in the offices of the Duveen building in the Place Vendome. His first duty was to inspect the Schickler Collection."[133]

On her return to wartime Paris after six weeks in Morocco, Wharton was "greeted by the bright sunny news from Italy." But her spirits soon drooped beneath "the usual hideous arrears of letters which punishes one for every absence nowadays, & I must crawl back to the horrid mountain & try to nibble away at a little more of it."[134] Her doctor ordered her to begin a period of complete rest for three or four months at the end of November. "It is nothing but a case of brain and nerve fatigue, but I really must stop for a while."[135]

Even worse, Wharton discovered that the state of her war charities had become "horribly complicated by our association with the Red Cross. . . . I dislike to be thrown to a still greater extent on the tender mercies of the Red Cross. I say nothing more because we receive assistance from them, but when this is all over and we meet," she promised Minnie, "I will tell you something of their methods in France."[136]

One example of their methods occurred when the ARC cleaned out the office of the *Oeuvre des Tuberculeux de la Guerre*. Many of the furnishings had been loaned by Wharton's friends, and when the ARC took over the operation, it removed not only the records but also a rolltop desk belonging to Madame Langweil. In the correspondence between Wharton and the Red Cross that went on for more than a month, it became apparent that the ARC's solution to the problem was simply to buy the desk. In her novel *The Custom of the Country* (1913), Wharton had portrayed an acquisitive American heroine who buys and sells heirlooms that had been in European families for generations. But this was not fiction, and the subtlety of satire, she felt, would be lost on the ARC. Wharton told them flatly, "It would be impossible to propose to her to buy it."[137]

In a more serious matter, she pointed to "outrageous negligence, to call it by no worse name," in the tuberculosis sanatoriums where she had discovered patients without blankets or adequate medical attention.[138] She threatened to expose these unsatisfactory conditions to the American public if they were not corrected immediately. To one of her biggest contributors she confessed: "The last five or six months have, in some respects, been the unhappiest of my life. We handed over our tuberculosis sanatoria to the Red Cross in . . . the full belief that . . . the Red Cross could not only give more efficient management than we could obtain, but control sums of money beyond our reach. . . . It would take many pages to tell you the gradual growth of our disillusionment and the bitter criticism to which I have been subjected by the French members of our

Committee who could not understand my submitting to such treatment at the beginning, or being unable, since then, to obtain the proper care for our patients."[139] By the end of the month she could report that the ARC had corrected some of its shoddy practices by giving the tuberculosis patients some warm clothing,[140] but she sought to discipline it with one of the few means at her disposal. Her note to Homer Folks, the director of Civil Affairs of the ARC, was written with icy clarity: "I write to ask if you will kindly transmit to the Committee of the Red Cross my request that my name be withdrawn from the Tuberculosis Sanitarium at Yerres which the Red Cross has proposed to name after me."[141]

Even more disheartening than the conditions at the sanatoriums was the callous treatment of staff members of the American Hostels. Among other things Wharton found that, in spite of their earlier agreement, the American Red Cross was showing favoritism.[142] Wharton had held back two of her rest houses because she argued that she and Elisina were more attuned to French customs than ARC workers were or could be expected to be. And when she turned over the American Hostels, it was with the stipulation that the ARC would keep her management team intact. What Wharton had not anticipated was that after she had left for Morocco, the ARC would release French volunteers for no cause. Despite earlier assurances, French workers who had been with Wharton's charities for three years were dismissed suddenly, without reason and without the customary French eight days' severance pay. Nurses and doctors were told that they could leave because "American money is for American nurses" and doctors. Home visits to severely ill refugees by medical personnel were deemed inefficient and were discontinued. The American doctor in charge told Elisina, "This is American money, and the people who give the money have the right to decide how it should be used." Such conditions, Wharton said, "have made me decide that it is impossible for me to collaborate longer with the Red Cross in any branch of my work [and] . . . I am quite determined not to give my name to organizations which, in the hands of the Red Cross, no longer represent my methods of dealing with the poor."[143]

Where she could, she immediately took hold of the operations of her remaining charities. She asked Walter Berry to use his influence with the minister of the interior to permit the immediate delivery of coal to her convalescent homes in Groslay, where 110 tubercular women and infants were housed.[144] She knew that she was on the right track with the convalescent homes because the French Ministry of the Interior had cabled a proposal that she and Elisina take over the management of three more houses modeled on their own at Groslay, the whole operation to be paid for by the French government.[145]

੬੦

Throughout November Wharton looked at photographs of property. She told a real estate agent that she was interested in a large house near a woods, like the forest of Fontainebleau. And as the trip to Morocco retreated in time, it grew more enchanting in her mind. In mid-November she wrote to William Roscoe Thayer: "I am just back from a wonderful trip to Morocco, where France is doing such great things under General Lyautey, that I am impatient to tell the American public about them. I wonder if we shall ever understand the magnificence of France? Unluckily she runs the risk of being judged by her miserable government; but she will come out of this ordeal as she has come out of so many others."[146] She told Alice Garrett that her trip to Morocco seemed like a mirage now that she was back. She was so physically tired that "I am going to try to drop out of all my war work by the end of this month, that is of active participation."[147]

Wharton sought to keep contributors who were in danger of defecting to the ARC. One of her earliest and most consistent benefactors was Moncure Robinson, a friend of many years and a close friend of Ogden Codman's, who had stopped by her Paris door in August of 1914 and handed her maid the first of his generous and regular gifts. Now he revealed his plan to shift his monthly contribution of $1,000 from Wharton's charities to the American Red Cross. In her letter asking him to stay with her, she was unsparing in her criticism of the ARC: "I feel I owe it to our poor tuberculous patients and to the public in America to let the Red Cross methods here be known."[148] To other friends she privately complained, "The Red Cross has been & is still—a perfect night-mare to me! I am sick to think of the mischief they have done, & the impression they are giving everywhere of incompetence and arrogance combined."[149] When Minnie wrote that their booth at a New York City charity fair had had only a moderate success, Wharton responded, "From my point of view $2,000 seems a decent sum for one stall so soon after the country has been sucked dry by the Red Cross."[150]

Minnie often bore the brunt of Wharton's temper, especially when engaged in the onerous duties of writing the periodic reports to the charity committees in America. On occasion she scolded Minnie: "You seem to think it is easier to write a report than it really is!! I have tried to train several of our workers to do this, but they never seem to have a sufficiently comprehensive vision. However, now that the raising of funds for the American Hostels is off my shoulders, Elisina Tyler hopes to be able to send you once a fortnight, or once a month, a bulletin of anecdotes about our patients from Groslay and Arromanches, and from the Children of Flanders Rescue Committee."[151]

Later Wharton promised to send "by the valise the fullest possible reports of Edith Wharton's War Charities, to December 1st, 1917." The promised pathetic human-interest cases had been delayed. When Minnie asked for them, Wharton exploded: "As for the individual pathetic stories it is hard for us here, on the edge of this awful tragedy, to understand why people in America do not understand that we are too busy to collect anecdotes. We work all day long every day trying to help as many people as we can, and until the horizon lightens it will be hard to see talking and collecting anecdotes."[152] Wharton, whose own health had suffered through overwork, closed her letter by insisting that Minnie hire a secretary out of the charity general funds and that she keep well.

Wharton's busy charity schedule left her unable to accept the invitation to dine with Colonel Edward M. House, President Wilson's aide and confidant, and Brand Whitlock, the former minister to Belgium, on November 26. But she did ask Whitlock about initiating an appeal to send clothing to Belgium. She was ready to send a cable to ask Mrs. Augustus Belmont to sign the appeal with Whitlock's signature and her own.[153]

House had come to France to hammer out the necessary military understanding with the French. He cabled Wilson, "If we send over a million actual fighting men by the autumn of 1918, they will continue to use their men for offensive operations and [we can] use ours for defensive purposes until then."[154] House played mediator between the French prime minister, Georges Clémenceau, and the British prime minister, David Lloyd George, in determining a plan that would coordinate military and political control over the Allied forces. Thus, when House asked to dine informally with Wharton during the first week of December, he had a great deal to say to her assembled guests: Berry, Berenson, Royall Tyler, and Polybe. After dinner they were joined by Morton Fullerton and an Alsatian doctor Bucher. There was good talk all around, and the American diplomat made a good impression on his audience of expatriates.

Colonel House was not the only new American in the city: "Paris literally swarms with compatriots." Wharton added that for her own tastes "there are too many women in the number. The R. C. [American Red Cross] seems to have shovelled them over by the 1000s & I hope some will get their passports home."[155] General Pershing agreed with Wharton's assessment, and in a confidential memo to his chief of staff in Washington insisted that the volunteers be carefully screened. Pershing said that not only did idle Americans coming to France put a drain of scarce food and shipping space, they posed a threat to morale and morals: "There is much criticism by the French and by resident Americans of [the] large influx of idle young Americans of both sexes. Most of them come to Paris and many enter the gay life here to the discredit of their more serious countrymen. They menace our good relations with the French who consider them as idle non-producers and undesirable." Pershing asked that passports be restricted to those volunteers approved in advance by American Red Cross officials operating in France.[156]

The Garretts, who assumed their new diplomatic post in the Hague, had liked *Summer*, Wharton's novella of desire set in New England. And Wharton noted that her English publisher, Sir Frederick Macmillan, told her that the novella was having a better sale in England than any of her other books.[157] On the other hand, "the Pittsfield Public Library has ruled it out!!"[158]

ঽ৯

The question of honors and medals for charity workers was always a contentious one for Wharton. She complained to the French secretary of health that his insistence that she distinguish between which of her workers should get silver medals and which bronze left her in a quandary. Among her four large organizations, it was nearly impossible to distinguish between the managers—*chefs d'emploi* to receive silver medals and workers, some of whom had key positions, to receive bronze medals—"without neglecting some collaborators whose work deserves recognition." She had similar difficulty distinguishing among her organizers of Edith Wharton committees in the United States. She would insist, of course, on a gold medal for Minnie, "who has raised over 500,000 francs, for me since the beginning of the war." And there was Miss Estelle Neuhaus, whose benefit concerts had brought in hundreds of thousands of francs. Under the circumstances Wharton thought it best to send along a tentative list.[159]

She used the American diplomatic bag (after an earlier misfire of trying to send her Christmas greetings by regular mail) to respond to the Garretts' telegram of Christmas greeting. Her own holiday was "a dark &

desperate day that swarmed from dawn to midnight with relations & refugees." She sent them a gift that would have been useful had they been in Paris rather than in neutral Holland: "I send a little electric night-light for Zeppelin nights, when the chandeliers in the Legation have to be extinguished!"[160]

5

≈

ARMISTICE AND WITHDRAWAL: 1918

THE FINAL YEAR OF THE WAR, 1918, FOUND WHARTON WITHDRAWING MORE and more from administrative and fund-raising duties with the charities. Several of the relief organizations (for example, the American Hostels for Refugees) had been turned over to the American Red Cross. Those that remained under her direction—the convalescent homes—were increasingly looked after by Elisina Tyler. Wharton insulated herself from petitioners by turning all of her correspondence over to secretaries, who pleaded Mrs. Wharton's latest illness to excuse her from public appearances or her injured wrist to explain unanswered letters. Meanwhile she sought closer emotional ties with Bernard Berenson and a new friend, Ronald Simmons. Even before the Armistice she had decided to move from Paris to the suburbs. And with the arrival of the delegates to the Peace Conference and many Americans in Paris, she retreated further and further into a private emotional and geographical space.

Wharton spent the Christmas holidays of 1917-1918 "submerged . . . by refugees and relations. The latter swam here," she told Mary Berenson, "all bright and beautiful in khaki." To Mary suffering with bronchitis in England, Wharton reported that Berenson, in Paris with her, was well and "manages in spite of his endless engagements, to be very kind to me."[1] Some of Wharton's frustration over Berenson's occasional inaccessibility was apparent one evening when she telephoned the Hôtel Ritz three times asking for him and was left waiting each time for five minutes in dead silence before hanging up and trying again.[2]

If Wharton had trouble getting her own calls through, others apparently had no trouble reaching her. The flood of letters and requests continued. She was hoping to "get away from letters and bothers" in the middle of February to spend ten days with friends near Marseilles. Throughout January, she prefaced each dictated business letter with the justification that her doctor had ordered her to write as little as possible.[3] To friends and contributors to her charities, she excused the dictated letters by saying that she had hurt her right hand.[4] Most who inquired were told by her secretary that Wharton was under strict doctor's orders to rest for several months, during which she was not allowed to receive visitors. Her secretary advised those few petitioners invited to make personal visits to call in the morning because Madame Wharton had been ordered to rest after five each afternoon.[5]

The rhythm of her written responses suggests that Wharton allowed letters to pile up for six or seven days, then called in her secretary and dictated her replies. At this time, in mid-January of 1918, she was turning down requests for donations of lace for New York charity exhibitions. With her refusal of one order she said that she was going to close her sewing *ouvroir* as soon as all of her workers found jobs.

Still much on her mind, of course, were the offenses of the American Red Cross, especially where the American Hostels' dispensary was concerned. She wrote a long letter to Lewis Cass Ledyard detailing her complaints. The ARC doctors and nurses had taken over the operation with no courtesy toward the French doctors, some of whom (such as her personal physician, Isch Wall) had given their services for free for more than a year. Most galling to Wharton, home care for old and epileptic patients had been abandoned, and those with wounds were expected to change their own dressings.

These and other ARC policy breaches led her to conclude that "it is impossible for me to collaborate longer with the Red Cross in any branch of my work." She went on: "The extent to which our organization had broken down since the Red Cross have taken it in hand is so humiliating and heart-breaking to me, and I receive such daily evidence of neglect and indifference, and of complete misunderstanding of the moral problem to be dealt with, that I do not wish to have my name associated with any work run on such principles."[6]

She also pointed out that Dr. White, the tuberculosis expert sponsored by her Boston committee, had transferred his services from the *Tuberculeux de la Guerre* to the Red Cross in August but was still drawing a salary of $10,000 a year from her Boston and New York committees. "I am curious to know," she asked with stinging innocence, "on what ground Dr. White is accepting a salary to represent a non-existing organization."[7]

Wharton had sent Minnie Jones a draft charities report highly critical of the ARC to publish in the American newspapers, but she held up publication pending decisions about the future of the American Hostels. She asked Ledyard if he and a few of his friends could guarantee the $18,000 a month necessary to keep her two independent convalescent houses operating. She concluded, "I can truly say that my own collaborators have done their utmost to avoid any friction, and try to make the war victims we are helping understand that the unfortunate changes brought about by the Red Cross methods are beyond our power to prevent."[8]

⁂

One of the most draining aspects of her charity work was arranging for the pitiable individual cases that friends and strangers brought to her attention. Where she could she made room for medical cases in her convalescent homes, but many of the needy cases continued to require special attention. For example, she sent her former secretary, Dolly Herbert, to the Paris suburb of St. Denis to inspect a possible house for an old woman she was trying to place.[9] In addition, she tried to find suitable housing in Châlons-sur-Marne for a seventy-nine-year-old widow from Verdun.[10] She soon began to deposit unspecified contributions in a personally controlled trust fund, drawing on the account for individual cases. Enclosed with checks drawn on the trust fund, Wharton would also frequently offer advice, for example: "I enclose a small check from my 'Trust Fund' for Mme Trichon in the hope that it will help her out a little; but please give it to her in very small amounts, or the bad woman with whom she lives will undoubtedly take the money from her. I speak from long experience of dealing with refugees."[11]

As more and more Americans began to arrive, she served as a conduit, an information service. When asked by French friends about how to entertain the newly arrived AEF officers, Wharton could be blunt and sweeping in her evaluations. She cautioned a group of French society women who were planning to entertain American servicemen, for example, that nobody in the entire American officer corps spoke French.[12] She advised Charles du Bos's father when he wanted to entertain American officers at a musical tea.[13] During the same period, she steadfastly refused to undertake new charity schemes suggested to her.

In early February she addressed the *Sociétié des Conférences*, composed of worthy members of the French Academy, on why America had entered the war. At the last moment she learned that she was expected to bring the American ambassador, and she was able to secure Ambassador Sharp. On the stage she was "'flanked' on the right by Mr. Sharp & Walter, to my left by Bourget & other Academics." She was supported in the back of the hall by Elisina and Royall Tyler, Ronald Simmons, "& by various other pals." Though "never before having uttered one word in public in any tongue!" she found that when her moment came she was not a bit nervous. "I felt I had such lots of interesting things to tell them that the speaking tube didn't matter much; & then I saw such heaps of friendly faces grinning at me from the 'salle' that I plunged in without a shiver." (She later jokingly told an audience of American soldiers that since she had to deliver the speech in French, she "was sustained by the thought that my audience probably didn't understand more than half of what I was saying."[14]) Her speech was enlivened by human interest stories provided by D'Arcy Paul, the mutual friend of the Garretts and hers. "His stories saved my conference from acting as a quick sleeping draught on an audience of 400 intellectuals."[15] She managed to keep everyone awake except "one old gentleman & an officer, whom I soothed into immediate slumber."[16]

ﾊ

As Wharton withdrew more and more from charity administration, she found that her remaining organizations moved on with a momentum of their own. After the new year began, Elisina met with Red Cross officials about aiding Groslay and Arromanches. If Wharton was ambivalent about staying with the fund-raising side of her charities, her able lieutenants were not. Elisina and Minnie were planning Elisina's trip to America to seek donations. Wharton was annoyed that Elisina, fearing criticism from sensitive American committees that recently had been swindled by bogus war charities, refused to book a first-class cabin for the voyage. Wharton sensed, however, that she should be careful about objecting to any aspect of the trip, "especially as all credit for the good management of our three charities belongs to her, and it would be very grudging of me to seem to oppose her going to America to tell the story of what she has accomplished."[17]

Wharton was about to leave Paris herself. In a flurry of activity on February 11, she made a number of domestic arrangements the day before her departure[18] and invited Berenson to join her "for a sun bask (outer and inner) at the delicious hotel at San Salvadeur near Hyères."[19] By late February she was back at the familiar Costebelle Hôtel in Hyères, chiding

Berenson for not writing her more frequently: "Who am I, to reproach my friends for not writing? But I do, all the same, when I love 'em! So there's no help for you . . . but don't let me languish so long again. I simply hate living, on the Bronte plan, 'without the aid of joy.'"[20] She still smarted over Geoffrey Scott's marriage to Sybil Cutting and was especially sympathetic to Mary Berenson, who had confessed her anguish in a recent letter. Scott was Berenson's secretary and Mary's personal favorite. Wharton's idea of personal solace extended to Berenson, whom she tried to entice to take the sleeping train south and join her. Promising to delay her departure if he should leave chilly Paris, she offered "peach and plum trees white and rosy, and the irises and hyacinths, and the golden showers of mimosa."[21]

≈

Meanwhile, on January 8, President Wilson had announced his Fourteen Points to end the war and to guide the peace. These noble aims were promulgated without any consultation with his European allies and with little discussion within his own cabinet. Even Wilson's close adviser Colonel House was taken completely off guard: "I never knew a man who did things so casually." Wilson's private secretary learned of the speech only two hours before the president delivered it, and three cabinet members discovered its contents only several hours afterward.[22]

≈

During the autumn of 1917, when Wharton had begun to receive frequent requests to serve on boards and to speak to American servicemen, she began to insist on being referred to as "Mrs. Wharton" on all public occasions. The preference for "Mrs. Wharton" rather than "Edith Wharton" or "Mrs. Edith Wharton" became firmer in 1918. For instance, after learning from Mrs. Sharp, wife of the ambassador, that she had been elected to the Honorary Board of the Women's War Relief Corps, Wharton instructed the secretary of that organization, "Will you kindly request that my name shall be entered on your Committee list as Mrs. Wharton, and not as 'Mrs. Edith Wharton'?"[23]

A fuller explanation of her preference came in her response to the nomination for her election to the prestigious National Institute of Arts and Letters. The secretary of the institute in the original letter of nomination (sent in care of Scribners) pointed out that while only one woman was presently a member (Mrs. Julia Ward Howe), the nominating committee was proposing Mrs. Margaret Deland and Mrs. Mary Wilkins Freeman as well as Wharton. Wharton responded to the proposed election by stipulating "If the honor is paid me, may I ask to be spoken of simply as 'Mrs. Wharton'? I sign my books, naturally, with my Christian name, but when it is prefix [prefaced] by a Mrs., I feel myself associated with vendors of patent medicines and other categories of females with whom I have no affiliation."[24] (Lydia Pinkham's popular home remedy and other patent medicines frequently carried the inventor's first name.)

A consequence perhaps of thinking of herself as a personage, rather than simply as a person, Wharton may have resented this less-than-august company of female writers and claimed the distinction she deserved. She felt that any form of public address that included her given name was too informal, that it smacked of those New England authors who used two or three names, and that it was not the form of address to be used with people of her social station. A related explanation comes from her position as a divorced woman. During her divorce in 1913 she had taken legal steps to insure that she could retain the name "Mrs. Wharton." For legal purposes her signature would have been "Edith Newbold Jones," but her registered professional name was "Mrs. Wharton."[25]

Wharton's insistence on her proper name grew more emphatic as the war drew to a close. In a dictated letter supporting Naval Ensign E. M. Pickman's request to his commander that his wife be allowed to come to Paris, Wharton's secretary obliged by saying that Mrs. Pickman had worked for the Children of Flanders Rescue Committee in the summer of 1915 and that Mrs. Wharton would be delighted to have her rejoin the work as soon as possible. But Wharton's secretary pointedly added: "In speaking of Mrs. Wharton in your statement to Admiral Sims, will you kindly call her 'Mrs. Wharton', and suppress the 'Edith'. Mrs. Wharton asks me to say that she particularly dislikes this use of her Christian name, although it always seems to be inflicted on 'femmes de lettres' in France."[26]

To a request that she speak to American soldiers and sailors, she broke her usual rule of refusing requests to speak in public but insisted, "If my name is announced in advance, will you kindly speak of me as Mrs. Wharton and not as Mrs. *EDITH* Wharton. I object very much to this use of my Christian name."[27] And a year after the Armistice, her secretary enclosed her by now common correction along with Wharton's donation to a Paris charity: "Mrs. Wharton hopes you will excuse her pointing out that her name has been put on your Committee list as Mrs. 'Edith Wharton'. She dislikes very much this use of her Christian name in a public way, and she would be much obliged if you would have it altered to 'Mrs. Wharton'."[28]

Her early engraved Paris notepaper has "Mme Edward Wharton" across the center and down below in the right hand corner in smaller type "53, rue de Varenne." When she moved to St. Brice after the war, her bookplates said simply "Mrs. Wharton."

Wharton's anxiety over how she was addressed was not entirely misplaced. Some people had (and have) trouble remembering that Wharton was a "Mrs." and not a "Miss." A charitable donor writing to the Paris edition of the New York Herald in the opening days of the war offered to contribute a large amount of money if the "Miss Wharton" collecting funds were the novelist. As recently as 1972, Stephen Longstreet, writing a history of Paris, entitled his twenty-first chapter "Society's Historian— Miss Wharton."[29]

The names of her fictional characters were always a matter of importance to Wharton. Despite her claim in A Backward Glance that her characters came to her with their names so firmly attached that it was impossible to change them "even with the aid of a hypodermic," her notebooks and manuscripts show that she frequently altered characters' names. Lily Bart in The House of Mirth was first called "Rose," and Ellen in The Age of Innocence went through the permutations of "Clementine" and "Clementina" in early outlines of the story. Wharton frequently used names as labels of obvious derision, as with "Indiana Frusk" in The Custom of the Country.

In Wharton's uncollected satire, "Writing a War Story," the American relief worker Miss Ivy Spang is looking for an opening for a war story she has been commissioned to write. She takes no consolation from the opening of the last story in the most recent number of the magazine, which began "A shot rang out—" "Its place on the list showed what the editor and his public thought of that kind of an opening, and her contempt for it was increased by reading the author's name. The story was signed 'Edda Clubber Hump.' Poor thing."[30] Wharton and Henry James loved to swap funny names drawn from the newspapers. After James's death, she included Lapsley in the game: "Of couse you've seen the Daily Mail that they've caught Mrs. Rachel Gobsweib, and sent her up. Her name alone makes the nature of her offense sufficiently clear."[31]

๛

During the second week of March, Wharton, still in the south of France, told the Garretts, "I've been away from Paris for a month 'resting.'" She anticipated her return to Paris in two days with "a quite unspeakable dread." The Garretts had praised her recent *Scribner's Magazine* article on French culture and customs, and she told them she was already projecting a book on the subject with the tentative title *French Ways and Their Meaning*. The editor of *Cosmopolitan* had asked her for five more articles just like the *Scribner's* piece. And "as people will think it will be good proppergander I'm buckling down to the task," she said, taking the measure of the magazine, "& you may seek my prose next summer among the 'ads' for motor tyres & noiseless w.c.s."[32]

Her opinion of American journalism was not high. When she was invited by General Pershing to edit a page of "The Stars & Stripes," the weekly AEF newspaper published at the front, she hesitated until Walter Berry promised to help. But she remained ambivalent about the assignment: "'God only knows how much I dread it—', as the Maine man said when he went to Portland on a spree!" "Still," she added, "it does seem a chance to lift the paper out its horrible base-ball & Ladies Home Journal atmosphere."[33]

๛

The American army had had a successful campaign, and Wharton thought "how clever of Clémenceau to go & tell them so! What a man!" She playfully told Alice Garrett that she was so impressed by the picture of the Garretts' grand house in the Hague "that I shall never dare ask you & John to come and stay at the little Louis XV pavilion I've just bought near Montmorency. It was built for a dancer, 'La Guimaso', and you'll see the appropriateness at once."[34]

Once back in Paris, she was submerged by the usual flood of business correspondence, despite the help of Mrs. Blair Fairchild, who frequently acted as her personal secretary after the beginning of March.[35] Wharton continued to be a clearinghouse for all those with "special cases" to be placed and problems to be solved. To complaints about conditions in a tuberculous hospital in Besancon, Wharton instructed the correspondent to write directly to Mr. Folks of the ARC.[36] A petitioner with a question about a blind boy was referred to Miss Winifred Holt of the Lighthouse that cared for the war blind in Paris.[37] In answer to another request,

Wharton would allow the Women's War Relief Corps to make photographs of the American Hostels and the Children of Flanders, but only if the pictures were clearly labeled with the names of her charities.[38]

ᨠ

On March 21 the Germans launched a broad offensive, their last of the war. With their new strategy of using storm troopers to penetrate the lines, they quickly reached the rear lines of the British Fifth Army. Using a massed force of sixty-two divisions along a forty-two-mile front, the Germans pushed the British back twenty-five miles in one week, taking a total of 90,000 prisoners.

The Germans also began shelling Paris, more than seventy-five miles away, with long-range guns, including Big Bertha. The huge gun, nicknamed for its inventor's wife, could propel a 240- pound shell more than ninety miles. In the United States an aged Henry Adams had commented to his nurse, "This is no world for an old man to live in when the Germans can shoot to the moon."[39]

Wharton herself was not spared the effects of Big Bertha. She wrote Alice Garrett:

> The chief interest of this letter will be due to the fact of its being written during an air raid—the first daylight one that Paris has been favored with since the famous attack in the beginning of the war, when the universe was nearly deprived, at one fell stroke, of Mr. Herrick & his Conseiller & Ambassade. It is now 9:45, & since 8 o'c there has been a good deal of booming in the banlieue, & sirening in Paris; but they have not stopped the circulation as they do at night—a fearful crash interrupted me here; probably a French camion close by, certainly not a bomb. But my household is in the cellar (by request, as the last bad raid absolutely encircled this house), all except dear old Gross, & my maid & I, who prefer bombs to pneumonia, & are all too busy to bother, anyhow.
> This quarter was badly frightened the last time, but probably by day there will be less "French flurry".[40]

In her request for a safe-conduct pass, Wharton collapsed events and time by more than a week when she told the security director of the Paris police that she had hurried her return from the south of France because of the aerial bombardments. The home for the Children of

Flanders at St Ouen had been so badly shaken that it was necessary to transfer the whole colony.[41] Wharton was still seeking advice on business matters from John Garrett. When the *Rotterdamsche Courant* newspaper wanted to serialize a Dutch translation of *Summer*, she at first thought the editor's offer of 250 francs absurdly low and responded that she would accept 500 francs, still well below her usual fee. But then she had second thoughts. She asked John to tell the editor that a patriotic Mrs. Wharton would allow publication only "if you can assure me that your political views are always in accord with those of the nations for whom my country is fighting."[42] Facing mounting expenses from her recent purchase of "a tiny place near Paris," she was willing in the end to accept the 250-franc offer if the newspaper's politics were right.

Despite Big Bertha's lobbing of shells into Paris during the spring of 1918, Wharton told several people that she was not in favor of moving the children out of the capital. This resistance may have been a reaction to what happened in September of 1914 when, with Wharton stuck in England, the manager of the *Foyer* abandoned her first workroom. Wharton felt responsible for not being present to straighten out the mess when thirty of her workwomen were thrown into the street without any money, an experience that left her devotedly loyal to all of her workers. Now, in late March of 1918, she was still trying to track down the twenty medals promised five months earlier to her war workers.[43]

In another effort to gain recognition for her charities, she made arrangements with the official in charge of the *Direction du Cinématographe de l'Armée* to make films of the convalescent homes at Groslay and Arromanches and several of the Children of Flanders colonies. The films would be carried by Justin Godart, former undersecretary of the Ministry of Health, who was to depart shortly for the United States, where he was to speak about Wharton's charities.[44] Through friends Wharton arranged speaking engagements for him in Washington and elsewhere.[45]

In April she made her first speech to the American soldiers. She began by telling the members of the AEF that she had never spoken in public until her speech delivered in French in February. Though she considered speaking in public to be a man's job, not a woman's, she continued, "I believe if I were dead, and anybody asked me to come back and witness for France, I should get up out of my grave and do it." The purpose of her talk was to acquaint American servicemen with the customs of France.

Her first lesson was a general one: They should try to learn from France rather than insist on teaching the French people their American ways. Different countries, she generalized, would have different customs. Then she commented dryly, "liking corn-beef hash for breakfast instead of a roll and butter is not a necessary proof of superiority." One lesson they needed to learn immediately was the courtesy of saying "Bonjour, Monsieur" or "Bonjour, Madame" when entering a shop or restaurant, which was sure to get them better treatment and better food. Further, they should take off their hats when a funeral passed, and in no circumstances should the drivers in her audience cut through a funeral procession.

She urged them to remember that the first people they met on landing were not a true gauge of the French. Using an argument from class consciousness that may have been lost on the army draftees who now replaced earlier volunteers, she encouraged them to "try to make friends with the best ones you would like your wives and mothers and sweethearts to know." She contrasted the beauty of the French cities, which "when they have any public improvement to make, they try to make it beautiful as well as useful," with American cities "full of factory chimneys and gas-works and bar-rooms." The French had proven that urban utility could coexist with beauty: "They don't allow hideous 'elevated' to straddle over their wide avenues, or overhead trolley wires to disfigure them."[46] There is no record of how her remarks were received.

As the spring progressed, her thoughts were turning more and more to the estate she would soon begin restoring in St. Brice, some twenty miles from Paris. It is clear that she planned to keep an apartment in Paris; she inquired about the possibility of a twelve-year lease on an unfurnished apartment near the Invalides.[47]

On May 12 she wrote Berenson that another "cardiac crisis" had led her doctor to order her to bed for two or three weeks. "No letters, no telephones, no talking. He seems rather anxious about my heart, but thinks it will get all right if I'm careful." The one activity Dr. Isch Wall would allow her on good days was to be driven "*pour une petite promenade en victoria*," a concession she thought absurdly funny because she would have a better chance of finding an airplane than such a splendid carriage. She was allowed to see Berenson and Berry but no one else.[48]

On May 13 her secretary, in a letter to Wharton's hostess in Marseilles, repeated the information that she had suffered another *crise cardiaque* and had been ordered to rest without writing or telephoning for two or three weeks. It was for this reason that Wharton would miss a wedding on the fifteenth.[49] Wharton was clearly annoyed to learn that her usually precise butler, White, had told Charles du Bos that she suffered from "nervous exhaustion." She explained, "This tiresome 'crise cardiaque' is no doubt the result of doing too much work of a too tiresome kind, but otherwise my nerves are as sound as ever, and I am very much bored at having to remain quiet."[50] She was still sending notes to her friends the Garretts through the American diplomatic pouch.[51]

In spite of having been ordered to remain inactive, she made arrangements during the final days of May for two American soldiers with an interest in landscape gardens to visit the garden of Vaux-le-Vicomte.[52] Her secretary was making reservations for her to return to the Hôtel Savoy in Fontainebleau, insisting there be fresh eggs and fish even on meatless days to satisfy the requirements of Wharton's diet.[53]

Job applicants were getting short shrift. When the American novelist Dorothy Canfield Fisher recommended that a special education teacher from California apply to Wharton's charities, Wharton's secretary curtly replied that because of Wharton's illness "she cannot occupy herself with business matters."[54] Wharton told all who wrote her that their schemes of adopting Belgian and French children in her charge ran counter to the wishes of the governments that had entrusted her with the children.

Friends got gentler treatment. To Lapsley, who had just lost a friend, she offered sympathy: "In this loneliest of worlds we must keep an even tighter clutch on each other." She went on to praise Elisina as well as Minnie Jones: "For nearly two years I haven't done any 'active management', though I know everything that is being done down to the last detail. My line has been money. Getting that means a good deal of steady work. But my very gallant sister-in-law Minnie Jones, who heads my N. Y. Committee, has been here for a month with me (she returned last week) looking over the ground, and preparing new plans for raising funds on her return, with the help of 'movies' of all our institutions."[55]

By May 27 the road to Paris was unprotected, and the French called in the American army. The Germans, moving forward at a rate of ten miles a day, were meeting light resistance. Not since the Battle of the Marne had Paris been in such peril. Hundreds of thousands of Parisians left the city, and the French government was ready to leave the capital once again. Following Pershing's orders that it might have to be evacuated, trucks were parked outside the American embassy. On June 4 the Americans troops got their baptism under fire at Belleau Woods. There they advanced in long rows without covering fire from artillery or tanks. They took the woods, but more than 5,000 of the 8,000 marines engaged were killed or wounded.

୬

By the first week of June, Wharton was well enough to dine with her doctor and Berenson. She planned a weekend excursion in her automobile to her children's colony at Montseult. An attraction of the trip was that it would take her past her recently purchased estate in St. Brice.[56] Though she had been distracted from her writing by night raids and daily shelling by Big Bertha, Wharton told Lapsley that her heart was better but that she was suffering the effects of "the rottenest kind of anaemia." She begged him to come so they could have talks about Henry James, and she promised him a welcome at "a tiny bungalow I have bought near Montmorency,"[57] which she optimistically hoped to have ready by the middle of August.

During June, recovering from what she termed the "insurrection" of her heart aided by anemia, Wharton was less than sympathetic with the low spirits of two of her contemporaries. Mary Berenson and Lizzie Cameron were both in England nursing illnesses brought on by grief— Lizzie over the recent death of her daughter Martha, and Mary over the loss of Geoffrey Scott.

In behavior that surely interested as well as chilled Wharton as an author of ghost stories, Lizzie occasionally slept on Martha's grave. She became obsessed with the thought that her daughter needed a monument, much like the one Henry Adams had erected for his wife, Clover. Lizzie's son-in-law implored Wharton to come over and visit Lizzie, and Wharton, though barely recovered herself, felt a sense of duty to her old friend. Only when Royall Tyler argued that she could not go because she was sure to be delayed at Le Havre or Southampton and because any such delay would work a hardship on her remaining refugee charities did Wharton, relieved, give up the trip. She grasped at the excuse of a broader public good and proposed to send in her stead a Mrs. Mead whom Lizzie had met in Paris. When Lizzie replied that she would refuse even to see Mrs. Mead, Wharton became furious. Lizzie's curt response "quite frankly has distressed and hurt me more than anything that has happened in a good many years."[58] Wharton scolded Lizzie for her self-indulgent, macabre self-pity, pointing out that though she had herself endured a great deal of sorrow in her life, she had found that "the only out was to do the next thing that came to hand, though so often it comes in the form of seeing someone one may not care to see or writing a letter when one wanted to hold one's peace!"[59]

In the summer Lizzie's niece Elizabeth Hoyt came from the United States to care for her. Wharton knew Miss Hoyt, since both had been frequent guests at Lizzie's Right Bank apartment. Luckily, Miss Hoyt, the first woman in New York State to get a driver's license, was self-sufficient and independent. She needed all her strength to deal with a despairing, grief-possessed Lizzie.

Wharton suggested that Lizzie return to Paris with Elizabeth Hoyt and take up her old work at the refugee centers. She sought the injunction of the dead daughter: "There is plenty of work for you too here. . . . Martha would have wanted that, wanted it above all things. I don't think I have ever written so outspokenly to anyone—but you will understand my doing so, I know."[60] Yet Lizzie would not budge. Miss Hoyt, fearing that she would harm herself, did not leave her alone during the day and during the night slept with the door open between their connecting rooms.

Wharton continued to write Elizabeth Hoyt letters of encouragement, telling her to keep her resolve. "You must not resign your job either. I don't believe it would be a good thing for Lizzie if you did. We all belong to the war now."[61] Like Elisina Tyler, like Mary Berenson, and others, Elizabeth Hoyt began to see Wharton in a new light: "I feel guilty about my feelings for Mrs. Wharton. I have always thought her hard and she has been *too* nice."[62] When Elizabeth Hoyt did return to Paris the first week of July, Lizzie remained at Stepleton in a cloud of grief and self-pity, cared for by servants. Later in the summer she was consoled by a visit from Elisina, and she underwrote the maintenance of a bed at one of Wharton's convalescent homes in Martha's memory.[63]

The convalescent homes had adopted a policy of taking in paying patients, whenever there was room. A woman named Frances Wharton, apparently no relation to Teddy, was paying a monthly subscription for a little girl to be cared for at Arromanches.[64] When Wharton left Paris in mid-June for several days of rest at Fleury,[65] her secretary assured the American committees "that Paris is calm and confident, and that the whole of France rings with praise of our splendid American soldiers."[66] Wharton's good works still found support in unexpected quarters. A subscriber to the Paris edition of the *New York Herald* sent a blind donation and asked the newspaper to contribute it to a worthy charity. The editor wrote Wharton, "The Management of the *Herald*, therefore, have decided to turn over to your admirable organization, 'Les Enfants en Danger', the said sum of 250 frcs, which you will receive with this note."[67]

Mary Berenson had been in England with her family for some time complaining of stomach and digestive troubles—troubles that Wharton thought stemmed from nerves. She encouraged Berenson not to become immersed in his wife's illnesses. In fact, drawing on her own struggle with her husband ten years earlier, Wharton encouraged Berenson to all but leave his wife. When he departed for a visit with Mary, Wharton lamented that she had "lost my best and most understanding friend." Writing from her bed, she was sad that, unlike Madame de Beaumont, "alas, no unfaithful lover seems likely to expatiate his cruelty by putting up a lovely bas-relief to me in St. Louis-des-Français."[68]

Her exaggerated (and literary) despair soon found an outlet in travel. Royall Tyler persuaded her that she should go off for three or four weeks of mountain air—a plan she had toyed with the previous summer when she proposed joining Lizzie in Chamonix but finally decided against it. She had already rejected an invitation to join the Bourgets at Reyat, where the large American hospitals meant the town "was simply swarming with American officers." She had not yet turned anti-American, but she did not want to be surrounded by her countrymen. She said, "Wherever our soldiers are I should *have* to see them."[69]

Mary had written to Wharton that her doctor had confirmed a serious infection of the bladder, but Wharton was skeptical. She advised Berenson: "Do manage to have a talk alone with her new specialist, and do, above all, make sure he is the *best* specialist and not a freak doctor." She encouraged him to make friends with the American ambassador Walter Hines Page, and with her friends Willie Buckler and Mary Hunter. She had recently attended a much diminished meeting of their Thursday lunch club, where only three other regulars were present.[70] Delivering a diagnosis from across the Channel, Wharton told Mary she was convinced that her problem was simply nerves and that when she got away from London, out into the fresh air of Surrey or Sussex, she would recover.[71]

Wharton gave Alice Garrett an account of her own recent health problems: "There have been painful moments, & I believe I felt them more than anyone, for I have been ill since early in March—my heart went kaput, & bad anemia helped it in its insurrection: so I have been chaise-lounging & vegetating through all the storm & stress." She rejected her doctor's suggestions that she try a cure in the Auvergne or Dauphiné. Her own rest at Fleury the previous week had lasted only three days, when, frantic for news of the war, she returned to Paris: "I decided there was no 'cure' for me except what I can get on my own balcony 'right here'!" She was encouraged by the war news, especially reports in the German papers that the American army was a significant force. "I wish you were here to hear the universal chorus of praise of the military qualities of our men. I mean *professional* praise from French officers & soldiers. It makes up for the old weary 'neutral days—' but thousands of American lives would have been spared if we had come sooner." The spirit of Paris was returning. She found the Printemps department store "packed with women grabbing bargains in the good old way."[72]

Her greatest anxiety was over Berenson. When he did not write, she found herself "in a state of such anxious suspense about you and your fate that I'm afraid this letter won't be worthy of a place in the E.W. archives—for anxiety makes me inarticulate."[73] With what must have sounded like hollow compensation, Wharton pointed out to Berenson that though the letters from Mary he had forwarded to her were bad, "my letters from Lizzie Cameron are worse." She concluded, "*nothing* matters in times like these but the sense of being the captain of one's soul!" Most of all she missed their daily conversations: "Talking to most people gives me the horrid feeling one has in nightmares of trying to move forward and feeling one's feet glued. The never-get-any-whereness of most human intercourse is enough to drive one to the desert."[74] Talking with Berenson was, by contrast, always a delight: "You're the only person who has given me, for a long time past, what I used to call 'a good swim'—and what, after all, if I honestly survey my past, I find I've really cared for more than anything else, and have always found the necessary ingredient in other joys."[75]

At the end of June she wrote Berenson that her spirits had drooped: "I didn't see how (though I thought I did) intensely I cared for the beautiful visible world (of man's making) and how this massacre of it ploughs into my soul." Part of her reaction may have been caused by "two sharp hail-storms" of German artillery the previous two nights. The house behind Walter Berry's had been badly damaged, but her own was safe.[76] She sought refuge in a concert of Beethoven sonatas.[77]

The first day of July she moved back to the rue de Varenne apartment. In days of silence and sunshine at Madame de Béarn's château in the country, she "hunted for myself in vain in the empty cells I used to inhabit."[78] Another source of frustration was that she was blocked on progress on her war novel *The Marne*. Her earlier draft of 8,000 words,

which she had read to her cousin Le Roy King in the evenings to get his
military view of the story, remained just that—8,000 words. Once back
in Paris, she shook off her torpor and poured out 2,000 words onto her
author's pad.

Wharton could take pleasure in the fact that, as reported in the
Herald of July 3, her special fund for *Les Enfants en Danger* received a
donation of 106 francs from the children of Longfellow School in Oak-
land, California. That brought the total for the fund to 77,000 francs. As
a measure of expenses, it took 2,000 francs to support a bed for a year at
one of the convalescent homes for children from the war zone.[79] She was
at the Fourth of July festivities in Paris from eight in the morning on. As
she wrote to Minnie and to Mary Berenson, the day's events thrilled her
and made her feel patriotic.[80] She told Minnie, "Our troops cover themselves daily with fresh glory. . . . The whole of France rings with their
praises—praise of their skill as well as their pluck."[81]

ﻬ

A week later Wharton was warning Berenson that Mary's sudden recovery should be regarded cautiously since she had experienced a similar
pattern of ups and downs with Teddy during his attacks of mania and
depression. She was sure that Mary's and Teddy's problems were the
same: "I am greatly troubled about your future, dearest Berenson and
frightened at the way it is developing in accordance with my own
experience."[82] She warned him that Mary's problems, unless attended to
with what is today called "tough love," would destroy them both. She
urged him to get Mary to a good American neurologist, who, she said,
would probably recommend an immediate separation. Such a separation
had been recommended for Elizabeth Hoyt in the troubling case of Lizzie
Cameron. For herself, Wharton was planning to go, at Isch Wall's
recommendation, to enjoy the mountain cure at St. Nectaire in the
Auvergne, where she had sent White, her butler, when his rheumatism
got bad. She had instructed him to negotiate with the manager for a
better price for her suite on the grounds that she was to stay for several
weeks.[83] As time went on, the trip to St. Nectaire became uncertain
because the manager of the hotel said that the present occupant of
Wharton's reserved room—only one of two in the entire hotel with a
bath and w.c.—was too ill to be moved.[84] Wharton felt too shaky to
attempt a trip to England, and with Elisina away in Burgundy, she was
waiting until the first of August to get away herself.[85]

Writing to Mary, Wharton said that she should see a specialist and that in the meantime she should count her blessings. Her bucking up of Mary included the advice "to decorate one's inner house so richly that one is content there, glad to welcome any one who wants to come and stay, but happy all the same in the hours when one is inevitably alone"— whereupon she caught herself and told Mary that she didn't want to sound like the ladies who "announce that they've discovered a bust-developer which they will impart free of charge to any one desiring to attract."[86] These earlier comments to Mary she described in a letter to Berenson as "a few home truths."[87]

Later Wharton said she was relieved to hear the doctors were sure that Mary's trouble was physical. She was concerned, however, to learn that Mary had fallen away from a belief in science and was now waiting for a miracle. "It throws a new light on the weakness of the mind fed on the belief in short cuts and providential improvisations—and *how* it explains the success of Mrs. Eddy, and mind-healing, and all the other 'Quantis' of that kind!"[88] To the names of people that Berenson mentioned having met in England, she replied that aside from a few friends, such as Percy Lubbock and Robert Norton, "the rest has faded for me strangely, now that Henry, who lit it all up, is gone."[89] And now she was not sure she ever wanted to return to England.

She remembered sitting alone with Royall Tyler one evening when they heard the rumble of distant cannon fire. Tyler, whose place with American intelligence in Paris made him privy to war plans, announced that it was the beginning of General Ferdinand Foch's big push.[90] By late July, in Fleury and with the Allies making progress, she told Berenson, "To hug you and jubil with you this morning would be a better heart-cure than all the springs at St. Nectaire can offer me!!" She was especially proud of the compliments that Foch, Pétain, and other French military leaders paid the American troops. Wharton was still telling Berenson, "Mary, don't forget, is a spoilt child!"[91] She continued the letter upon returning to Paris the following day. She had been reading the notebooks of Samuel Butler, which had been praised by Shaw, Arnold Bennett, and others, and she concluded, "It isn't *grown up*, any of it; and only the ungrown-up and the un-read (like Wells, Bennett and co) could have taken such an exaggerated view of Butler's place as a 'thinker.'"[92]

By July 15 Wharton was back at Fleury,[93] but at the end of the month her heart was playing tricks on her again. She canceled her trip to St. Nectaire in disgust over the manager having given her room to someone else[94] and instead crawled down to the Hôtel Savoy in Fontainebleau. She was staggered by the medical treatment Berenson reported from England: "'Isolating' a patient with a nervous break-down in the same house with her husband—*cela dépasse la mesure* of idiocy!—Of course it won't work, and you will have to leave if Mary doesn't." In July of 1910, when Teddy Wharton had threatened to leave a clinic in Kreuzlingen, Switzerland, and return to Paris, Isch Wall wrote him a stern letter saying that what his wife needed more than anything else was to be "isolated from her family," meaning that she should be spared the extra burden of caring for Teddy.[95] Wharton agreed with the separation treatment then and now, and she closed by flirting with Berenson: "How I wish you would come back and nurse *me* for a while." She asked him to join her in Fontainebleau where, with her secretary on holiday for a month, she would "have to deal 'in person' with all my *courrier!*"[96]

During the first week of August, plans went forward for a mass meeting of the Allied Women on War Service in France. Wharton did not attend either of the two planning sessions. Her name was suggested ("subject to her acceptance") as chair of the hospitality committee, but in minutes of the meeting the suggestion was penciled through. In the final printed program "Mrs. Wharton" was listed as a member of the Executive Committee of the Congress of Allied Women on War Service. She missed the elaborate ceremony that took place on August 21 at the Théâtre des Champs-Elysées.[97]

By the middle of the month she was encouraging Berenson to "steal away softly, but resolutely" as soon as Mary was installed in a cottage and surrounded by her grandchildren. She told him that "every week you stay with her is just so much self-destruction, and of no use whatever to her—on the contrary." Referring to Lizzie Cameron's "barbarous ostentation of grief," Wharton said that such cases were only helped by the resoluteness of those surrounding the self-pitying soul. Of the two patients, she observed, "In both there is a real sorrow, and a great deal of indiscipline, and the absence of certain experiences that make women really grow up."[98]

Part of this black mood was undoubtedly brought on by having to deal with her own grief over the recent death of Ronald Simmons, a young Yale graduate whom Wharton had come to know a year earlier through tuberculosis work. When America entered the war, Simmons volunteered for duty and was assigned to a position in intelligence in Marseilles, where he died of pneumonia on August 12. Wharton was devastated for weeks by his loss. Writing to Berenson immediately after his death, she confided, "I don't believe anyone but his own mother will feel it quite as you and I will—for we both had the same sense of his exquisite quality."[99] Ten days later she was still mourning the death of Simmons. Some of her friends thought that she was in love with the young man. According to R.W.B. Lewis, Lapsley felt that she may have loved Ronald Simmons: "But Lapsley, looking back, thought that on Edith's side there had been something of an Indian-summer romance. Lapsley was normally the least trustworthy witness to Edith Wharton's emotional life; in this instance, however, his intuitions may have been sound. Certainly about no other of her male friends in 1917 and 1918 did Edith speak with so warmly intimate a tone."[100] Wharton dedicated her short war novel *The Marne* and her much longer war novel *A Son at the Front*, published five years later, to Simmons. Such dedications were unusual for her, and a double dedication was unheard of. Her reaction to losing Simmons frightened her, especially since she realized "how incapable I am of filling such a gap as he has left."[101]

෪

As August wore on she worked steadily at *The Marne*. She still maintained that Berenson was making himself worse by staying with Mary, "and nothing is so destructive as being vampired by a person one loves and who is in Mary's state, poor, poor dear." Wharton had enjoyed her refuge in the Fontainebleau forest with her books. She claimed that she would have enjoyed being with Berenson on his visit to Santayana, though she said of the philosopher, "he flees me sedulously; though he is studiously kind at a distance." In the meantime General Pershing had sent a lieutenant, "just a little liaison ass" who mixed his words in French and English, to invite her to visit an AEF camp. She had only the highest praise, on the other hand, for the American troops, whom she called "the real thing at the front."[102]

The writing of business letters had left her "kaput," and she had to stay in bed for a day or two. On one of her periodic day trips to Paris to attend to business, she found Walter Berry looking "played out." When Mary planned a visit to her family in the country, Wharton begged Berenson, "Do seize the chance and leave, for both your sakes."[103]

Despite being ill with the grippe during the first two weeks of September, Wharton attended to the business correspondence of finding a suitable artificial arm for an amputee[104] and telling other petitioners that she would forward their requests to an appropriate charity.[105] Late in the month she was forced to tell the wife of her own physician, concerned that an old woman was receiving only eighty francs a month and a furnished room, that the woman was in far better shape than most of the hostels' refugees.[106]

When Wharton wrote Berenson after a silence of several days, it was from a bed at Mrs. Lee Childe's country home in Loiret. She was forced to admit, "Country cures don't seem to have helped much this year." By now Bernard and Mary Berenson had settled in Sussex at Littlehampton. The name brought Wharton an immediate flood of memories of Henry James and the people and places in the area. Though she grudgingly acknowledged that Berenson had "stuck to the job" and that Mary was recovering some of her vitality, she herself was still unable to reconcile herself to the loss of Simmons: "I feel it more and more as the weeks pass."[107] Yet if there was grief on the personal front, news from the wider war front was more optimistic. She made a distinction between her "poor carcass" and her "indomitable soul," and her soul was buoyed by the war communiqués. She expected to return to Paris on September 17.[108]

かめ

Try as she might, she could not divorce herself from her charities, many now under the control of the American Red Cross. She put the best face on the situation in a letter to Mrs. Charles Scott, a volunteer who had run the hostel clothing depot since its beginning four years earlier: "The question of relations between the Red Cross and the Hostels (as far as the clothing of the Hostels' refugees was concerned) was settled without difficulty and I see no reason why there should be any principal difference in the working arrangement of the Vestiaire, or why things should not go on as smoothly and pleasantly as in the past."[109] As much as she tried to extricate herself from the administration of the charities, by the end of the month she was back in Paris "riding the whirlwind, as usual in Elsina's absence" and being treated with injections to fight off another onset of the grippe.[110]

In early October she was thinking back to her problems of the spring, her heart attack, the shelling of her neighborhood two or three days a week, and raids every moonlit night. Her little war novel *The Marne* and her article on Morocco, she told Robert Grant, would soon be published. She was glad that he too was writing: "It is a good thing not to be entirely steeped in philanthropy." But the war charities were never far from her mind, especially now that the high prices of materials and rents were beginning to affect them. She added, "I hope Minnie Jones will take her films to Boston and make some money for us."[111]

ᘓ

The American Expeditionary Force fought bravely again at the Aisne-Marne in September. It undertook the large operation of the St. Mihiel salient on its own, and owing to the confusion within the German command captured 16,000 German prisoners and 443 guns. The AEF soldiers were then shifted some sixty miles, many in all-night marches, to be in place for the big push on the Meuse. Under cover of darkness the Americans moved more than 500,000 troops. The battle opened September 26. By October 10 the Americans had taken the Argonne Forest. While casualties included more than 26,000 American dead, the war was effectively over.

ᘓ

While Wharton could tell Mrs. Scott that relations between the American Red Cross and the clothing depot of the hostels had been regularized, she was not ready herself to accept an invitation to join the board of governors of the Paris District Chapter of the ARC, even though she was assured that the board would have only advisory power during the war. Wharton refused the invitation on the grounds of health: "After four years of rather steady war-work I am feeling the need of as much rest as I can get; and therefore, to my regret, it will not be possible for me to accept your very kind suggestion."[112]

She thanked her good friend in Washington, Marian Bell, for raising more than $2,000. She was already worried about the exposure of the weakened civilians in the repatriated French provinces to the Spanish flu, which would soon grip those fortunate to survive the war and the occupation. She urged Bell, "Now that victory is in sight we must not let people at home forget that the retreating Germans are leaving in their wake scenes of devastation and horror more complete than anything of the same kind that they have yet perpetrated." And with remarkable, if grim, foresight she could forecast, "I look forward to a year during which the demands on our hospitals at Groslay and Arromanches will be greater and more urgent than ever before."[113]

By the middle of the October she had other concerns. She apologized to Mrs. Scott for missing a little ceremony at her house, "but I am very sad over the disappearance of my young cousin, Newbold Rhine-lander, who was shot down over the German lines a short time ago, and do not feel like participating in any festivities."[114] To Berenson she wrote, "My dearest and youngest of all cousins, a golden-haired young Rhine-lander (aviator) was shot down Sept. 26 over German lines, and we know no more yet."[115]

Though she was pleased with American soldiers generally, when Private Victor Solberg sent her some of his verses to comment on, she delivered a tart criticism: "I must tell you sincerely that in your case I do not find the influences you suggest [Wordsworth, Shelley, Tennyson], but rather those of the poet's corner of a daily newspaper." She advised him, "You must prepare yourself for so noble a mission by reading the best, and only the best, and by studying the grammar and etymology of your language as well as the history of its rhythms. It takes a great deal of the deepest kind of culture to write one little poem."[116]

Wharton still tried to find help for individuals whom former workers brought to her attention, though she was forced to admit "the expense of living has increased so much that I am anxious about the future."[117] And on the last day of October she wrote Berenson acknowledging the receipt of a book and asking if he would go to talk to some of the less severely wounded American soldiers in the hospital. Visitors from home, she said, helped the wounded soldiers adjust but were in short supply.[118]

By the beginning of November, life both at home and abroad had settled into a wartime pattern. The AEF men began to be called "Yanks" instead of "Sammies" in the newspapers and in public.[119] The influenza outbreak, which was to kill more people over the next few months than the war did in four bloody years, had reached the United States. In New York regulations on where and how to cough were posted everywhere. Chicago health officials advised closing skating rinks, theaters, lodges, and all public meeting places.[120] A more immediate health concern for Wharton was Alfred White, her butler of thirty years, whose rheumatism now made it imperative that he move to a warm climate. She asked Lewis Cass Ledyard to try to find him a confidential post with one of his wealthy friends in Florida or in California. She concluded her letter of reference for White and appeal to Ledyard, "These are great days in France."[121]

Wharton's independent convalescent homes were receiving more and more official attention. The day before the signing of the Armistice agreement, Mrs. Sharp, wife of the American ambassador, welcomed Madame Poincaré, wife of the president of France, to one of the convalescent homes at Groslay, where she was also received by Wharton and Elisina Tyler.[122] A few days after the signing Wharton wrote a friend, "I wish you were in Paris to see the wonder and the glory of these great days."[123]

The day of the Armistice found Wharton and her household on the balcony listening first to the bells of nearby Sainte Clotilde and then the answering bells from all of the other churches in Paris: "We had fared so long on the thin diet of hope deferred that for a moment or two our hearts wavered and doubted. Then, like the bells, they swelled to bursting, and we knew the war was over."[124]

The same day a letter of appeal for funds for shoes for the Children of Flanders appeared in the Herald. In a similar appeal the previous year Wharton had raised 15,000 francs, but she explained that with the higher prices this year she was setting her goal at 20,000 francs.[125] Within two days she had received 1,500 francs, and by the end of the week a generous gift from Mr. and Mrs. John Lalor (whose earlier gift had established a braille press in the charity where Dorothy Canfield Fisher worked) brought the total to 4,000 francs.[126] By the end of the month the shoe fund topped 7,000 francs.

✿

More and more Americans were reaching Paris to join the American volunteers and servicemen already there. When students and alumni from Ohio State University organized an evening gathering on November 30, the turnout (including alumnus Ambassador William Sharp) was so large that the party had to be moved from the reserved hotel banquet room to an open-air café on the boulevard des Italiens. Hotel space became acutely short with an influx of visitors to participate in the peace conference. With the coming of one group, another group was soon departing, as the Herald reported: "'Dollar-a-Year' Experts Return to Private Life."[127] A grimmer leave-taking was also under way: American war casualties were reported at 262,700, with 58,478 killed.[128]

Wharton reappeared in the pages of the Herald when she renewed her appeal for funds to buy shoes for the Flemish children. Anticipating the appearance in Paris in two days of the king and queen of Belgium, Wharton said that children would not return to their "ravaged towns for so many months to come."[129] Indeed, a picture of King Albert riding in an open car with French President Poincaré from the station did appear in the newspaper two days later. With the arrival of Woodrow Wilson in mid-December, all front-page articles focused on him and his efforts to broker a peace.

To raise funds for the convalescent homes at Groslay, Wharton turned once again to musicians to present a benefit concert at the Théâtre Fémina on the Champs-Elysées. The purpose was to re-create the popular camp concerts that had been given during the last months of the war. The artists were to be supported by an American military band that performed in camp concerts at the front. The first performer was to be a singer from the Odeon Theatre.[130] The concert was a great success, attended by Mrs. Sharp accompanied by several guests from the diplomatic community, plus Wharton and Elisina.[131]

Wharton planned to leave Paris shortly after the concert to take up her suite at the Hôtel du Parc in Hyères on December 31 or January 1.[132] She was going to motor down by a route that included a stop at the Hôtel de la Poste in Beaune, with later stops in Lyon and Avignon. At all of the hotels she requested for herself a room with fireplace and bath and additional rooms for her maid and chauffeur. She explained to the hotel director that she was driving because she could not get space on a train.[133] She was accompanied by Robert Norton: "I shall have with me an English friend, Mr. Robert Norton, of the Admiralty, who is just recovering from double pneumonia after the grippe."[134] As a parting shot at her landlord, she wrote that she was having to leave Paris because it was impossible to keep her apartment warm. Even with fires burning in her bedroom, the temperature never got above fourteen degrees Celsius (57 degrees Fahrenheit) and frequently dropped to ten (50 degrees Fahrenheit). All of the other rooms were simply too cold to use. "In these conditions it is impossible for me to continue to live in my apartment, and I want you to meet next Monday at 11 with Mr. Knight [her architect] to see if these conditions cannot be corrected."[135]

She again celebrated the holiday, as she had for the previous four Christmases, in the noisy company of the refugees. The American philanthropists Mr. and Mrs. Lalor gave a party on Christmas Eve for the American Hostel's children's colony. After the lighting of the tree, films of the convalescent homes at Groslay and Arromanches were shown.[136] Wharton did manage a quiet Christmas evening with Berenson, and the two talked of the joy of their all being together before long at I Tatti. Wharton confessed to Mary Berenson, "I have felt myself sliding steadily down hill again, as I did last spring, and this time, as there seems to be no danger of being called back by an air-raid, I am hoping to get a solid 2 months' rest in the South." Of Mary's visit to Lizzie Cameron, she added, "Poor Lizzie! I'm glad you are going to see her, and I hope that the sight of some one who has been very ill, and has fought a way back to normal activities, will wake her out of her evil lethargy." Then, reflecting on her own life, Wharton offered this philosophy: "Life has not been particularly tender to me, but I consider it so great and inexhaustible a gift that the real unpardonable sin to me is its denial, its 'reneging,' even by those whom its mailed fist has belaboured. There is no end to it in its mercy and its pain, but the mercies are more wonderful and immeasurable than the pain, and when I see women behaving as poor Lizzie has for the last months I wonder when our sex is coming out of the kindergarten."[137]

ʔ☙

CONCLUSION
THE END OF THE AGE OF INNOCENCE

THE WAR WAS OVER, BUT ITS EFFECTS WOULD BE WITH EDITH WHARTON FOR the rest of her life. Through the months following the Armistice, she gradually disengaged herself from the remaining charities. She was able to return to her first love—writing. She established a rhythm: St. Brice during the summer and fall and Hyères during the winter and spring, and a book every year. The noise and human bustle of Paris during the peace conference and into the 1920s with the arrival of Americans from "the lost generation" poisoned the city for her. She made her separate peace with the world and withdrew to her homes and gardens and friends.

☙

Early in January of 1919, Wharton made her way with Robert Norton by slow stages down to the Hôtel du Parc in Hyères. Her daily plan for recuperation included "seven hours of blue-&-gold & thyme & rosemary & roses every day that the Lord makes; & in the evenings, dozing over a good book!"[1] Despite Berenson's entreaties from Paris, she was not sorry to be missing the crush of the peace conference. Even when she would return north, she told Alice Garrett, she planned to stay well away from the commotion in the capital: "The bliss of being away from the Paris of the Conference has cured me of ever much wanting to be in any Paris again, & as soon as possible after arriving I shall pop into my little chateaulet at St. Brice which is getting itself ready for me. And all my winters to come, please the Lord, I shall spend in the sun. There's my political programme."[2]

To complete her program, she and Norton during their desultory tours around Toulon and Hyères searched for her place in the sun. They came across the former convent Ste. Claire du Vieux Château, named for the nuns of the order of Ste. Claire, high above the main town of Hyères. She took the property on a long-term lease. It would require a great deal of renovation, but she fell into the project with renewed energy, telling Royall Tyler, "I feel as if I am going to get married—to the right man at last."[3]

While Wharton was negotiating for property on the Mediterranean and recovering from the bone-tiredness brought on by war relief work, her able lieutenants were busy in New York. Elisina Tyler had gone to the United States to plead for money to continue the work of the convalescent homes. When she and Wharton announced plans to withdraw from their work, the French government urged them to carry on the fight against tuberculosis. The French Department of the Interior worked with Wharton's group to establish a model tuberculosis sanatorium in one of the poorer parts of Paris. Wharton and Elisina believed that if the American open-air cure could be demonstrated successfully in France, then the French people might stop regarding tuberculosis as an incurable disease. Help had already come from the American Red Cross, which, in scaling down its work in France, turned over 300 beds, 200,000 francs, and a great deal of medical equipment to Wharton's convalescent homes. Now Elisina was in the United States trying to raise $200,000 to meet a challenge grant of $100,000 offered by two anonymous friends.[4]

By June Minnie and Elisina had raised enough money in America for 400 more beds. Wharton, back in Paris, had renewed her fund-raising efforts, this time soliciting sheets and pillow cases from Lizzie Cameron for the new convalescent homes. She told Lizzie that her own plans for her future were firm: "Paris is too much of a whirlwind for me, and in a few months I hope to transplant [myself] to Hyères, & spend my remaining winters in sunshine. Still, I shall be near Paris for 1/2 the year, for my little shanty at St Brice (into which I am moving next week) is only thirty minutes from Paris."[5]

≥●

To those who wrote expressing disgust that American soldiers took their holidays in Germany, Wharton explained: "Many Germans speak English, and it is useless to deny that German villages are much better kept than those in France. These are without doubt the principal reasons of the ignorant American point of view about the two countries. I think the American propaganda is also much to blame for not having sent better educated people to the camps to talk to the soldiers about France and try to make them understand the French character and all that France means to civilization."[6] She had tried. She had written a series of essays, *French Ways and Their Meaning* (1919), extolling French intellectual and cultural values. Her inherent social conservatism was well matched to the qualities of reverence, taste, intellectual honesty, and continuity, each of which was accorded a chapter. Her announced intention was "to help the American fresh from his own land . . . overcome [his] initial difficulties, and to arrive at a quick comprehension of French character."[7] The resulting essays, however, were less of a handbook for American Expeditionary Force soldiers trying to understand France than Wharton's most unequivocal defense of her preference for France. She was especially sympathetic to the intellectual independence of the French woman: "Compared with the women of France the average American woman is still in the kindergarten."[8]

≈

The children of Flanders returned to Belgium in July of 1919, but contributions to any and all of Wharton's charities were still welcome. Wharton was still helping individual cases brought to her attention. A Mlle Martinière, who "has been doing the most beautiful work for [the] Ouvroir ever since the beginning of the war," needed 300 francs, for instance, for a surgical corset to correct a disease of the spine.[9] Wharton told one contributor that she was holding her donation until she found the highest exchange rate; then she would use the money to buy a gramophone for the convalescent homes at Groslay and toys for the children.[10]

Still on a personal basis, she took up the cause of four young Belgian boys named Herrewynn. Their mother had abandoned the family in Calais for another man, and when their father reached Paris to join his army unit, he had turned the boys over to the care of a charity. The father was severely gassed during the war, and when it became apparent that he could not care for the children, Wharton spent a great deal of time placing the boys in schools and following their progress.[11] She lodged the two younger boys in Paris, where she personally paid 300 francs every three months for their care and education. The older boys were being prepared at the Institut St. Michel in Poperinghe, and Wharton wrote to the reverend mother in charge, "I hope that things are going well for the little Herrewynn, and will you ask the good sisters to send me news of them from time to time."[12]

Well after the end of the war, she frequently used unspecified gifts to support the four boys: "The eldest, as I wrote your committee last spring, are at present being educated in Belgium, and the two youngest are at a charming little home for boys, near here, where they are as well and happy as possible. I went to see them the other day and was delighted with their appearance and manners. The board for these two children costs 50 frs. a month per child at present, but if the cost of living continues to increase it will probably go up."[13] She went so far as to sign a formal agreement with the father making her responsible for their education. And when one of boys died of typhoid in 1921, she paid to have the family brought together for the funeral service in northern France and later provided a headstone for the grave.[14]

Despite her distaste for the crowds in Paris, Wharton was still making business appointments through the autumn of 1919 to meet people at 53 rue de Varenne,[15] and she was keeping up her rent on a garage in the city.[16] Her secretary generally answered all inquiries, such as those from persistent former charity workers wondering where their promised medals for service were.[17] Wharton personally handled a few requests from former employees. She wrote a character reference for a Dr. Konechowsky, a Russian subject about to have her French permit of visit revoked. Wharton testified that she had known the doctor for twelve years and that she had been dedicated since 1914 to the health of refugees at the American Hostels, which had given aid during the last five years to 5,000 refugees, to the infants from Flanders, and to the patients in the American Convalescent Homes.[18] Elisina Tyler and Walter Berry were asked to write character letters for Dr. Konechowsky as well.

After Wharton found her refuge in St. Brice, she conspired with coworkers to get Elisina to join her there: "She will never rest until she gets away from Paris, and no amount of determination to do so will protect her from telephone and door bell; so do use your influence to persuade her to come."[19] Safely tucked away from the hubbub of Paris, Wharton was free to accept or decline invitations. She turned down an invitation to become a board member of the American Library Association in Paris, having her secretary reply that "for over a year her health has obliged her to decline all similar requests, and she does not feel it possible to make an exception." As she frequently did when refusing such invitations, she

promised to send a contribution within a few days.[20] Closer to home, she
sent the Curé of St. Brice a liberal donation of three hundred francs and
asked him to come for a cup of tea. She also subscribed to several war
charities[21] and sent a subvention to have one of her stories set in Braille
for blind soldiers.[22]

By mid-November of 1919 Wharton, Elisina, and Minnie had raised
sufficient funds to carry on the work of the convalescent homes until the
French government would assume their operation two years later. Two of
the homes, Belle Alliance and Bon Accueil at Groslay near St. Brice, still
cared for more than a hundred women and children.[23] Wharton planned
to leave them "as a permanent memorial of American work for the
tuberculous in France."[24] Her organization planned to open yet another
new home with an additional 200 beds in the spring.[25] Funds continued
to flow in from far-flung sources; the Patriotic Society of American
Women in Buenos Aires, Argentina, sent 250 francs, and the French
Heroes Memorial Fund sent liberal checks.[26] Her secretary told one of
Wharton's most loyal individual contributors, "Mrs. Wharton now has
about $1000 to carry on her assistance to individual cases through the
winter, and the Convalescent Homes are fully provided for."[27]

ﾞﾑ

With the beginning of 1920, Wharton began to set her personal financial
house in order. She found a new trust company to look after her New
York properties and asked for an estimate of her monthly income on her
trust property accounts once all expenses were deducted. She explained,
"As a great part of my time is spent in Europe it is important for me to
know in advance on what monthly income I can count, and I should be
much obliged if, after having looked into the conditions of my property
in and out of trust, you would write me making any suggestions as to the
possibility of selling certain buildings that may require constant repairs,
and investing the money in more up-to-date real estate, the income of
which would not be subject to such frequent changes."[28] Her French
income for 1918 was only 13,781.30 francs, and with mounting costs
associated with renovating two homes in France, she wanted to be sure
that she was not taxed twice on her income. Throughout the spring she
was busy changing the trustees of her estate.[29]

Also during the opening weeks of 1920 she was finishing the final
chapters of *The Age of Innocence* at le Bocage, the rented villa in Hyères
where she was spending the winter.[30] Jeanne Duprat, her secretary in

Paris, acted as intermediary between Wharton and the professional typing service hired to ready the manuscript for Appleton in New York. By mid-February the final chapters were ready, and Duprat took the manuscript to Walter Berry, who entrusted it, as during the war, to a ship's passenger, a Mr. M. L. Schmitt, who would deliver it to Mr. Jewett, her editor at Appleton.[31] Duprat's letters to Wharton in the south of France concerned mostly domestic matters: seeds delivered to St. Brice, the health of Gross, letters received at 53 rue de Varenne, and so forth. They were date-marked about every three days, so the two were in fairly constant touch with each other.

Already she was embracing a new outlet for her novels. She considered a film offer for a remake of The House of Mirth, this time suggesting the title Lily Bart. "A film has already been made from the House of Mirth, but it was taken from the play which I wrote in collaboration with Clyde Fitch many years ago. Apparently the Company who made the film have no idea that the play was taken from a novel, and that I was the person to apply to, for they applied to the heirs of Clyde Fitch for permission to use the play. I gave my consent and received half the proceeds, the whole business being carried on between the producer of the film, the Fitch's heirs and my publisher."

"I hope this does not invalidate my power to authorize a film to be made directly from my novel."[32]

Wharton returned to Paris during the second week of May in 1920. Again she was concerned about individual cases of need. When she passed a man begging in the rue de Varenne, who looked as if he were in the last stages of tuberculosis, she had only a franc to give him. She sent her former secretary, Dolly Herbert, to try to find him, "as I am haunted by the idea that the poor man has no place in which to lodge."[33] Moved though she was by individual appeals of charity, she frequently refused to lend her name to written appeals: "I made it a rule during the war not to beg for any 'Oeuvre de Guerre' except my own, as I was obliged to make so many appeals that I feared my name would become a terror to the charitable."[34]

Her loyal contributors and committees back in America continued to raise money for her charities. As late as July 20, 1920, the Rhode Island Committee of Edith Wharton's War Charities was still sending its annual contribution, and in her acknowledgment Wharton noted that the donation had reached her "opportunely" because "the cost of living has become a severe strain on the work of our Convalescent Homes."[35]

੨ѧ

Wharton used the war as a background in three of her novels: *The Marne*, published in 1918; *A Son at the Front*, published in 1923; and *The Mother's Recompense*, published in 1925. These novels have been variously labeled by literary historians of the war as sentimental or bloodthirsty. Stanley Cooperman in his survey *World War I and the American Novel* places Wharton in the company of Mary Raymond Shipman Andrews and Temple Bailey and dismisses her as one of the women novelists who "seriously portrayed God-fearing boys blondly [sic] carrying the banners of Christian faith against a simian foe."[36] Commenting on *The Marne*, Cooperman accuses her of "combin[ing] gentility with bloodthirst, the manners of the social novelist with the matter of a recruiting poster;"[37] and he was no fonder of *A Son at the Front*: "As late as 1923 Miss [sic] Wharton could repeat every political and military cliché, every atrocity-inflated statement of the War to Preserve Civilization."[38]

Cooperman's reading of the war novels seems narrow, ignoring as it does subjects other than propaganda. He overlooks the theme of incest, for example, which preoccupied Wharton before, during, and after the war. During the war, her limited fictional production dealt repeatedly with the taboo of incest. The incest may be familial, as that between Beatrice Palmato and her father in the "Beatrice Palmato" fragment,[39] but more frequently it involved an intergenerational advance by a much older male guardian toward a female ward, as was the case between Charity and Lawyer Royall in *Summer*, or between the orphaned Yvonne Malo and her guardian in "Coming Home" or between Kate Clephane's former lover and Kate's daughter in *The Mother's Recompense*. The incest also took the form of a homoerotic attraction, as that between John Campton and his son George in *A Son at the Front*.[40] How much of this welling up of forbidden sexual matters was caused by residual memories of her affair with Morton Fullerton and how much was caused by the general disloca-tion of values resulting from the war is difficult to say. Paul Fussell has shown that British war literature from the same period is full of homo-erotic suggestions.[41]

Wharton also may have used incest as a symbolic action in her fiction to displace the frustration she felt in having two devoted male friends of her own generation, Walter Berry and Bernard Berenson, prefer much younger women for their intimate companionship. Many of Wharton's younger male friends were inaccessible to her because they were either married or homosexual. Certainly her teasing state-ments in her letters about wanting to be married again or about finding the right man at last lead us to wonder if she was looking for someone. Her grief over the death of Ronald Simmons seems to indicate that she wanted someone to mourn, even if she could not have him as a life companion.

Another theme in Wharton's war fiction is her satire of those society women who became involved in relief agencies. Their scramble for medals and decorations in the wake of the churning of the war charities was obviously grist for Wharton's mill. She began her satire of American society women and their less-than-pure motives in *The Marne*. Troy Belknap's mother greets the opening of the war as an opportunity for pleasant diversion: "She thought it would be delightful to take convalescent officers for drives in the Bois in the noiseless motor."[42] When Troy's father insists that the teenage boy return to school in the United States, Mrs. Belknap gives up her war work, but not before delivering supplies (like Wharton): "Meanwhile, having quite recovered, she rose from her cushions, donned a nurse's garb, poured tea once or twice at a fashionable hospital, and on the strength of this effort, obtained permission to carry supplies (in her own motor) to the devastated regions."[43]

Wharton was no less scathing in her presentation of the actions and motives of women in America who delighted in the combination of social activity and a good cause: "'It makes us so happy,' beaming young women declared with a kind of ghoulish glee, doing up parcels, planning war tableaux and charity dances, rushing to 'propaganda' lectures given by handsome French officers, and keeping up a kind of continuous picnic on the ruins of civilization."[44]

When Troy wrenches permission from his parents to return to France to drive an ambulance, he finds the young American volunteers on the steamer to France naive and self-absorbed.

> The steamer seethed with wrangles and rivalries between their various organizations, and now and then the young crusaders seemed to lose sight of the object of their crusade—as had been too fre-quently the case with their predecessors. Very few of the number knew much about the history or customs of France or could speak French, and most of them were full of the importance of America's mission. This was Liberty's chance to enlighten the world; and all

these earnest youths apparently regarded themselves as her chosen
torch-bearers.

"We must teach France efficiency," they all said with a glow-
ing condescension.

The women were even more sure of their mission; and there
were plenty of them, middle-aged as well as young, cocked-hatted,
badged, and gaitered—though most of them, apparently, were going
to sit in the offices of Paris war charities; and Troy had never noticed
that Frenchwomen had donned khaki for that purpose.

"France must be purified," these young Columbias proclaimed. "Frenchmen must be taught to respect Women. We must
protect our boys from contamination . . . the dreadful theatres . . .
and the novels . . . and the Boulevards. . . Of course, we mustn't be
hard on the French, . . . for they've never known Home Life of the
Family, but we must show them . . . we must set the example . . ."[45]

Wharton addressed this smug missionary attitude in *French Ways and
Their Meaning*. She pointed out in those essays that rather than teach the
French about American methods of production, the young soldiers and
relief workers could learn a lesson from their hosts about style and what
matters in life.

When *A Son at the Front*, Wharton's second war novel, appeared in
1923, the reviewers reacted in one of two ways. Many thought that five
years after the end of the war, Wharton was raking dead coals. Others
thought that her war story was worth telling. The novel, again dedicated
to Ronald Simmons, tells the story of the American artist John Campton
trying to save his son, George, from military service. The novel is four
times as long as *The Marne*, and the characters are more richly drawn.
There are really two wars: the one at the front, which we never see, and
the one at the rear between Mr. and Mrs. Brant (George's stepfather and
mother) and John Campton fighting to protect of a son who does not
want to be protected. The backdrop is not that of the trenches but the
gilded halls of the hotel luxes where a war between rival charities and
relief organizations is played out.

After the war begins, Campton observes many other Americans
engaged in war charities:

Other people, he knew, had found jobs: most of his friends had been
drawn into some form of war-work. Dastrey, after vain attempts to

enlist, thwarted by an untimely sciatica, had found a post near the front, on the staff of a Red Cross Ambulance. Adele Anthony was working eight or nine hours a day at a Depot which distributed food and clothing to refugees from the invaded provinces; and Mrs. Brant's name figured on the committees of most of the newly-organized war charities. Among Campton's other friends many had accepted humbler tasks. Some devoted their time to listing and packing hospital supplies, keeping accounts in ambulance offices, sorting out refugees at the railway stations, and telling them where to go for food and help; still others spent their days, and sometimes their nights, at the bitter-cold suburban sidings where the long train-loads of wounded stopped on their way to the hospitals of the interior. There was enough misery and confusion at the rear for every civilian volunteer to find his task.[46]

Through a friend of George's, young Boylston, Campton is introduced to a new charity, "The Friends of French Art," which helps the families of mobilized artists. Previously Campton had always worried that the women organizing charity bazaars would ask him for his paintings to auction off. Now he is approached by a Mlle Davril, who makes the appeal that the money raised through his gift to "The Friends of French Art" was to be spent only "in giving employment, not for mere relief."[47] This program sounds very much like Wharton's own criteria for a useful war charity. As Mlle Davril says, "'At any rate, it would mean work and not stagnation; which is all that most charity produces.'"[48]

Campton's old friend Paul Dastrey, after being tested at the front for three months, is one of the few people Campton can talk to about the war. In discussing keeping George out of the war "by any honourable means," Campton reddens self-consciously at the word "honourable," but Dastrey foreshadows Hemingway's Frederic Henry in A Farewell to Arms in observing "'I wasn't thinking of that: I was considering how the meaning had evaporated out of lots of our old words, as if the general smash-up had broken their stoppers. So many of them, you see,' said Dastrey smiling, 'we'd taken good care not to uncork for centuries. Since I've been on the edge of what's going on fifty miles from here a good many of my own words have lost their meaning, and I'm not prepared to say where honour lies in a case like yours.'"[49]

Wharton satirizes the sentimental appeals that raise large sums of money in the United States. There is more than a touch of farce in the quick conversion of Mr. Mayhew, a former peace delegate, who, after being briefly imprisoned in Germany, now lectures widely and with great effect on atrocities he has never witnessed:

> He had therefore, with an expenditure of eloquence which Campton thought surprisingly slight, persuaded Boylston to become his understudy, and devote several hours a day to the whirling activities of the shrimp-pink Bureau of Atrocities at the Nouveau Luxe. Campton, at first, could not understand how the astute Boylston had allowed himself to be drawn into the eddy; but it turned out that Boylston's astuteness had drawn him in. "You see, there's an awful lot of money to be got out of it, one way and another, and I know a use for every penny—that is, Miss Anthony and I do," the young man modestly explained; adding, in response to the painter's puzzled stare, that Mr. Mayhew's harrowing appeals were beginning to bring from America immense sums for the Victims, and that Mr. Mayhew, while immensely gratified by the effect of his eloquence, and the prestige it was bringing him in French social and governmental circles, had not the cloudiest notion how the funds should be used, and had begged Boylston to advise him.[50]

An interesting related question is Mr. Meyhew's frequent "need for rest," which may reflect some residual guilt on Wharton's part for the many rest breaks she took, leaving Elisina or Lizzie in charge.

Campton's son, George, goes to the front, comes back wounded, is patched up, and returns to the front, where he is soon killed. Some of Wharton's least considered and emotionally charged propaganda comes out in these pages. She was perhaps reflecting on her own discouragement in 1915 when she wrote:

> But his excitement and Boylston's exultation [over America's outrage at the sinking of the *Lusitania*] were short-lived. Before many days it became apparent that the proud nation that had flamed up overnight at the unproven outrage of the *Maine* was lying supine under the flagrant provocation of the *Lusitania*. The days which followed were, to many Americans, the bitterest of the war: to Campton they seemed the ironic justification of the phase of indifference and self-absorption through which he had just passed. He could not go back to Mrs. Talkett and her group; but neither could he take up his work with even his

former zeal. The bitter taste of the national humiliation was perpetually on his lips: he went about like a man dishonoured.[51]

Reflecting her own feelings, Wharton wrote of John Campton: "The people about him—Miss Anthony, Boylston, Mlle Davril, and all their band of tired resolute workers—plodded ahead, their eyes on their task, seeming to find in its fulfillment a partial escape from the intolerable oppression."[52] The wave of preparedness, she said, "had spread like a prairie fire, sweeping away all the other catchwords of the hour, devouring them in one great blaze of wrath and enthusiasm."[53]

The novel examines forms of fund raising for the charities. For instance, there is a veiled reference to Wharton's arranging concerts to raise money for the American Hostels in 1915: "Campton had gone to Mrs. Talkett's that afternoon because she had lent her apartment to 'The Friends of French Art' who were giving a concert organized by Miss Anthony and Mlle Davril, with Mme de Dolmetsch's pianist as their leading performer."[54]

The character Boylston allowed Wharton to comment on some of the nasty political intrigues involved in the war charities: "Boylston outlined the situation which his astuteness had detected while it developed unperceived under Campton's dreaming eyes. Mr. Mayhew was attending all their meetings now, finding fault, asking to have the accounts investigated, though they had always been audited at regular intervals by expert accountants; and all this zeal originated in the desire to put Mme de Dolmetsch in Miss Anthony's place, on the plea that her greater social experience, her gift of attracting and interesting, would bring in immense sums of money ... ," but Boylston suspects that Madame de Dolmetsch is really interested in getting her hands on the large balance "The Friends of French Art" already have in the bank. "'I mean that lots of people are beginning to speculate in war charities—oh, in all sorts of ways. Sometimes I'm sick to the point of chucking it all. But Miss Anthony keeps me going.'"[55]

The final section of the novel includes a philosophical analysis of France by Campton that sounds very much like Wharton in *French Ways and Their Meaning:*

> An Idea: they must cling to that. If Dastrey, from the depths of his destitution, could still feel it and live by it, why did it not help Campton more? An Idea: that was what France, ever since she had

existed, had always been in the story of civilization; a luminous point about which striving visions and purposes could rally. And in that sense she had been as much Campton's spiritual home as Dastrey's; to thinkers, artists, to all creators, she had always been a second country. If France went, western civilization went with her; and then all they had believed in and been guided by would perish. That was what George had felt; it was what had driven him from the Argonne to the Aisne. Campton felt it too; but dully, through a fog. His son was safe; yes—but too many other men's sons were dying. There was no spot where his thoughts could rest: there were moments when the sight of George, intact and immaculate—his arm at last out of its sling—rose before his father like a reproach.[56]

In *The Mother's Recompense*, written during 1924-1925 and published in 1925, Wharton again satirized rich American women who volunteered for war charities. The expatriate Kate Clephane remembers that during the war there was a flurry of charity activity, but the motives of the American women involved were not always as selfless as they might have been. Kate's reflections tell us something about her past: "She had her 'set' now in the big Riviera town where she had taken refuge in 1916, after the final break with Chris, and where, after two years of war-work and a 'Reconnaissance Française' medal, she could carry her head fairly high, and even condescend a little to certain newcomers."[57] War work was a path of social legitimacy for the socially tarnished or sexually suspect of the expatriate community. In the same novel we learn a little more about the rich, distracted Americans who used war work as a respectable diversion.

૨ઢ

Wharton's interest in philanthropy extended to the last years of her life. One of her final projects was to raise money for a "new hospital which is being started in Paris for educated people of small means, who . . . go to the charity hospitals of Paris if they cannot afford to pay the prices of the very expensive private clinics."[58] Drawing on her war experience that money is more easily raised from a few rich donors than hundreds of poorer ones, she asked Max Farrand to put her in touch with philanthropist Edward Stephen Harkness. Wharton saw the Paris hospital as a way of memorializing those whom she loved: "I am so much interested in the undertaking that I have, with the generous help of Walter Berry's friends and relatives, funded a room in his memory in the hospital; and a number of other private people have also funded rooms."[59] Until the end of her life Wharton answered those in need with her strong sense of *noblesse oblige*.

᠉

Edith Wharton's experiences in the First World War grew out of events that she could not control. For a woman who created imaginative worlds in her fiction and who designed living spaces and gardens, this loss of control was traumatic. Both Wharton and Henry James thought that if Germany won, the cataclysm would bring the end of civilization.

Wharton's response to the war was to get involved. At first glance she showed amazing executive abilities—"amazing," that is, until one considers her earlier administration of a large household, her creation of her own writing career, and her designing and building of The Mount in Massachusetts. Her talents were those of a general officer in the war on homelessness and tuberculosis. Wharton raised large sums of money and coordinated the energies of others. She was an executive who never donned a nurse's uniform and whose appearances at the hostels and at the homes for the Children of Flanders became increasingly administrative and ceremonial. Her idea of charity is close to modern workfare. The emphasis was always on restoring temporarily displaced individuals to employment and self-sufficiency as soon as possible. Her talent was to inspire and direct the work of others.

Throughout the long years of the war she was rarely physically healthy. She suffered from heart problems. Her bouts of bronchitis, influenza, and pneumonia during the fall and winter were matched by chronic hay fever and allergies during the spring and summer. Health crises were followed by trips and periods of rest that never lasted long enough to restore her energies. In the end her health was permanently affected by the cycles of strain caused by overwork.

Her personal relations during the war were also in upheaval. On the positive side, her divorce from Teddy Wharton was final, and she began a long and close friendship with Bernard Berenson. But the war years also saw the deaths of Henry James and Egerton Winthrop, two of her closest friends. At times she imagined that the perfect man might find his way into her life. Some of her comments were merely flirtatious, as when after meeting Livingston Farrand, she asked Minnie if there were any more Farrand brothers available. When a unknown man bought a manuscript one of her poems at an auction, she asked her sister-in-law if the successful bidder would not like to take the poet in the bargain. Was she simply flirting on these occasions or did her comments reveal a wish to be part of a relationship? Did she hope for a reprise of the physical passion that she experienced briefly with Morton Fullerton? At times Wharton's appeals for companionship seem less innocent: She insisted that Berenson all but abandon his sick wife and come "jubil" with her. Wharton's sustained grief over the death of Ronald Simmons points to a deep, unmet need in her busy life.

With her executive abilities came a certain amount of impatience with her own sex. Wharton was quick to accuse Elisina, Lizzie, and Mary Berenson of self-indulgence in extending their grief over the loss of children and former loves. And Wharton could be especially hard on her women colleagues, demanding levels of performance from Elisina, Minnie, and Lizzie that she rarely asked of Charles du Bos or Royall Tyler.

Above all things Edith Wharton was a writer. Her trip early in 1914 to North African left her with a strong fascination for the region and the germ of a story. That story was never written—the first of several blocked attempts to get back to writing fiction after the war began. She could not get a strong hold on the projected novel *Literature*, and even a humorous sketch about the snobbery of a count had to be abandoned. Her best writing during the war was reportage from various points on the front and from Paris. She did produce the wonderful novella *Summer*, and we are left wondering from what deep wellsprings that story of New England emerged. Did the desolation of the houses on the Mountain in *Summer* symbolize what she observed in her tours of the front? Her war stories have been dismissed by critics and most readers. However, the best of them, "Coming Home," explores the theme of an independent French woman facing the German army. More than a typical revenge plot, the story is rich with hints of incest and the struggle an independent woman artist. Wharton's war novels, *A Son at the Front* and *The Marne*, dramatize life at the rear, the squabbling and office politics of war charities and the loss of personal control.

Wharton lived through the passage of one world into another. After the Armistice she could no longer count on a meritocracy of the elite. No longer was philanthropy based on the private model of *noblesse oblige*; during a few short weeks in 1917 it shifted to the corporate model of the American Red Cross, with economies of scale and huge amounts of money raised through advertising and coordinated public appeals. The character of the world had changed. With the coming of the First World War, Edith Wharton experienced the end of the age of innocence.

NOTES

The following abbreviations of major collections of Edith Wharton's Letters and Papers have been used throughout the notes.

Evergreen House: The John Work and Alice Garrett Collection, Evergreen House, Johns Hopkins University (includes unpublished letters from Edith Wharton and from John and Alice Garrett)

Harvard: The Houghton Library, Harvard University (includes unpublished letters from Edith Wharton and others in various manuscript collections)

Harvard University Archives: Harvard University Archives, Harvard University (includes unpublished letters from Elisina Tyler, Mildred Bliss, and others in the Bliss and Tyler Papers)

Indiana: The Lilly Library, Indiana University (includes unpublished letters from Edith Wharton and from Elisina and Royall Tyler)

Letters: Edith Wharton, *The Letters of Edith Wharton*, eds. R.W.B. and Nancy Lewis, Charles Scribner's Sons, 1988.

Library of Congress: Nelson Miles Papers, Manuscript Division, The Library of Congress (includes unpublished letters from Edith Wharton and from Elizabeth Cameron)

Rockefeller Archives: Rockefeller Foundation Archives, Rockefeller Archive Center (includes unpublished letters from Edith Wharton and others)

Special Collections, Princeton: Manuscript Division, Department of Rare Books and Special Collections, Princeton University (includes unpublished letters from Edith Wharton and from Charles Scribner and members of the Scribner firm)

Villa I Tatti: The Berenson Archives, The Harvard University Center for Italian Renaissance Studies, Villa I Tatti (includes unpublished letters from Edith Wharton and from Bernard and Mary Berenson)

Yale: The Wharton Papers, Yale Collection of American Literature, The Beinecke Rare Book and Manuscript Library, Yale University (includes unpublished letters from Edith Wharton and others)

PREFACE

1. This number is an estimate offered by Dorothy and Carl J. Schneider, *Into the Breach: American Women Overseas in World War I* (New York: Viking Press, 1991), 11, and Appendix A, 287-289.

2. Ibid., 2.

   Other sources break down the deaths this way: 1 million French, 722,000 British, 2 million German, 600,000 Italian, 1.8 million Russian. In terms of the percentage of those who served who were killed, France "led" the way with 17 percent, Germany 16 percent, Britain, 12 percent, Russia 12 percent, and the United States 3 percent. J. M. Winter, *The Experience of World War I* (New York: Oxford University Press, 1989), 202, 206.

   The most recent statistic comes from John Steele Gordon: "At 11:00 A.M. on November 11, 1918, as the guns fell silent after fifty-one months and 8,538,315 military deaths. . . ." in "What We Lost in the Great War," *American Heritage* (July/August 1992): 89.

3. Wharton to Mary Cadwalader Jones, October 19, 1918. This letter and all other quoted unpublished correspondence from Wharton to Minnie Jones is held in the Wharton Papers, Collection of American Literature, Beinecke Rare Book and Manuscript Library, Yale University. The literary rights to Wharton's letters are held by Ambassador William R. Tyler. I am grateful to Ambassador Tyler and to the Beinecke Library for permission to quote from Wharton's unpublished correspondence.

   Subsequent references to letters held in the Wharton Papers in the Beinecke Library will be indicated in the notes by a closing reference to "Yale."

4. Blake Nevius, *Edith Wharton: A Study of Her Fiction* (Berkeley: University of California Press, 1953), 161.

5. Stanley Cooperman, *World War I and the American Novel* (Baltimore: Johns Hopkins University Press, 1967), 41.

6. Peter Buitenhuis, *The Great War of Words: British, American, and Canadian Propaganda and Fiction, 1914-1933* (Vancouver: University of British Columbia Press, 1987), xvii.

7. Interview published in the *New York Times Magazine*, March 21, 1915, 4. Also quoted in Buitenhuis, *The Great War of Words*, 61.

8. Wharton to Bernard Berenson, Esquire, notes on the morning of November 14, 1914, Villa I Tatti. I am grateful to the Harvard University Center for Italian Renaissance Studies at Villa I Tatti and to Ambassador William R.

Tyler and the Edith Wharton Estate for permission to quote from Edith Wharton's unpublished correspondence in the Bernard Berenson Papers held at Villa I Tatti.

Subsequent references to letters from Wharton to Bernard and Mary Berenson held at Villa I Tatti will be indicated in the notes by a closing reference to "Villa I Tatti."

9. Wharton to Elisina Tyler, April 12, 1916. I am grateful to the Lilly Library of Indiana University and to Ambassador William R. Tyler and the Edith Wharton Estate for permission to quote from Edith Wharton's unpublished correspondence in the Wharton Papers at the Lilly Library.

Subsequent references to letters from Wharton to Elisina and Royall Tyler held at the Lilly Library will be indicated in the notes by a closing reference to "Indiana."

10. Robert A. Martin, "The Salons of Wharton's Fiction: Wharton and Fitzgerald," *Wretched Exotic: Essays on Edith Wharton in Europe*, eds. Katherine Joslin and Alan Price (New York: Peter Lang, 1993), 97-103.

11. The story is recounted in Gide's *Journals*, translated and annotated by Justin O'Brien (New York: Alfred A. Knopf, 1951), and in R.W.B. Lewis, *Edith Wharton: A Biography* (New York: Harper & Row, 1975), 399.

12. Edith Wharton, *Fighting France: From Dunkerque to Belfort* (New York: Charles Scribner's Sons, 1915), 152-154.

13. Shari Benstock, *No Gifts from Chance: A Biography of Edith Wharton* (New York: Charles Scribner's Sons, 1994), 151. The quotation from Wharton about relationships among the classes comes from a letter to Dr. Morgan Dix, December 5, 1905, in *The Letters of Edith Wharton*, eds. R.W.B. and Nancy Lewis (New York: Charles Scribner's Sons, 1988), 99. Subsequent references to this collection will be abbreviated in the notes as *"Letters."*

14. Percy Lubbock, *Portrait of Edith Wharton* (New York: D. Appleton and Company, 1947), 29.

15. Ibid., 35.

16. Janet Flanner, "Dearest Edith," *The New Yorker*, March 2, 1929, 27-28.

INTRODUCTION

1. Many of the details describing this day have been drawn from reports in the European edition of the *New York Herald*, July 4 and 5, 1918, pp. 1, 2.

Published in Paris, this edition had the largest circulation of any English-language newspaper on the Continent.

2. "Huge, Cheering Crowds Attend Avenue Président Wilson Ceremony and See Franco-American Troops on March," *New York Herald*, July 5, 1918, p. 1.

3. "General Pershing Sends America Stirring 'Fourth' Message," *New York Herald*, July 4, 1918, p. 1.

4. Wharton to Bernard Berenson, July 5, 1918, Villa I Tatti.

5. Wharton to Mary Cadwalader Jones, July 7, 1918, Yale. A slightly different version of this letter may be found in R.W.B. Lewis and Nancy Lewis, eds. *The Letters of Edith Wharton* (New York: Charles Scribner's Sons, 1988), 406-408. Minnie Jones edited the letter and passed it along to the *New York Times*, where it appeared on July 30, 1918, p. 10.

6. Wharton to Mary Berenson, July 7, 1918, Villa I Tatti.

7. Ibid.

8. "Monster Parade Features Fourth in New York City," *New York Herald*, July 5, 1918, p. 1.

9. Wharton to Bernard Berenson, July 1, 1914, Villa I Tatti.

10. Ibid. The last quotation is my translation of Edward Rousse's comment, quoted by Wharton, *"Je me cherche et je ne me retrouve pas."*

11. Wharton to Bernard Berenson, a continuation of the earlier letter of the same date but marked *same day: later. rue de V.*, July 1, 1918, Villa I Tatti.

CHAPTER 1

1. Wharton to Charles Scribner, February 23, 1914, Scribner Archives, Box 167, Folder 5, Princeton University Libraries. Published with permission of the Manuscripts Division, Department of Rare Books and Special Collections, Princeton University Libraries. I am grateful to the firm of Charles Scribner's Sons and to the Princeton University Libraries and to Ambassador William R. Tyler and the Edith Wharton Estate for permission to quote from the unpublished correspondence in the Scribner Archives.

   Subsequent references to letters held in the Scribner Archives at the Princeton University Libraries will be indicated in the notes by a closing reference to "Special Collections, Princeton."

2. Wharton to Charles Scribner, March 28, 1914, Special Collections, Princeton. For a full discussion of the plot, characters, and theme in the

seventy-page draft manuscript of "Literature," see Nancy R. Leach's article "Edith Wharton's Unpublished Novel," *American Literature* 25 (November 1953): 334-353.

3. Wharton to Bernard Berenson, April 16, 1914, *The Letters of Edith Wharton*, eds. R.W.B. Lewis and Nancy Lewis (New York: Charles Scribner's Sons, 1988), 317. Hereafter cited as *Letters*.

4. Ibid, 318.

5. Wharton to Edward L. Burlingame, May 10, 1914, Special Collections, Princeton.

6. Robert Bridges to Wharton, June 2, 1914, Special Collections, Princeton.

7. Wharton to Charles Scribner, June 27, 1914, Special Collections, Princeton.

8. Percy Lubbock, *Portrait of Edith Wharton* (New York: D. Appleton and Company, 1947), 123.

9. Wharton to Bernard Berenson, March 12, 1914, Villa I Tatti.

10. Edith Wharton, *A Backward Glance* (New York: D. Appleton and Company, 1934), 337.

11. Henry James to Wharton, June 5, 1914, *Henry James and Edith Wharton, Letters: 1900-1915*, ed. Lyall H. Powers (New York: Charles Scribner's Sons, 1990), 287.

12. John Sutherland, *Mrs. Humphry Ward* (Oxford: Oxford University Press, 1990).

13. Wharton, *A Backward Glance*, 336-337.

14. *New York Herald*, July 7, 1914, p. 3; and July 20, 1914, p. 1. The letters to the editor column for July 1914 were full of anguished cries from American citizens living in Paris.

15. Herrick, after turning down the positions of ambassador to Italy and secretary of the treasury offered him by President McKinley, finally accepted President Taft's appointment as ambassador to France in 1912. He resigned the post when Democrat Wilson was inaugurated in March of 1913, but at Wilson's request stayed on performing the duties of ambassador until December of 1914. During the early weeks of the war he assumed responsibility for the interests in France of the belligerents Germany, Austro-Hungary, Serbia, Turkey, and Japan. He stayed in Paris during those fateful days in late August of 1914 when the French government decamped for Bordeaux, a decision that endeared him to the French people. And he received the Grand Cross of the Legion of Honor in 1914. (Until 1929 Herrick and Edward Tuck were two of only eight Americans to receive this award. After the war Herrick was reappointed ambassador

to France by President Harding, and when Herrick died in France in 1929, he was given a state funeral.)

16. For a description of Berry's background and his friendships with Wharton, James, and Proust, see Leon Edel, "Walter Berry and the Novelists," *Nineteenth-Century Fiction* 38 (March 1984): 514-528.

17. Like Wharton, Berry was engaged in refugee work, playing a part in establishing the Union of Foreign Colonies in France to help war victims. Proust would dedicate *Pastiches et mélanges* to Berry: "To Monsieur Walter Berry, lawyer and *littérateur*, who from the first day of the war, before a hesitant America, pleaded the cause of France with incomparable talent and energy—and won it." Berry received the Legion of Honor, and the Paris *Figaro* called him "the most eminent representative of the American colony in France."

18. Wharton to Elizabeth Cameron, December 30, 1916, Library of Congress. The correspondence between Wharton and Elizabeth Cameron is held in the Nelson Miles Papers, Manuscript Division, Library of Congress. I am grateful to Ambassador William R. Tyler and the Edith Wharton Estate for permission to quote from the correspondence between Edith Wharton and Elizabeth Cameron held in the Library of Congress.

    Subsequent references to Wharton's letters to Elizabeth Cameron in the Nelson Miles Papers (letters that detail the long and frequently challenging friendship between these two strong-minded individuals) will be indicated in the notes by a closing reference to the "Library of Congress."

19. Wharton, *A Backward Glance*, 336.

20. James R. Mellow, *The Charmed Circle: Gertrude Stein and Company* (New York: Avon Books, 1974), 265-274.

21. Wharton to Bernard Berenson, July 26, 1914, *Letters*, 325-326.

22. *New York Herald*, June 26, 1914, p. 1.

23. Wharton, *A Backward Glance*, 338.

24. Edith Wharton, *Fighting France: From Dunkerque to Belfort* (New York: Charles Scribner's Sons, 1915), 3-6.

25. Ibid., 9-10.

26. *The Journals of Andre Gide*, vol. 2, 1914-1927, translated and annotated by Justin O'Brien (New York: Alfred A. Knopf, 1951), 45.

27. Wharton, *A Backward Glance*, 340.

28. R.W.B. Lewis, *Edith Wharton: A Biography* (New York: Harper & Row, 1975), 27.

29. Wharton, *Fighting France*, 12-13.

30. Wharton to Bernard Berenson, August 11, 1914, *Letters*, 333.
31. *New York Herald*, July 30, 1914, p. 3.
32. H. Pearl Adam, *Paris Sees It Through: A Diary 1914-1919* (London: Hodder & Stoughton, 1919), 17.
33. Edward Fowles, *Memories of Duveen Brothers* (London: Times Books, 1976), 85.
34. Adam, *Paris Sees It Through*, 17.
35. *New York Herald*, August 2, 1914, p. 3.
36. Wharton, *A Backward Glance*, 339-340.
37. Charles Inman Barnard, *Paris War Days* (Boston: Little, Brown and Company, 1914), 9.
38. Ibid., 48, 66-67.
39. Adam, *Paris Sees It Through*, 20.
40. Cables: Wharton to Charles Scribner, sent 5:03 P.M. August 4 and received by Scribner's in New York on August 5, 1914; Charles Scribner to Wharton, sent care of Munroe & Company Bankers, Paris, August 6, 1914, Special Collections, Princeton.
41. Barnard, *Paris War Days*, 29, 72.
42. Shari Benstock, *No Gifts from Chance: A Biography of Edith Wharton* (New York: Charles Scribner's Sons, 1994), 152.
43. Wharton to Bernard Berenson, August 22, 1914, *Letters*, 334.
44. The Comtesse Pauline-Eulalie-Eugénie d'Haussonville was president of the *comité central des dames de la Société de secours aux blessés militaires* from 1907 until 1922. She received the Legion of Honor for her war work in 1920.
45. Barnard, *Paris War Days*, 40.
46. "Orders for Dresses Would Help French Working Women," *New York Herald*, August 20, 1914, p. 3.
47. J. M. Winter, *The Experience of World War I* (New York: Oxford University Press, 1989), 170.
48. Charles Barnard says in his entry of Tuesday, August 25, "I met Mrs. Wharton who remains in Paris, and who is doing good work with her ouvroir, or sewing circle, which, with Mrs. Thorne, she has organized in the Rue Vaneau. This ouvroir is to supply work to unmarried French women and widows. Among those who have liberally subscribed to this are Mrs. William Jay, Mrs. Elbert H. Gary, Mrs. Breach Grant, and Mrs. Griswold Gray," Barnard, *Paris War Days*, 113-114.
49. Wharton, *A Backward Glance*, 341.
50. Ibid., 209, 341.

51. Alan Albright, "American Volunteerism in France" in *Les Américains et la Légion d'Honneur: 1853-1947*, ed. Véronique Wiesinger (Chateau de Blérancourt: Musée national de la Coopération franco-américaine, 1993), 126.

52. Mrs. Edward Tuck gave 1,000 francs; Mrs. Hazen Chase, 300; Wharton herself, 300; her friend Comtesse Rosa de Fitz-James, 200.

53. *New York Herald*, August 27, p. 3; August 31, p. 2.

54. Wharton to Sara Norton, September 2, 1914, *Letters*, 335.

55. Henry James to Wharton, August 6, 1914, in James, *Letters*, 289.

56. *New York Times*, September 2, 1914, pp. 1, 2.

57. Wharton to Bernard Berenson, c. September 3, 1914, *Letters*, 336.

58. Wharton, *A Backward Glance*, 342-343.

59. Sutherland, *Mrs. Humphry Ward*, 130.

60. Wharton, *A Backward Glance*, 343.

61. Wharton to Robert Grant, August 31, 1914. I am grateful to the Houghton Library of Harvard University and to Ambassador William R. Tyler and the Edith Wharton Estate for permission to quote from the correspondence between Edith Wharton and Grant held in the Robert Grant Papers at the Houghton Library.

    Subsequent references to the Grant Papers at the Houghton Library will be indicated by a final reference in the note to "Harvard."

62. Wharton to Bernard Berenson, c. September 3, 1914, *Letters*, 336.

63. Wharton to Sara Norton, September 2, 1914, *Letters*, 335.

64. Wharton to Robert Grant, August 31, 1914, Harvard.

65. Patricia R. Plante writes of Wharton's expatriation and her determination that the German invasion should be repelled: "Her problem was not merely one of escaping the plutocrats, but of finding another brownstone atmosphere. Hence, having once discovered it among the French, she was not prepared to lose it again. Every sacrifice had to be made for its preservation. The German invasion of France, therefore, was for Wharton a re-enactment of the vulgar attack of the nouveaux-riches upon New York society. The latter had lacked the strength to ward off the barbarians, and this renewal of the struggle was an opportunity—a second chance—to defeat the 'Goths.'" "Edith Wharton and the Invading Goths," *Midcontinent American Studies Journal* 5 (Fall 1964): 19.

66. Wharton to Robert Grant, August 31, 1914, Harvard.

67. Mrs. Herman Harjes, "Boys with Hands Cut Off," *New York Times*, September 2, 1914, p. 2.

68. Wharton to Sara Norton, September 2, 1914, *Letters*, 335.

69. Ibid.
70. Wharton to Sara Norton, September 27, 1914, *Letters*, 340.
71. Fowles, *Memories of Duveen Brothers*, 87.
72. Wharton to Mary Cadwalader Jones, September 7, 1914, Yale.
73. Wharton to Bernard Berenson, early September 1914, *Letters*, 328.
74. Wharton to Gaillard Lapsley, September 8, 1914, Yale.
75. Barnard, *Paris War Days*, 175.
76. Wharton, *A Backward Glance*, 345.
77. Wharton to Bernard Berenson, "Off to Paris tomorrow," September 23, 1914, Villa I Tatti.
78. Wharton to Bernard Berenson, September 30, 1914, *Letters*, 341.
79. *New York Herald*, September 26, 1914, p. 2.
80. Wharton to Sara Norton, September 27, 1914, *Letters*, 338.
81. *New York Times Magazine*, November 28, 1915, p. 1.
82. Wharton to Royall Tyler, October 11, 1914, Indiana.
83. Elisina Tyler to Mildred Barnes Bliss, December 1, 1913, Pusey Library, Harvard University. I am grateful to the Harvard University Archives, Harvard University, and to Ambassador William R. Tyler and the Edith Wharton Estate for permission to quote from the correspondence between Elisina Tyler and Mildred Bliss held in the Royall Tyler Papers in the Harvard University Archives.

      Subsequent references to letters and documents in the Harvard University Archives will be noted by "Harvard University Archives."
84. Elisina Tyler to Mildred Barnes Bliss, December 3, 1914, Harvard University Archives.
85. Elizabeth Dryden, *Paris in Herrick Days* (Paris: Dorbon-Aine, 1915), 121-122.
86. Wharton to Elizabeth Gaskell Norton, February 1, 1915, Harvard.
87. Quoted in Mrs. Winthrop Chanler, *Autumn in the Valley* (Boston: Little, Brown and Company, 1936), 177.
88. Quoted in the *New York Times*, September 16, 1914, p. 2.
89. Scribners to Wharton, October 13, 1914, Princeton.
90. Wharton to Charles Scribner, October 24, 1914, Princeton.
91. Wharton to Gaillard Lapsley, November 8, 1914, Yale.
92. Quoted in Roger Burlingame, *Of Making Many Books* (New York: Charles Scribner's Sons, 1946), 314.
93. Quoted in ibid., 315-316.
94. Gide, *Journals*, 53.
95. Ibid., 62.

96. Ibid., 68.

97. Ibid., 70.

98. The *Foyer Franco-Belge* seems to have been operating by August 26, for in an entry on that date Gide mentions Mme Theo's directing a Belgian woman to the competent relief agency with which she herself has registered.

99. Barnard, *Paris War Days*, 122-123, 144.

100. Wharton to Gaillard Lapsley, November 8, 1914, *Letters*, 342.

101. Charles du Bos said that after his marriage, "between Edith and my wife a friendship sprang up immediately that for thirty years, until Edith's death, never knew a shadow, and thus my marriage strengthened also my personal link with Edith herself." Quoted in Lubbock, *Portrait of Edith Wharton*, 99.

102. Wharton to Sara Norton, November 26, 1914, Harvard.

103. Ernest Samuels, *Bernard Berenson: The Making of a Legend* (Cambridge, MA.: The Belknap Press of Harvard University Press, 1987), 189.

104. Wharton to Bernard Berenson, November 14, 1914, note marked 8:30 A.M., Villa I Tatti. Wharton and Berenson exchanged early-morning notes through White, her butler. At the end of this note, she writes insistently, "Tell me quick, for I'm beginning 'right now'!"

105. Wharton to Bernard Berenson, November 14, 1914, marked 9 A.M., Villa I Tatti.

106. Wharton to Mary Berenson, November 27, 1914, Villa I Tatti.

107. Samuels, *Bernard Berenson*, 194.

108. Gide, *Journals*, 91-92.

109. Paul Fussell observes: "No one can calculate the number of Jews who died in the Second War because of the ridicule during the twenties and thirties of Allied propaganda about Belgian nuns violated and children sadistically used. In a climate of widespread skepticism about any further atrocity stories, most people refused fully to credit reports of the concentration camps until ocular evidence compelled belief and it was too late." *The Great War and Modern Memory* (New York: Oxford University Press, 1975), 316.

On the appetite for atrocity stories and the unreliability of the Bryce Report, Peter Buitenhuis writes:

> The Bryce Report continued to exert a powerful influence on American public opinion throughout the war. And yet the report, as is now generally acknowledged, was largely a tissue of invention, unsubstantiated observations by unnamed witnesses and second-hand eyewitness reports, depending far more on imagination than any other factor. The witnesses

were not put on oath, nor were they cross-examined. There was no attempt at scholarly investigation and evaluation of this evidence. Most significant of all, the documents and testimony of the witnesses disappeared from British records at the end of the war, so it has been impossible to make a subsequent check of the evidence.

The Bryce Report was the origin of most of the gruesome stories which had such effective currency throughout the war—stories of mass rapes, the spitting of babies on bayonets, the cutting off of children's hands and women's breasts, hostage murders, Germans excreting on private possessions, and so forth.

The Great War of Words: British, American, and Canadian Propaganda and Fiction, 1914-1933. (Vancouver: University of British Columbia Press, 1987), 27.

Wharton's friends were clearly influenced by the report. Daisy Chanler noted in her autobiography: "We all read Lord Bryce's report on the German atrocities in Belgium. Coming from him, the distinguished historian, the kindly and hospitable English gentleman whom we had known as Ambassador in Washington, this Report carried conviction and filled us with zealous indignation." Chanler, *Autumn in the Valley*, 160.

110. "Clearing House for American Relief," *New York Herald*, November 26, 1914, p. 2.

111. Ibid., p. 2.

112. Benstock, *No Gifts from Chance*, 143. Professor Benstock tells the author in a letter, "I believe EW knew the Warder sisters as far back as the 1880s" (22 March 1994).

113. Wharton to Alice Garrett, December 7, 1914, John Work Garrett Papers. I am grateful to Evergreen House of the Johns Hopkins University and to Ambassador William R. Tyler and to the Edith Wharton Estate for permission to quote from the Wharton letters in the John Work and Alice Garrett papers.

In subsequent notes references to this collection will be indicated by "Evergreen House."

114. Wharton to Mary Berenson, December 20, 1914, *Letters*, 344.

115. Elisina Tyler to Mildred Barnes Bliss, December 3, 1914, Harvard University Archives.

116. The hostels then in operation were located at 4 rue Pierre Nicole, 18 rue Taitbout, and 5 rue du Colisée. The following committees were listed:

medical, clothing, "the committee on collecting money in hotels and banks." The members of the general committee included Mrs. Walter Gay, Mrs. Edith Wharton, Mrs. Edward Tuck, Comtesse de Berthier, M. Charles du Bos, Mr. George Monroe, M. Henri Dupuis, M. Boccon Gibon, and Miss Spofford.

117. Charles Scribner to Wharton, December 8, 1914, Special Collections, Princeton.

118. Wharton to Charles Scribner, December 29, 1914, Special Collections, Princeton.

119. Referred to in Plante, "Edith Wharton and the Invading Goths," 20, drawing on a quotation in Arthur M. Schlesinger, *Political and Social Growth of the American People 1865-1940* (New York: Macmillan Company, 1941), 400-401.

    Charles A. Fenton has described World War I as "a literary fracture" between Wharton's generation, as exemplified by the members of the National Institute of Arts and Letters in 1914, and the generation that followed: Hemingway, Dos Passos, Fitzgerald, Faulkner. See Fenton, "A Literary Fracture of World War I," *American Quarterly* 12 (1960): 119-132.

120. "Mrs. Wharton Asks for Funds to Aid Refugees," *New York Sun*, January 18, 1915, p. 2.

121. Wharton to Gaillard Lapsley, December 23, 1914, Yale.

122. Wharton to Beatrix Farrand, c. December 1914, quoted in Eleanor Dwight, *Edith Wharton: An Extraordinary Life* (New York: Abrams, 1994), p. 287.

123. *New York Herald*, December 27, 1914, p. 2.

124. *New York Times*, September 22, 1914, p. 2.

125. *New York Times*, September 5, 1914, p. 3.

126. Letter of December 21, 1914, to A. F. Jaccaci in Paris from Mr. Frederic R. Coudert of 2 Rector Street in New York City, Harvard University Archives.

127. Wharton to Mrs. Whitney Warren, December 29, 1914; and Wharton to Mr. Whitney Warren, undated, Harvard.

CHAPTER 2

1. Wharton to Mary Berenson, January 12, 1915, *Letters*, 345.

2. Wharton to Mrs. Woodward Haven, January 1, 1915, Louis Auchincloss folio II, Yale.

3. Wharton to Charles Scribner, January 30, 1915, Special Collections, Princeton.

4. Wharton to Bernard Berenson, February 10, 1915, Villa I Tatti. The income tax had been introduced in the United States in 1913. In 1914 an income tax on resident aliens was adopted in France. Throughout the spring and summer of 1914 the *Herald* was full of articles and letters to the editor from American expatriates in France regretting that soon they would have to pay income taxes to two governments.

5. R.W.B. Lewis, *Edith Wharton: A Biography* (New York: Harper & Row, 1975), 378.

6. Wharton to Mary Berenson, January 12, 1915, *Letters*, 346.

7. Entry for January 7, 1915, by Helen Coolidge in John Gardner Coolidge, *A War Diary in Paris, 1914-1917* (Cambridge, MA: Riverside Press, 1931), 23.

8. Wharton to Alice Garrett, undated note marked "Thursday morning," c. December 1914, Evergreen House.

9. Wharton to Alice Garrett, unpublished letter dated only "Wednesday morning," c. early 1915, Evergreen House.

10. Wharton to Mary Berenson, January 12, 1915, *Letters*, 346.

11. The unsettling juxtaposition between moments of intense aesthetic beauty and scenes of human devastation was to overwhelm other Americans as well that winter. Helen Coolidge, wife of John Coolidge, experienced a similar reaction during a concert at Mildred Bliss's the following week. Whether it was caused by the music or her visit to wounded soldiers in Val de Grace hospital before the concert, or the combination, she admitted in her diary, "I felt so depressed I left early and walked home in the darkness." Quoted in Coolidge, *A War Diary in Paris*, entry for January 14, 1915, 25.

12. Edith Wharton, *Fighting France: From Dunkerque to Belfort* (New York: Charles Scribner's Sons, 1915), 41.

13. Wharton to Mary Berenson, January 12, 1915, *Letters*, 347.

14. Wharton to Bernard Berenson, January 27, 1915, Villa I Tatti.

15. Quoted in Shari Benstock, *No Gifts from Chance: A Biography of Edith Wharton* (New York: Charles Scribner's Sons, 1994), 310.

16. Letter to the *New York Herald,* February 25, 1915.

17. "Mrs. Wharton Asks for Funds to Aid Relief," *New York Sun*, January 18, 1915, p. 2.

18. Charles Scribner to Wharton, January 19, 1915, Special Collections, Princeton.

19. Wharton to Lily Norton, February 1, 1915, Harvard.

20. André Gide, *The Journals of André Gide*, vol. 2, translated and annotated by Justin O'Brien (New York: Alfred A. Knopf, 1951), 103.
21. Wharton to Bernard Berenson, January 27, 1915, Villa I Tatti.
22. Wharton to Bernard Berenson, February 10, 1915, Villa I Tatti.
23. Wharton cable to Charles Scribner, February 20, 1915, Special Collections, Princeton.
24. Wharton to Mary Berenson, January 12, 1915, *Letters*, 346.
25. Wharton to Mary Berenson, February 24, 1915, Villa I Tatti.
26. Wharton, *Fighting France*, 49-50.
27. Wharton to Robert Grant, February 13, 1915, Harvard.
28. Gide, *Journals*, 128.
29. The *Nation*, February 11, 1915, 175.
30. "Mr. Roosevelt's Advice Is Not to Go to Europe. He Says Americans Should Not Go Abroad to View Suffering in Spirit of Curiosity," *New York Herald*, March 26, 1915, p. 1.
31. Wharton, *Fighting France*, 34.
32. Wharton cable to Scribners, March 3, 1915, Special Collections, Princeton.
33. Wharton to Henry James, March 11, 1915, *Letters*, 351.
34. *Letters*, 353.
35. James E. Sait, "Charles Scribner's Sons and the Great War," *Princeton University Library Chronicle* 48 (Winter 1987): 178.
36. Wharton to John Work Garrett, March 5, 1915, Evergreen House.
37. Wharton to Robert Grant, February 13, 1915, Harvard.
38. The composition and publication of that story, "Coming Home," is described in my article "Edith Wharton's War Story," *Tulsa Studies in Women's Literature* 8, no. 1 (Spring 1989): 95-100.
39. Wharton to Sara Norton, March 16, 1915, Yale.
40. Wharton to Robert Bridges, March 24, 1915, Special Collections, Princeton. Also quoted in Roger Burlingame, *Of Making Many Books* (New York: Charles Scribner's Sons, 1947), 311.
41. Wharton to Mary Berenson, March 13, 1915, Villa I Tatti.
42. *New York Times Magazine*, November 28, 1915, p. 2.
43. "Dire Need of Poor Children of Ypres," *New York Herald*, March 24, 1915, p. 2.
44. Wharton to Robert Grant, April 8, 1915, Harvard.
45. *New York Herald*, April 27, 1915.
46. Wharton to Robert Bridges, April 22, 1915, Special Collections, Princeton.

47. *New York Herald*, May 4, 1915, p. 2.
48. Elisina Tyler to Mildred Bliss, April 19, 1915, Harvard University Archives.
49. Elisina Tyler to Mildred Bliss, April 27, 1915, Harvard University Archives. Paul Fussell comments on this tendency to see the war in literary terms in *The Great War and Modern Memory* (New York: Oxford University Press, 1975), chapter 5.
50. Wharton to Elizabeth Gaskel Norton, April 24, 1915, Harvard.
51. Elisina Tyler to Mildred Bliss, May 17, 1915, Harvard University Archives.
52. Wharton to Bernard Berenson, May 4, 1915, Villa I Tatti.
53. Coolidge, *A War Diary in Paris*, 69-70.
54. Elisina Tyler to Mildred Bliss, June 6, 1915, Harvard University Archives.
55. Scribners to Wharton, cable, April 30, 1915, Special Collections, Princeton.
56. Wharton to Scribners, cable, May 2, 1915, Princeton.
57. Wharton to Daisy Chanler, May 10, 1915, Yale.
58. Wharton to Daisy Chanler, June 8, 1915, Yale.
59. Edith Wharton, *A Backward Glance* (New York: D. Appleton and Company, 1934), 330.
60. Ibid., 346.
61. Wharton to Daisy Chanler, May 19, 1915, Yale.
62. Wharton to Daisy Chanler, June 8, 1915, Yale.
63. Wharton, *Fighting France*, 113.
64. Ibid., 114-115.
65. Wharton to William Crary Brownell, May 21, 1915, Special Collections, Princeton.
66. Wharton to Scribners, cable, May 24, 1915, Special Collections, Princeton.
67. Wharton to Robert Bridges, May 27, 1915, Special Collections, Princeton.
68. Wharton to Scribners, cable, May 29, 1915, Special Collections, Princeton.
69. Wharton to Robert Bridges, May 27, 1915, Special Collections, Princeton.
70. Quoted in Burlingame, *Of Making Many Books*, 311.
71. Wharton to Gaillard Lapsley, May 22, 1915, Yale.
72. Wharton to Bernard Berenson, June 11, 1915, Villa I Tatti.
73. Wharton, *Fighting France*, 151-154.
74. Ibid., 156-157.
75. Ibid., 161.
76. Ibid., 168.

77. "In one of those villas for nearly a year, two hearts at the highest pitch of human constancy have held up a light to the world. It is impossible to pass that house without a sense of awe. Because of the light that comes from it, dead faiths have come to life, weak convictions have grown strong, fiery impulses have turned to long endurance, and long endurance has kept the fire of impulse. In the harbour of New York there is a pompous statue of a goddess with a torch, designated as 'Liberty enlightening the World.' It seems as though the title on her pedestal might well, for the time, be transferred to the lintel of that villa in the dunes." Ibid., 177.

78. Quoted in Burlingame, *Of Making Many Books*, 312.

79. "Edith Wharton's Work: She Wants Money to Buy Motors for the French Red Cross," *New York Times*, June 25, 1915, p. 10.

80. *New York Herald*, July 9, 1915, p. 2.

81. Wharton to Elizabeth Gaskell Norton, July 4, 1915, Harvard.

82. Wharton to Mary Berenson, July 22, 1915, Villa I Tatti.

83. Wharton to Henry James, August 11, 1915, Harvard.

84. Wharton to Bernard Berenson, July 16, 1915, Villa I Tatti.

85. Elisina Tyler to Mildred Bliss, August 21, 1915, Harvard University Archives.

86. Wharton to Charles Scribner, October 21, 1915, Special Collections, Princeton.

87. Wharton, *A Backward Glance*, 349.

88. I have described the creation and editorial politics surrounding this beautiful gift book in "The Making of Edith Wharton's *The Book of the Homeless*," *Princeton University Library Chronicle* 47, no. 1 (Autumn 1985): 5-21.

89. Wharton to Robert Bridges, July 19, 1915, Special Collections, Princeton.

90. Edith Wharton to Alice Garrett, dated only "Monday night," c. mid-July-August, 1915, Evergreen House.

91. Wharton to Bernard Berenson, July 24, 1915, Villa I Tatti.

92. Wharton to Bernard Berenson, August 5, 1915, Villa I Tatti.

93. Wharton to Mary Berenson, August 27, 1915, Villa I Tatti.

94. Henry James to Wharton, July 19, 1915, Yale. See also Henry James, *Henry James and Edith Wharton, Letters: 1900-1915*, ed. Lyall H. Powers (New York: Charles Scribner's Sons, 1990), 345-346.

95. Wharton to Charles Scribner, July 19, 1915, Special Collections, Princeton.

96. Wharton to Charles Scribner, July 22, 1915, Special Collections, Princeton.

97. Daniel Berkeley Updike, "Notes on the Press and Its Work," *Updike: American Printer and His Merrymount Press* (New York: American Institute of Graphic Arts, 1947), 21.

98. Charles Scribner to Wharton, cable, August 3, 1915, Special Collections, Princeton.

99. Charles Scribner to Wharton, August 3, 1915, Special Collections, Princeton.

100. Wharton to Charles Scribner, July 22, 1915, Special Collections, Princeton.

101. Joseph Conrad to Henry James, July 24, 1915, Yale.

102. Several of these letters are in *The Book of the Homeless* file in the Wharton Papers (Yale Collection of American Literature, Beinecke Rare Book and Manuscript Library) at Yale University.

103. Charles Scribner to Wharton, August 16, 1915, Special Collections, Princeton.

104. Wharton to Robert Grant, September 7, 1915, Yale.

105. Wharton to Henry James, August 11, 1915, Harvard.

106. Wharton, *Fighting France*, 183.

107. Ibid., 200.

108. Wharton to Mary Berenson, August 27, 1915, Villa I Tatti.

109. Wharton to Charles Scribner, September 10, 1915, Special Collections, Princeton.

110. Wharton to Mary Cadwalader Jones, October 26, 1915, Yale.

111. André Suarès, "Song of the Welsh Women," *The Book of the Homeless* (New York: Charles Scribner's Sons, 1916), 147.

112. Wharton to Charles Scribner, August 30, 1915, Special Collections, Princeton.

113. Wharton to Charles Scribner, September 23, 1915, Special Collections, Princeton.

114. Wharton to Charles Scribner, October 15, 1915, Special Collections, Princeton.

115. Quoted in Sait, "Charles Scribner's Sons and the Great War," 163.

116. Charles Scribner to Wharton, August 30, 1915, Special Collections, Princeton.

117. Wharton to Charles Scribner, September 30, 1915, Special Collections, Princeton.

118. Charles Scribner to Wharton, October 22, 1915, Special Collections, Princeton.

119. Charles Scribner to Wharton, September 23, 1915, Special Collections, Princeton.
120. Wharton to Mary Cadwalader Jones, November 10, 1915, Yale.
121. *New York Times*, January 30, 1916, p. 21.
122. Wharton to Sara Norton, September 10, 1915, Yale.
123. *New York Herald*, September 12, 1915, p. 2.
124. Wharton to Elizabeth Cameron, September 23, 1915, Library of Congress.
125. Arline Boucher Tehan, *Henry Adams in Love: The Pursuit of Elizabeth Sherman Cameron* (New York: Universe Books, 1983), 236.
126. Ibid., 11.
127. Ibid., 243-244.
128. Wharton to Elizabeth Cameron, September 25, 1915, Library of Congress.
129. Gide, *Journals*, 100-101.
130. Wharton to Gaillard Lapsley, October 5, 1915, Yale. After her return, Wharton would receive regular reports on James's health from his nurse and housekeeper, Miss Theodora Bosanquet, beginning with a typewritten letter on November 4, 1915, Harvard.
131. Wharton to Elisina Tyler, October 6, 1915, Indiana.
132. Quoted in Coolidge, *A War Diary in Paris*, 80.
133. Wharton to Theodore Roosevelt, October 19, 1915 (uncataloged letter in the Ethel Derby files of the Roosevelt papers at the Houghton Library), Harvard.
134. Wharton to Mary Cadwalader Jones, October 26, 1915, Yale.
135. Wharton to Sara Norton, October 27, 1915, Yale.
136. Charles Scribner to Wharton, August, 9, 1915, Special Collections, Princeton.
137. Charles Scribner to Robert Grant, August 10, 1915, Harvard.
138. Charles Scribner to Robert Grant, August 31, 1915, Harvard.
139. Charles Scribner to Wharton, August 30, 1915, Special Collections, Princeton.
140. Charles Scribner to Wharton, October 8, 1915, Special Collections, Princeton.
141. Wharton to Sara Norton, on letters lost on the *Arabic*, October 27, 1915, Yale.
142. Charles Scribner to Edith Wharton, November 26, 1916, Special Collections, Princeton.
143. Wharton to Elizabeth Cameron, October 31, 1915, Library of Congress.
144. Wharton to Elizabeth Cameron, November 16, 1915, Library of Congress.
145. Tehan, *Henry Adams in Love*, 9-10.

146. Quoted in ibid., 257.

147. *New York Herald*, November 17, 1915, p. 2.

148. "American Hostels Ask for Aid for Their Refugees: Funds Are Urgently Needed to Purchase Coal for 3,000 Fugitives from Invaders," *New York Herald*, November 20, 1915, p. 2.

149. *New York Herald*, December 8, 1915, p. 2.

150. Wharton to Mary Cadwalader Jones, December 11, 1915, Yale.

151. Daisy Chanler, a child of her privileged class, describes such wartime rummage sales and the inappropriate way the poor spent their money: "Great rummage sales were organized by ladies who in times of peace devoted their energies to giving and going to parties. These sales assumed such proportions that the police had to be called in to keep order and establish one-way circulation for the dense and often unruly crowds that came to buy. The sidewalk was jammed for hours before the doors were opened, and then there would be a wild rush for the high-piled clothes counter where fur coats, handsome gowns, and all manner of luxurious garments were offered for a song. The very poor, who for their few dollars could have fitted themselves out with warm and substantial tweeds, would be sorely tempted by some gauzy, glittering creation wholly inappropriate to an East Side tenement." Chanler, *Autumn in the Valley* (Boston: Little, Brown and Company, 1936), 162.

152. Wharton to Sally Fairchild, November 17, 1915, Yale.

153. Wharton to Elizabeth Cameron, letter marked only "Sat. Eve," Library of Congress. Wharton's contact at the newspaper, which had always been very generous with space for her appeals, was through a Miss Birkhead.

154. Wharton to Elizabeth Cameron, letter marked "Wed. 24" [November 1915], Library of Congress.

155. Wharton to Elizabeth Cameron, November 29, 1915, Library of Congress.

156. Wharton to Elisina Tyler, November 30, 1915, Indiana.

157. Gide, *Journals*, 111.

158. Wharton to André Gide, December 8, 1915, Yale.

159. Wharton to Elizabeth Cameron, November 29, 1915, Library of Congress.

160. Wharton to Elizabeth Cameron, December 1, 1915, Library of Congress.

161. Wharton to Elizabeth Cameron, December 2, 1915, Library of Congress.

162. Wharton to Gaillard Lapsley, December 17, 1915, Yale.

163. Wharton to Elizabeth Cameron, December 4, 1915, Library of Congress.

164. Wharton to André Gide, December 8, 1915, Yale.

165. Charles Scribner to Wharton, December 10, 1915, Special Collections, Princeton.

166. Wharton to Charles Scribner, December 26, 1915, Special Collections, Princeton.
167. Wharton to Elizabeth Cameron, December 25, 1915, Library of Congress.
168. Charles Scribner to Wharton, November 8, 1915, Special Collections, Princeton.
169. *New York Times Book Review*, November 5, 1916, p. 465.

CHAPTER 3

1. Wharton to Mary Cadwalader Jones, January 7, 1916, *Letters*, 367.
2. Wharton to Elizabeth Cameron, January 1, 1916, Library of Congress.
3. Charles Scribner to Wharton, January 27, 1916, Special Collections, Princeton.
4. Charles Scribner to Wharton, January 27, 1916, Special Collections, Princeton.
5. Charles Scribner was able to buy so heavily at the auction because the firm was having a very good Christmas season. He wrote his London agent: "The holiday trade is excellent and I hear nothing but praise of the retail floor and I think the clerks are doing better than usual. The wholesale demand is also very good now and we are quite sold out of the 'Men of the Old Stone Age' and 'Beautiful Gardens in America,' which two seem to be purchased largely as holiday gifts. I think we go into the New Year in pretty good shape." Quoted in James E. Sait, "Charles Scribner's Sons and the Great War," *Princeton University Library Chronicle* 48 (Winter 1987): 159.
6. Wharton to Mary Cadwalader Jones, February 11, 1916, Yale.
7. Wharton to Elizabeth Cameron, April 3, 1916, Library of Congress.
8. The New York Committee of the Edith Wharton Charities, *Report of Edith Wharton's War Charities in France* (1916), 17.
9. Wharton to Royall Tyler, c. March 1916, Indiana.
10. Charles Scribner to Wharton, April 21, 1916, Special Collections, Princeton.
11. Wharton to Mary Cadwalader Jones, January 14, 1916, Yale.
    A year later the accounting department at Scribners reported to Minnie Jones that the publisher had paid out $1,500 in advances on expected sales of the book but that they still had a number of copies on hand, which they were hoping to sell at a reduced price. Wharton, now preoccupied with other projects, advised Scribners, "With regard to the copies of The Book

of the Homeless which remain unsold, of course, it would be best to sell them at a reduced price."

So the total sales of the book, set against an extremely high production cost for its exceptional quality of printed text and reproduced art, netted only $1,500. With the receipts of the auction, the entire project netted about $9,500. Edith Wharton, who regretted missing the pre-Christmas sale that would have brought even bigger receipts, never regretted undertaking the project nor the financial results. She wrote to Scribner, "The book is certain to become very valuable some day, and I have no fear of its future." She was right. Collectors still prize *The Book of the Homeless*, with the $5 trade edition wholesaling at recent book auctions for $70 and listed in booksellers' catalogs for $100.

12. Wharton to Mary Cadwalader Jones, January 7, 1916, *Letters*, 367.
13. Wharton to Theodora Bosanquet, January 17, 1916, Houghton Library, Harvard.
14. Wharton to Mary Cadwalader Jones, January 7, 1916, *Letters*, 366.
15. Ibid., 366.
16. Ibid., 367.
17. Wharton to Mary Cadwalader Jones, April 15, 1916 (from Beauvallon-sur-Mer), Yale.
18. Minutes of April 6, 1916, meeting of the New York Committee of the Edith Wharton Charities, Yale.
19. Minutes of April 18, 1916, special meeting of the New York Committee of the Edith Wharton Charities, Yale.
20. Minutes of the April 24, 1916, meeting of the New York Committee of the Edith Wharton Charities, Yale. After a conference of the members by telephone, "it was decided that in view of the difficulty of selling the $100 boxes, in such a short time, it would be more prudent to give up the benefit." Mr. Kahn released the committee from its earlier agreement with the Metropolitan.
21. Wharton to Beatrix Farrand, June 22, 1916, Yale.
22. Wharton to Mary Cadwalader Jones, January 7, 1916, *Letters*, 368.
23. Wharton to the editor of the *New York Times*, January 9, 1916, Yale.
24. Shari Benstock, *No Gifts from Chance: A Biography of Edith Wharton* (New York: Charles Scribner's Sons, 1994), 288.
25. Wharton to Mary Cadwalader Jones, January 14, 1916, Yale.
26. Apparently the Baltimore firm engaged by John Work Garrett's parents to represent Wharton's war charities in Baltimore was pleased to be relieved of the duty. A letter of January 25, 1916, from B. Howell Griswold,

Jr. (on stationery from Alexander Brown & Sons, Founded 1800, Foreign and Domestic Bankers) to Wharton explained: "Mrs. Garrett asked me to organize a Committee to serve for what we understood was to be a comparatively brief time, to receive contributions, and we made our appeal without results. All the members of our Committee, however, are professional beggars. We are all engaged in work for Baltimore charities, for the Red Cross, for hospitals, etc. None of us has been immune.

"If a Committee can be formed in Baltimore which would devote special attention to your work, you would get much better results." Wharton Papers, Yale.

27. Wharton to Mary Cadwalader Jones, January 14, 1916, Yale.
28. André Gide, January 23, 1916, The Journals of André Gide, vol. 2, translated and annotated by Justin O'Brien (New York: Alfred A. Knopf, 1951), 119.
29. Ibid., January 25, 1916, 120.
30. Wharton to Mary Cadwalader Jones, January 22, 1916, Yale.
31. The second page of a letter from Wharton to Royall Tyler, Hôtel Costebelle, Hyères, stationery. The first page with the address and date are missing, but obviously the letter was written after the publication date of The Book of the Homeless in January 1916, Indiana.
32. Wharton to Elizabeth Cameron, March 21, 1916, Library of Congress.
33. L. C. Dolly Herbert (Wharton's secretary) to Mary Cadwalader Jones, January 2, 1916, Yale.
34. Wharton to Mary Cadwalader Jones, January 23, 1916, Yale.
35. Wharton to Elizabeth Cameron, March 18, 1916, Library of Congress.
36. Wharton to John Garrett, [February] 10, 1916, Evergreen House.
37. "Mrs. Wharton's Charity: She Makes a New Appeal for the American Hostels in Paris," New York Times, March 18, 1916, p. 10. The letter is datelined Paris, February 28, 1916.
38. Wharton was persistent in the personal cases in which she took an interest. Two months later she asked John Garrett to jog the memory of Mr. Grew in Berlin about the case of Odette Lesne. Wharton to John Work Garrett, April 15, 1916, Evergreen House.
39. Wharton to John Garrett, February 26, 1916, Evergreen House.
40. Wharton to John Garrett, March 5, 1916, Evergreen House.
41. Wharton to John Garrett, March 10, 1916, Evergreen House.
42. Wharton to Monsieur Garrett, Chancellerie de L'Ambassade des Etats Unis, March 10, 1916, Evergreen House.
43. Wharton to Elizabeth Cameron, March 1, 1916, Library of Congress.
44. Wharton to Gaillard Lapsley, January 10, 1916, Letters, 369.

45. Wharton to Theodora Bosanquet, March 1, 1916, Houghton Library, Harvard. *Henry James and Edith Wharton Letters: 1900-1915* ed. Lyall H. Powers (New York: Charles Scribner's Sons, 1990), 391.
46. Wharton to Alice Garrett, March 3, 1916, Evergreen House.
47. Wharton to Elizabeth Cameron, picture postcard and note from the Hôtel Costebelle in Hyères, both dated March 14, 1916, Library of Congress.
48. Wharton to Elizabeth Cameron, March 15, 1916, Library of Congress.
49. Wharton to Elizabeth Cameron, March 17, 1916, Library of Congress.
50. Wharton to Elisina Tyler, c. March 1916 from the Hôtel Costebelle in Hyères, Indiana.
51. A copy of the Citation of the Legion of Honor for Wharton is held in the archives of the Legion of Honor Museum in Paris, opposite the Musée D'Orsay. In French it reads:

Le Président de la République Française, Vu la Déclaration de Conseil de l'Ordre en Date du 20 Mars 1916. Sur la proposition du Président du Conseil.

Ministre des Affairs Etrangères,

Décrète:

Art. 1er — Mme. Edith Wharton, citoyenne americaine, femme de lettres est nominée Chevalier de l'Ordre National de la Légion d'Honneur. (Par sa parole, par ses écrits et par ses publications a su, depuis le Début de la guerre, gagner de nombreuses sympathies à la cause française et s'est signalée par sa charité et son dévouement aux oeuvres de bienfaisance).

Art. II _____ Le Président du Conseil, le Ministre des Affaires Etrangeres, et le Grand Chancelier de l'Ordre sont chargés, chacun en ce qui le concerne, de l'exécution du présent décret.

Fait à Paris, le 28 Mars 1916

Signé: R. Poincaré

Contresigné: A. Briand

Pour ampliation:

Le Ministre Plénipotentiaire, Chef du Service du Protocole

And by a declaration of the council of the order on August 3, 1923, she was promoted to the rank of officer of the order of the Legion of Honor. In the decree, she was joined in the promotion on that day by two Dutchmen (an architect and a diplomat), a Mexican collector of art, and an Italian who was the head of service at the Institut Pasteur. This time the order was signed by A. Millerand and countersigned by R. Poincaré.

52. Wharton to Elizabeth Cameron, March 29, 1916, Library of Congress.
53. Wharton to Elizabeth Cameron, April 3, 1916, Library of Congress.
54. Egerton Winthrop cable to Wharton, April 5, 1916, Yale.
55. Wharton to André Gide, April 7, 1916, Yale.
56. Nicky Mariano, *Forty Years with Berenson* (New York: Alfred A. Knopf, 1966), 180-181.
57. Wharton to Elizabeth Cameron, April 3, 1916, Library of Congress.
58. Ibid.
59. Wharton to Elizabeth Cameron, April 9, 1916, Library of Congress.
60. Wharton to Mary Cadwalader Jones, April 15, 1916, Yale.
61. Obituary, *New York Times*, April 7, 1916, p. 11.
62. Wharton to Max Farrand, April 12, 1916, Yale.
63. These two leaves were laid in among the letters in the John Work and Alice Garrett papers to and from Wharton, Evergreen House. The last word is blurred and unrecoverable.
64. Wharton to Elizabeth Cameron, April 10, 1916, Library of Congress.
65. Wharton to Elizabeth Cameron, April 19, 1916, Library of Congress.
66. Wharton to Elizabeth Cameron, April 9, 1916, Library of Congress.
67. Wharton to Robert Grant, April 17, 1916, Yale.
68. Wharton to Elisina and Royall Tyler, April 19, 1916, Indiana.
69. Wharton to Elizabeth Cameron, undated, Golf Hôtel stationery, Library of Congress.
70. Wharton to Cameron, a note marked "Wednesday," Library of Congress.
71. Wharton to Elizabeth Cameron, June 5, 1916, Library of Congress.
72. Wharton to Elizabeth Cameron, June 19, 1916, Library of Congress.
73. Wharton to John Work Garrett, June 9, 1916. A pair of receipts from September 9, 1916, shows that Garrett used the American embassy in Berlin to send the money. Evergreen House.
74. Wharton to Elizabeth Cameron, July 7, 1916, Library of Congress.
75. Wharton to Elizabeth Cameron, July 13, 1916, Library of Congress.
76. Wharton to Elizabeth Cameron, July 31, 1916, Library of Congress.
77. Wharton to Elizabeth Cameron, August 7, 1916, Library of Congress.
78. Wharton to Elizabeth Cameron, August 9, 1916, Library of Congress.
79. Wharton to Elizabeth Cameron, August 9, 1916, Library of Congress.
80. Wharton to Elizabeth Cameron, undated letter, Library of Congress.
81. Wharton to Mrs. Harrison Garrett, July 27, 1916, Evergreen House.
82. Wharton to Elizabeth Cameron, August 23, 1916, Library of Congress.
83. Wharton to Mary Cadwalader Jones, August 29, 1916, Yale.
84. Wharton letter to Robert Grant, August 25, 1916, Yale.

85. Wharton to Mary Cadwalader Jones, December 14, 1916, Yale.
86. Wharton to Elizabeth Cameron, August 28, 1916, Library of Congress.
87. Wharton to Bernard Berenson, September 4, 1918, Villa I Tatti.
88. Wharton to John Work Garrett, September 6, 1916, Evergreen House.
89. John Work Garrett to Wharton, September 7, 1916, Evergreen House.
90. Wharton to Mary Cadwalader Jones, September 13, 1916, Yale.
91. Wharton to Bernard Berenson, September 11, 1916, Villa I Tatti. She closed her letter of September 19, 1916, to Berenson: "Now I must go back to Chap. IX (this is not an allusion to a new attachment, but a reference to my daily literary task!)"
92. Wharton to Robert Grant, September 17, 1916, Yale.
93. Wharton to Gide, September 26, 1916, transcription at Yale.
94. Wharton to Mary Cadwalader Jones, March 9, 1916, Yale.
95. Wharton to Mrs. Ellen Barlow, March 10, 1916, Rockefeller Foundation Archives, RG 1.1, Series 500T, Box 25, Folder 247. I am grateful to the Rockefeller Archive Center and to Ambassador William R. Tyler and the Edith Wharton Estate for permission to quote from the unpublished correspondence in the Rockefeller Foundation Archives.

Subsequent references to letters held in the Rockefeller Foundation Archives will be indicated in the notes by a closing reference to "Rockefeller Archives."
96. Mrs. Ellen Barlow to Mr. John D. Rockefeller, Jr., April 1, 1916, Rockefeller Archives. In a postscript, Mrs. Barlow explained that she was the mother of Mrs. Pierre Jay: "Mr. and Mrs. Jay have the pleasure of knowing you and Mrs. Rockefeller."
97. J. Grant Forbes to Warwick Greene, July 4, 1916, Rockefeller Archives.
98. Wallace Sabine to Rockefeller Foundation, November 16, 1916, Rockefeller Archives.
99. Wharton to Elizabeth Cameron, August 23, 1916, Library of Congress.
100. Wharton to Mary Cadwalader Jones, August 5, 1916, Yale.
101. Wharton to Mary Cadwalader Jones, October 28, 1916, Yale.
102. Wharton to Mary Cadwalader Jones, September 14, 1916, Yale.
103. Wharton to Mary Cadwalader Jones, October 28, 1916, Yale.
104. Wharton to Bernard Berenson, September 2, 1918, Villa I Tatti.
105. Wharton to Bernard Berenson, September 11, 1916, Villa I Tatti.
106. Wharton to Bernard Berenson, September 19, 1916, Villa I Tatti.
107. For the correspondence that tells the story of this grim accident, see the Royall Tyler Papers in the Pusey Library at Harvard University.
108. Wharton to Mary Cadwalader Jones, September 13, 1916, Yale.

109. Elisina Tyler to Mildred Bliss, September 20, 1916, Harvard.

110. Wharton to Bernard Berenson, September 19, 1916, Villa I Tatti.

111. Wharton to Mary Cadwalader Jones, September 28, 1916, Yale.

112. Wharton to John Garrett, October 15, 1916, Evergreen House.

113. Wharton to Elisina Tyler, September 15, 1916, Indiana.

114. Wharton to Mary Cadwalader Jones, September 28, 1916, Yale.

115. Wharton to Robert Grant, September 17, 1916, Yale.

116. Wharton to Mary Cadwalader Jones, October 13, 1916, Yale.

117. Wharton to Mary Cadwalader Jones, October 6, 1916, Yale.

118. Wharton to Mary Cadwalader Jones, October 13, 1916, Yale.

119. Wharton to John Garrett, October 15, 1916, Evergreen House.

120. Gide, October 21 and October 26, 1916, *Journals*, 103, 104. Apparently the sensitivities of du Bos had to be considered at every turn. In an earlier journal entry of September 1915, Gide admitted that he was hesitant to reorganize the restaurant at the rue Taitbout because "I fear that Charlie du Bos might be hurt," 99.

121. Wharton to Elizabeth Cameron, undated note marked "Saturday," Library of Congress.

122. Gide, October 24, 1916, *Journals*, 161.

    "A letter from Mme Theo gives me news of Charlie du Bos, from whom the attribution of the financial grants has finally been taken away. I sent a telegram to Mme Theo offering to resume work at the Foyer for three weeks, for I fear they may be overtaxed."

123. Wharton to Mary Cadwalader Jones, December 20, 1916, Yale.

124. Wharton to Bernard Berenson, November 10, 1916, Villa I Tatti.

125. Wharton to Robert Grant, November 10, 1916, Yale.

126. Quoted in Samuels, 208.

127. Quoted in Arline Boucher Tehan, *Henry Adams in Love: The Pursuit of Elizabeth Sherman Cameron* (New York: Universe Books, 1983), 258.

128. John Gardner Coolidge, *A War Diary in Paris, 1914-1917* (Cambridge, MA: Riverside Press, 1931), 160-161.

129. Wharton to Robert Grant, November 10, 1916, Yale.

    This is a surprising statement since manuscripts of most of Wharton's books can be found among her papers in the Yale Collection of American Literature in the Beinecke Rare Book and Manuscript Library at Yale University. Other Wharton manuscripts are held in the Rare Book Room at the Princeton University Library and in the Lilly Library at Indiana University.

130. Wharton to Bernard Berenson, November 13, 1916, Villa I Tatti.

131. See the letters and notes from Wharton to Bernard Berenson, November 22, 23, 24, 26, 27, 1916, Villa I Tatti.

132. Wharton to the editor of the *New York Times*, December 1, 1916. The letter was transmitted by Mary Cadwalader Jones and published in the issue of December 18, 1916, p. 10.

133. Wharton to Bernard Berenson, December 2, 1916, Villa I Tatti.

134. Wharton to Mary Cadwalader Jones, December 6, 1916, Yale.

135. Wharton to Robert Grant, December 10, 1916, Yale.

136. Wharton in a letter to the *New York Times*, December 10, 1916, though published January 14, 1917, sec. 2, p. 4.

137. Wharton to the *New York Times*, December 16, 1916, though published January 26, 1917, p. 8.

138. Quoted by Wharton in a letter to the *New York Times*, December 22, 1916, though published February 13, 1917, p. 10.

139. Wharton to Alice and John Garrett, Christmas Day [December 25, 1916], Evergreen House.

140. Wharton to Elizabeth Cameron, December 22, 1916, Library of Congress.

141. Wharton to Elizabeth Cameron, Christmas Eve, 1916, Library of Congress.

142. Coolidge, *A War Diary in Paris*, 92.

143. Wharton to D'Arcy Paul, December 26, 1916, Evergreen House.

144. Wharton, "Christmas Tinsel," *The Delineator* (December 1923): 11. My description of the "celebration" is drawn from Wharton's article.

145. Wharton to D'Arcy Paul, December 26, 1916, Evergreen House.

CHAPTER 4

1. Wharton to Sara Norton, January, 1917, Harvard.

2. Wharton to John Jay Chapman, January 10, 1917, *Letters*, 386.

3. Wharton to Bernard Berenson, February 24, 1917, Villa I Tatti.

4. She would, for example, ask the French *conseiller* in New York to telephone Minnie when the valise arrived with sewing work done by refugees for a New York charity bazaar. "*Avec l'autorisation de Monsieur de Margerie je vous envoie une petite valise.*" Wharton to le Conseiller Général de France in New York City, November 9, 1917, Yale.

5. Wharton to Sara Norton, January, 1917, Harvard.

6. Wharton to Mary Cadwalader Jones, January 12, 1917, Yale.

210   THE END OF THE AGE OF INNOCENCE

7. Wharton to Mary Cadwalader Jones, January 3, 1917, Yale.
8. Wharton to Mary Cadwalader Jones, January 12, 1917, Yale.
9. Wharton to Mary Cadwalader Jones, November 29, 1917, Yale.
10. Wharton to Mary Cadwalader Jones, January 3, 1917, Yale.
11. Ibid.
12. Ibid.
13. Ernest Samuels, *Bernard Berenson: The Making of a Legend* (Cambridge, MA: The Belknap Press of Harvard University Press, 1987), 210.
14. Wharton to Bernard Berenson, January 5, 1917, Villa I Tatti.
15. Wharton to Bernard and Mary Berenson, January 18, 1917, Villa I Tatti.
16. Ibid.
17. Wharton to Mary Cadwalader Jones, January 27, 1917. Yale.
18. Wharton to Mary Cadwalader Jones, February 9, 1917, Yale.
19. Wharton to Bernard Berenson, January 28, 1917, Villa I Tatti.
20. Wharton to Mary Cadwalader Jones, February 2, 1917, Yale.
21. Wharton to Mary Cadwalader Jones, March 23, 1917, Yale.
22. Roger Asselineau, "Edith Wharton—She Thought in French and Wrote in English," in *Wretched Exotic: Essays on Edith Wharton in Europe*, eds. Katherine Joslin and Alan Price (New York: Peter Lang, 1993), 356.
23. Wharton to Mrs. Kingsbury Waterman, November 14, 1917, Yale.
24. Wharton to Mary Cadwalader Jones, February 9, 1917, Yale.
25. Wharton to Bernard Berenson, January 28, 1917, Villa I Tatti.
26. Mildred Aldrich to Gertrude Stein and Alice Toklas, January 16, 1917, Yale.
27. Wharton to Mary Cadwalader Jones, February 2, 1917, Yale.
28. Wharton to Bernard Berenson, January 5, 1917, Villa I Tatti.
29. Wharton to Bernard Berenson, January 29, 1917, *Letters*, 388.
30. Wharton to Bernard Berenson, February 4, 1917, *Letters*, 389.
31. Wharton to Bernard Berenson, February 9, 1917, *Letters*, 391.
32. Wharton to Bernard Berenson, February 13, 1917, Villa I Tatti.
33. Ibid.
34. Wharton to Bernard Berenson, February 24, 1917, Villa I Tatti.
35. Wharton to Mary Cadwalader Jones, March 9, 1917, Yale.
36. Wharton to Mary Cadwalader Jones, undated response to Minnie's letter of July 12, 1917, Yale.
37. Wharton to Bernard Berenson, March 10, 1917, Villa I Tatti.
38. Wharton to Comte de Pagan, March 6, 1917, Yale.
39. Wharton to Mary Cadwalader Jones, March 9, 1917, Yale.
40. Wharton to Mary Cadwalader Jones, March 23, 1917, Yale.

41. Wharton to Bernard Berenson, March 10, 1917, Villa I Tatti.
42. Coolidge, 204.
43. Mildred Aldrich to Gertrude Stein, January 21, 1917, Yale.
44. Wharton to Bernard Berenson, March 10, 1917, Villa I Tatti. She had probably been reading Renan's *Antichrist, Including the Period from the Arrival of Paul in Rome to the End of the Jewish Revolution.*
45. Wharton to Mary Cadwalader Jones, March 23, 1917, Yale.
46. Wharton to Mary Cadwalader Jones, March 31, 1917, Yale.
47. Wharton to Miss Reubell, April 4, 1917, Yale.
48. Wharton to Bernard Berenson, April 15, 1917, Villa I Tatti.
49. Robert H. Ferrell, *Woodrow Wilson and World War I, 1917-1921* (New York: Harper & Row, 1985), 8.
50. Ibid., 1-3.
51. Wharton to Mary Cadwalader Jones, April 6, 1917, Yale.
52. Wharton to the editor of the *New York Times*, April 8, 1917, Yale.
53. Wharton to Mrs. Garrett in Baltimore, June 17, 1917, Evergreen House.
54. Wharton to Mary Cadwalader Jones, April 6, 1917, Yale.
55. Wharton to Bernard Berenson, April 15, 1917, Villa I Tatti.
56. Elisina Tyler to Mildred Barnes Bliss, April 9, 1917, Royall Tyler Papers, Harvard University Archives.
57. Wharton to Mary Cadwalader Jones, May 11, 1917, Yale.
58. Wharton to Mary Cadwalader Jones, August 8, 1917, Yale.
59. Wharton to Mary Cadwalader Jones, November 14, 1917, Yale.
60. *New York Times*, May 6, 1917, sec. 2, p. 3.
61. Wharton to Sara Norton, May 5, 1917, Yale.
62. Wharton to Mary Cadwalader Jones, June 22, 1917, Yale.
63. Wharton to Sara Norton, June 22, 1917, Yale.
64. For an account of Wharton's evolving difficulties with the American Red Cross, see my article "Edith Wharton at War with the American Red Cross," *Women's Studies: An Interdisciplinary Journal* 20, no. 2 (Spring 1991): 120-131.
65. Merle Curti, *American Philanthropy Abroad: A History* (New Brunswick, NJ: Rutgers University Press, 1963), 237.
66. Elizabeth Brown Pryor, *Clara Barton: Professional Angel* (Philadelphia: University of Pennsylvania Press, 1987), 332.
67. Foster Rhea Dulles, *The American Red Cross: A History* (New York: Harper and Row, 1950), 68.
68. Quoted in ibid., 95.
69. Quoted in ibid., 80.

70. Gustave R. Gaeddert, *The Boardman Influence, 1905-1917*, vol. 3 of *The History of the American National Red Cross* (Washington, D.C.: American National Red Cross, 1950), 275.

71. "A movement was also started to place all the war relief societies started here under the direct control of the Red Cross." *New York Herald*, November 28, 1915, p. 2.

72. Robert H. Bremner, *American Philanthropy*, 2nd ed. (Chicago: University of Chicago Press, 1988), 122.

73. Henry P. Davison, *The American Red Cross in the Great War* (New York: Macmillan, 1919), 7.

74. Dulles, *American Red Cross*, 146-147.

75. Thomas W. Lamont, *Henry Davison: The Record of a Useful Life* (New York: Arno Press, 1965), 287.

76. Quoted in ibid., 286.

77. Wharton to Mary Cadwalader Jones, June 5, 1917, Yale.

78. Wharton to Mrs. Garrett, June 17, 1917, Evergreen House.

79. Wharton to Nathalie Boynton, letter with a receipt for a contribution of $80, June 22, 1917, Yale. Boynton was the chair of the Edith Wharton War Charities Committee in Washington, D.C.

80. Wharton to Miss Clark, June 4, 1917, Yale.

81. Wharton to Captain Kipling of the American Ambulance, May 12, 1917, Yale.

82. Wharton to Mrs. Scott, June 14, 1917, Yale.

83. Mrs. Winthrop Chanler, *Autumn in the Valley* (Boston: Little, Brown and Company, 1936), 167.

84. *New York Herald*, June 15, 1917, p. 2.

85. July 19, 1917. Quoted in Roger Burlingame, *Of Making Many Books* (New York: Charles Scribner's Sons, 1946), 312-313.

86. Wharton to John J. Pershing, July 22, 1917, *Letters*, 394-395.

87. The *Herald* noted Mrs. Wharton and Mr. and Mrs. W. R. Tyler were among the guests. For a full description of the parade, see the *New York Herald*, July 5, 1917, p. 1.

88. Elisina Tyler to Mildred Bliss, July 21, 1917, Harvard University Archives.

89. Wharton to James Perkins of the ARC, July 27, 1917, Yale.

90. Wharton to James Perkins, July 24, 1917, Yale.

91. Ruth Gaines, *Helping France: The Red Cross in the Devastated Areas* (New York: E. P. Dutton & Company, 1919), 48-49.

92. *New York Herald*, July 6, 1917, p. 2.

93. *New York Times*, July 30, 1917, p. 8.

94. *New York Herald*, July 22, 1917, p. 2.

95. William A. Gamson, *The Strategy of Social Protest* (Homewood, IL: Dorsey Press, 1975), 28-29.

96. *New York Herald*, July 22, 1917, p. 2.

97. Wharton to Elisina Tyler, July 27, 1917, Indiana.

98. Wharton to Mary Cadwalader Jones, August 8, 1917, Yale.

99. Wharton to Dr. Williams in New York, August 1, 1917, Yale.

100. *New York Herald*, August 7, 1917, p. 2.

101. Wharton (per secretary) to Miriam Fisher, August 27, 1917, Yale. "Mrs. Wharton asks me to say that her name was put by mistake on the Women's War Relief Corps. She was asked to head one of the Committees, but was obliged to decline as she is not well enough to undertake any new war-work."

102. *New York Herald*, August 15, 1917, p. 3.

103. Wharton to Louis Cass Ledyard, August 20, 1917, Yale. Ledyard was a prominent New York attorney dealing in trusts and estates. He was a director of many charitable and civic boards, including the Morgan Library and the New York Public Library. He and Payne Whitney had donated a convalescent hospital in the name of Wharton's charities.

104. Wharton to Elisina Tyler, August 31, 1917, Indiana.

105. Wharton to Mrs. William Eustis of Rhinecliff, NY, August 26, 1917, Yale.

106. Wharton to Bernard Berenson, September 4, 1917, *Letters*, 398-399.

107. Wharton to Robert Grant, September 4, 1917, Harvard.

108. Wharton to Dr. White of the ARC on a request she made of Homer Folks, September 4, 1917, Yale.

109. Gaines, *Helping France*, v.

110. *New York Herald*, September 9, 1917, p. 2.

111. Ferrell, *Woodrow Wilson and World War I*, 104.

112. *New York Herald*, September 13, 1917, p. 2.

113. *Letters*, 401, n.1.

114. Edith Wharton, *A Backward Glance*, (New York: D. Appleton and Company, 1934), 358.

115. Wharton to Mrs. William Payne Thompson of Blight Cottage, Newport, RI, September 14, 1917, Yale.

116. Wharton to Dr. Homer Folks, memorandum of understanding, September 15, 1917, Yale.

117. Wharton to Elisina Tyler, September 15, 1917, Yale. Wharton wrote to Elisina in French and English interchangeably.

118. Wharton to Mr. L. C. Ledyard, a receipt for 40,000 francs for the convalescent homes, c. September 1917, Yale. She told him, "But I shall strain

every nerve to keep the Maisons de Convalescence independent as long as the refugees continue to pour in."

119. Wharton to Homer Folks, November 15, 1917, Yale.
120. Wharton to Lewis Cass Ledyard, November 16, 1917, Yale.
121. Wharton to S. Smitney, secretary pro tem of the Refugees Relief Fund, November 2, 1917, together with an acknowledgment for two checks of $500 each, Yale.
122. Wharton to Captain W. Reed of the General Staff, marked "confidential," September 15, 1917, Yale.
123. Wharton to Bernard Berenson, September 13, 1917, Villa I Tatti.
124. Wharton to Mary Cadwalader Jones, September 26, 1917, Letters, 399-400.
125. Wharton to Bernard Berenson, October 2, 1917, Letters, 401-403.
126. Wharton to Mrs. James Burden, October 15, 1917, Yale.
127. Wharton to Max Farrand, March 14, 1917, Yale.
128. Wharton to Thomas Newbold Rhinelander, October 6, 1917, Yale.
129. Wharton to Mary Cadwalader Jones, October 25, 1917, Yale.
130. Samuels, Bernard Berenson, 226.
131. Bernard Berenson, Sketch for a Self-Portrait (New York: Pantheon, 1949), 84-85.
132. Quoted in Samuels, Bernard Berenson, 227.
133. Colin Simpson, Artful Partners: Bernard Berenson and Joseph Duveen (New York: Macmillan, 1986), 152.
134. Wharton to Alice Garrett, November 2, 1917, Evergreen House.
135. Wharton to Mary Cadwalader Jones, November 14, 1917, Yale.
136. Wharton to Mary Cadwalader Jones, November 29, 1917, Yale.
137. Wharton to Miss Bertha Laws, secretary to Dr. White, Department of Civilian Relief, American Red Cross, December 3, 1917, Yale. For the history of this imbroglio, see also Wharton's letter of November 7, 1917.
138. Wharton to Mr. Robinson, December 7, 1917, Yale.
139. Wharton to Louis Cass Ledyard, December 7, 1917, Yale.
140. Wharton to Louis Cass Ledyard, December 28, 1917, Yale.
141. Wharton to Homer Folks, December 29, 1917, Yale.
142. Wharton to Mary Cadwalader Jones, December 6, 1917, Yale: "[It] seems unfair that the Red Cross should have given assistance to one group, and should completely ignore another which is doing exactly the same kind of work with much less money at its disposal."
143. Wharton to Louis Cass Ledyard, January 4, 1918, Yale.
144. Wharton to Walter Berry, December 1, 1917, Yale.

145. Wharton to Mary Cadwalader Jones, November 14, 1917, Yale.
146. Wharton to William Roscoe Thayer, November 12, 1917, Harvard.
147. Wharton to Alice Garrett, November 2, 1917, Evergreen House.
148. Wharton to Mr. Robinson, December 7, 1917, Yale.
149. Wharton to Alice Garrett, December 2, 1917, Evergreen House.
150. Wharton to Mary Cadwalader Jones, December 21, 1917, Yale.
151. Wharton to Mary Cadwalader Jones, November 14, 1917, Yale.
152. Wharton to Mary Cadwalader Jones, December 21, 1917, Yale.
153. Wharton to Brand Whitlock, November 26, 1917, Yale.
154. Quoted in *The Intimate Papers of Colonel House*. vol. 3 of *Into the War*, ed. Charles Seymour (Boston: Houghton Mifflin Company, 1928), 260.
155. Wharton to Mary Cadwalader Jones, December 21, 1917, Yale.
156. John Pershing to his Chief of Staff in Washington, memorandum (No. 312-S) of November 25, 1917, Harvard University Archives.
157. Wharton to Mary Cadwalader Jones, November 14, 1917, Yale.
158. Wharton to Alice Garrett, December 2, 1917, Evergreen House.
159. Wharton to Mr. Griggs, secrétaire de Monsieur de Piessac, Cabinet du Sous-Secrétaire d'Etat au Service de Santé, December 5, 1917, Yale.
160. Wharton to Alice Garrett, December 28, 1917, Evergreen House.

CHAPTER 5

1. Wharton to Mary Berenson, January 3, 1918, Villa I Tatti.
2. Wharton to Bernard Berenson, January 25, 1918, Villa I Tatti.
3. Wharton to Madame M. M. Sallandrouze de Lamornaix, January 3, 1918, Yale.
4. Wharton to Miss Alice R. Pattee, with a receipt for $50, January 11, 1918, Yale. She used this same excuse with Madame la Comtesse de Brigode, January 12, 1918, Yale.
5. Wharton (per secretary) to Madame la Comtesse de Cherisey, January 10, 1918, Yale.
6. Wharton to Lewis Cass Ledyard, January 4, 1918, Yale.
7. Ibid.
8. Ibid.
9. Wharton to Mrs. L. C. Herbert, January 16, 1918, Yale.
10. Wharton to Mrs. Corbin, January 18, 1918, Yale.
11. Wharton to Mrs. Corbin, February 11, 1918, Yale.

12. Wharton to Madame de Corbeiller, February 4, 1918, Yale.
13. Wharton to Mrs. McCook, February 9, 1918, Yale.
14. Wharton, "Talk to American Soldiers," typescript with handwritten corrections (pp. 4-7 missing), p. 1, Yale.
15. Wharton to Alice Garrett, March 23, 1918, Evergreen House.
16. Wharton to John and Alice Garrett, March 11, 1918, Evergreen House.
17. Wharton to Walter Berry, undated, commenting on a letter of February 7, 1918, from Elisina Tyler, Yale.
18. She ordered blue-and-white linoleum for the apartment bathroom (Wharton [per secretary] to Bon Marché, February 11, 1918, Yale); saw to the repair of a clock, and redirected a number of appeals to more suitable charities; she declined an invitation to give a public reading at the Hostess Home (Wharton to Miss Edith A. Granger, February 12, 1918, Yale); and returned the photographs made for her *sauf-conduit* pass with pointed criticisms (Wharton to Messieurs Boissons & Taponier, February 13, 1918, Yale).
19. Wharton to Bernard Berenson, February 12, 1918, Villa I Tatti.
20. Wharton to Bernard Berenson, February 26, 1918, Villa I Tatti.
21. Ibid.
22. Robert H. Ferrell, *Woodrow Wilson and World War I, 1917-1921* (New York: Harper & Row, 1985), 125.
23. Wharton (per secretary) to the secretary of the War Relief Board, November 19, 1917, Yale.

    Some of Wharton's prickliness over correct forms of address may have been simple snobbery. Berenson's secretary/companion Nicky Mariano described a scene where Wharton refused a verbal invitation to join Marie-Laure de Noailles for lunch: "Edith declared that an invitation sent by word of mouth was an insult to her and that it should have been a written one. This was clearly Gaillard Lapsley's doing. He had anyhow little use for the Noailles and, being a rigid upholder of protocolled behaviour, had persuaded Edith to refuse the invitation. It was an easy thing to do as she had a sort of complex about not being treated as an equal by French titled society."
    Nicky Mariano, *Forty Years with Berenson* (New York: Alfred A. Knopf, 1966), 177.
24. Wharton to A. H. Thorndike, Secretary of the National Institute of Arts and Letters, December 18, 1917, Yale.
25. See Shari Benstock, *No Gifts from Chance: A Biography of Edith Wharton* (New York: Charles Scribner's Sons, 1994), 279; and R.W.B. Lewis, *Edith Wharton: A Biography* (New York: Harper & Row, 1975), 362.

26. Wharton (per secretary) to Naval Ensign Pickman, May 18, 1918, Yale.
27. Wharton to Mr. Norman Kimball, April 19, 1918, Yale.
28. Wharton (per secretary) to Mrs. Stern, the director of *Oeuvre de l'Enfants en la Famille*, November 3, 1919, Yale. Wharton enclosed her annual subscription of 250 francs to this charity.
29. Stephen Longstreet, *We All Went to Paris: Americans in the City of Light* (New York: Macmillan, 1972).
30. *The Collected Short Stories of Edith Wharton*, vol. 2, ed. R.W.B. Lewis (New York: Charles Scribner's Sons, 1968), 362. The satire was not collected by Wharton in any of her volumes of short stories during her lifetime.
31. Wharton to Gaillard Lapsley, September 21 [1921], Yale.
32. Wharton to John and Alice Garrett, March 11, 1918, Evergreen House.
33. Wharton to Alice Garrett, March 23, 1918, Evergreen House.
34. Wharton to John and Alice Garrett, March 11, 1918, Evergreen House.
35. See the folder marked "Fairchild, Blair and Edith" at Yale, which has typed letters in English and French from as early as March 3, 1918, from Madame Blair Fairchild. In letters of May 13 and 18, 1918, she signed Wharton's business letters "Pr. Mrs. Wharton; Secretaire."
36. Wharton to Madame Chicoteau of Vevey, March 15, 1918, Yale.
37. Wharton (per secretary) to Miss M. McCandless, March 15, 1918, Yale. The Lighthouse was the first charity for which Dorothy Canfield Fisher worked when she arrived in Paris with her young family. She established a Braille press for blinded soldiers.
38. Wharton to the Women's War Relief Corps, March 17, 1918, Yale.
39. Arline Boucher Tehan, *Henry Adams in Love* (New York: Universe Books, 1983), 264.
40. Wharton to Alice Garrett, March 23, 1918, Evergreen House.
41. Wharton to Monsieur Paul Guichard, Directeur de la Sureté Municipale, Préfecture de Police, Paris, March 15, 1918, Yale.
42. Wharton to Alice Garrett, March 23, 1918, Evergreen House.
43. Wharton to Monsieur de Piessac, *Service de Santé, Ministère de la Guerre*, March 1918, Yale.
44. Wharton to Lieutenant Pierre Marcel, March 19, 1918, Yale.
45. Wharton to Marian Bell, April 25, 1918, Yale.
46. Wharton, "Talk to American Soldiers," typescript with handwritten corrections (pp. 4-7 missing), p. 1, Yale.
47. Wharton to Commandant de Chaumont Quitry, May 10, 1918, Yale.
48. Wharton to Bernard Berenson, May 12, 1918, Villa I Tatti.
49. Wharton's secretary to Madame la Comtesse Pastré, May 13, 1918, Yale.

50. Wharton to Charles du Bos, May 13, 1918, Yale.
51. Wharton to Robert Woods Bliss at the American Consulate, May 14, 1918, Yale.
52. Wharton (per secretary) to Private V. P. King, May 15, 1918, Yale.
53. Wharton (per secretary) to Madame Lamperti of the Hôtel Savoy , May 25, 1918, Yale.
54. Wharton's secretary to Miss Lynn Weill of Bakersfield, California, May 26, 1918, Yale. Miss Weill was a trained Montessori teacher who had worked successfully with subnormal and nervous children.
55. Wharton to Gaillard Lapsley, May 27, 1918, Yale. On May 10 she acknowledged a note from the Ministry of War that the film of Arromanches had been completed and that Minnie had taken it to the United States.
56. Wharton to Bernard Berenson, June 6, 1918, Villa I Tatti.
57. Wharton to Gaillard Lapsley, May 27, 1918, Yale.
58. Quoted in Tehan, Henry Adams in Love, 268. For a full account of this period of strain between Wharton and Lizzie Cameron, see ibid., 267-270.
59. Quoted in ibid., 268.
60. Wharton to Elizabeth Cameron, June 15, 1918, Library of Congress.
61. Wharton to Elizabeth Hoyt, June 12, 1918, Yale.
62. Quoted in Tehan, Henry Adams in Love, 268.
63. Tehan, Henry Adams in Love, 270.
64. Wharton to "Dear Winifred," May 24, 1918, Yale.
65. Wharton to Captaine Brimond, June 14, 1918, Yale.
66. Wharton (per secretary) to the Boston Committee, June 20, 1918, Yale.
67. Percy Mitchell of the New York Herald to Wharton, June 14, 1918, Yale.
68. Wharton to Bernard Berenson, June 20, 1918, Villa I Tatti.
69. Ibid.
70. Wharton to Bernard Berenson, June 21, 1918, Villa I Tatti.
71. Wharton to Mary Berenson, June 21, 1918, Villa I Tatti.
72. Wharton to Alice Garrett, June 22, 1918, Evergreen House.
    On June 22, 1918, she also wrote to Frederick King, LeRoy's brother: "Every one in Paris is feeling very cheerful and confident, especially since the complete failure on Rheims and the Austrian attack on Italy. We all know there will be difficult days for the next few weeks, but very soon the Americans will be here in such numbers that they will make their weight felt in a way that the Germans will not like." Yale.
73. Wharton to Bernard Berenson, June 26, 1918, Villa I Tatti.
74. Ibid.

75. Wharton to Bernard Berenson, July 1, 1914, Villa I Tatti.
76. Wharton to Bernard Berenson, June 28, 1918, Yale.
77. Wharton to Bernard Berenson, June 29, 1918, Yale.
78. Wharton to Bernard Berenson, July 1, 1918, Villa I Tatti.
79. "Mrs.Wharton's Fund for 'Les Enfants en Danger,'" *New York Herald*, July 3, 1918, p. 2.
80. A description of the parade and events celebrating this Fourth of July and Wharton's own account of them are presented in the introduction to this book.
81. Wharton to Mary Cadwalader Jones, July 7, 1918, Yale.
82. Wharton to Bernard Berenson, July 12, 1918, Villa I Tatti.
83. Wharton to White, July 9, 1918, Yale.
84. Wharton to Bernard Berenson, July 28, 1918, Villa I Tatti.
85. Wharton to Bernard Berenson, July 5, 1918, Villa I Tatti.
86. Wharton to Mary Berenson, July 6, 1918, Villa I Tatti.
87. Wharton to Bernard Berenson, July 13, 1918, Villa I Tatti.
88. Wharton to Bernard Berenson, July 20, 1918, Villa I Tatti.
89. Ibid.
90. Edith Wharton, *A Backward Glance*, (New York: D. Appleton and Company, 1934), 359.
91. Wharton to Bernard Berenson, July 28, 1918, Villa I Tatti.
92. Wharton to Bernard Berenson, July 29, 1918, marked "*Back in Paris July 29th*," Villa I Tatti.
93. Wharton to Gaillard Lapsley, July 15, 1918, Yale; the rue de Varenne address is crossed through and a handwritten address added: Château de Fleury en Bière.
94. Wharton to the director of the Hôtel des Bains at St. Nectaire, July 27, 1918, Yale.
95. Benstock, *No Gifts from Chance*, 239.
96. Wharton to Bernard Berenson, August 1, 1918, Villa I Tatti.
97. Minutes of the Executive Committee in charge of the mass meeting of Allied Women on War Service, August 3 and August 7, 1918, Bliss Archives, Harvard University Archives.
98. Wharton to Bernard Berenson, August 15, 1918, Villa I Tatti.
99. Ibid.
100. R.W.B. Lewis, *Edith Wharton: A Biography* (New York: Harper & Row, 1975), 411.
101. Wharton to Bernard Berenson, August 15, 1918, Villa I Tatti.
102. Wharton to Bernard Berenson, August 24, 1918, Villa I Tatti.

103. Wharton to Bernard Berenson, August 25, 1918, Villa I Tatti.
104. Wharton to Monsieur Huiet, September 7, 1918, Yale.
105. Wharton (per secretary) to numerous requests for help with individual cases, September 9, 1918, Yale. In the Yale papers there are perhaps a hundred letters saying Mrs. Wharton will forward their request to an appropriate charity.
106. Wharton (per secretary) to Mrs. Isch Wall, September 27, 1918, Yale.
107. Wharton to Bernard Berenson, September 11, 1918, Villa I Tatti.
108. Wharton to Alice Garrett, September 11, 1918, Evergreen House.
109. Wharton to Mrs. Scott, September 16, 1918, Yale.
110. Wharton to Alice Garrett, September 28, 1918, Evergreen House.
111. Wharton to Robert Grant, October 2, 1918, Harvard.
112. Wharton to H. D. Gibson, Commissioner for France of the American Red Cross, October 9, 1918, Yale.
113. Wharton to Mrs. Gordon Bell, October 14, 1918, Yale.
114. Wharton to Mrs. Scott, October 16, 1918, Yale.
115. Wharton to Bernard Berenson, Tuesday (acknowledging his letter of October 4, 1918), Villa I Tatti.
116. Wharton to Private Victor Solberg, October 19, 1918, Yale *Letters*, 411.
117. Wharton to Miss Emily Hoppin, October 22, 1918, Yale.
118. Wharton to Bernard Berenson, October 31, 1918, Villa I Tatti.
119. "Where 'Yanks' May Go Visiting in Paris," *New York Herald*, November 1, 1918, p. 2.
120. *New York Herald*, November 3, 1918, p. 1.
121. Wharton to Lewis Cass Ledyard, carried by hand by Alfred White, November 8, 1918, Yale.
122. *New York Herald*, November 10, 1918, p. 2.
123. Wharton to Madame la Vicomtesse d'Osmoy addressed as "Dear Susie," November 14, 1918, Yale.
124. Wharton, *A Backward Glance*, 360.
125. *New York Herald*, November 11, 1918, p. 2.
126. *New York Herald*, November 16, 1918, p. 2.
127. *New York Herald*, November 30, 1918, p. 4.
128. *New York Herald*, December 2, 1918, p. 1.
129. *New York Herald*, December 4, 1918, p. 2.
130. *New York Herald*, December 19, 1918, p. 4.
131. *New York Herald*, December 21, 1918, p. 2.
132. Wharton to the director of the Hôtel du Parc, Hyères, December 12, 1918, Yale.

133. Wharton to the director of the Hôtel de la Poste, Beaune, December 17, 1918, Yale. She sent follow-up letters to hotels in Beaune and Avignon on December 21, 1918.

134. Wharton to Mr. Carrigan (a friend of Walter Berry's in Lyon), December 21, 1918, Yale.

135. Wharton to Monsieur Gérant, December 27, 1918, my translation from the French, Yale.

136. Wharton to Mr. Barbour, December 23, 1918, Yale.

137. Wharton to Mary Berenson, December 26, 1918, Villa I Tatti.

CONCLUSION

1. Wharton to Bernard Berenson, January 27, 1919, Yale, also in *The Letters of Edith Wharton*, eds. R.W.B. Lewis and Nancy Lewis. New York: Charles Scribner's Sons, 1988, 421.

2. Wharton to Alice Garrett, March 27 [1919], Evergreen House.

3. Quoted in the introduction by R.W.B. Lewis and Nancy Lewis, "Part Six: The Costs of Energy, 1919-1927." *The Letters of Edith Wharton*, eds. R.W.B. Lewis and Nancy Lewis. New York: Charles Scribner's Sons, 1988, 417.

4. "Plea for Hospital Aid: Money Needed to Keep Up Tuberculosis Work in France," *New York Times*, March 23, 1919, sec. 2, p. 1.

5. Wharton to Elizabeth Cameron, June 27, 1919, Library of Congress.

6. Wharton to Miss Kate Brousseau of Mills College in California, thanking her for sending 100 francs from Mills College, August 7, 1919, Yale. In the letter she writes, "all the children of Flanders went back to Belgium last month."

7. Edith Wharton, *French Ways and Their Meaning*, (New York: D. Appleton and Company, 1919), 16-17.

8. Ibid., 100-101.

9. Wharton to Miss Kate Brousseau, August 7, 1919, Yale.

10. Wharton to Miss Clark acknowledging a check for $250, October 17, 1919, Yale.

11. See the correspondence in a file marked "1920 Personal" at Yale.

12. Wharton (my translation) to Mère Colette, Institut St. Michel, Poperinghe, September 20, 1920, Yale.

13. Wharton to Mrs. Huntington, the treasurer of the Patriotic Society of American Women of Buenos Aires, acknowledging their check of 4,000 francs, August 27, 1920, Yale.

14. Shari Benstock, *No Gifts from Chance: A Biography of Edith Wharton* (New York: Charles Scribner's Sons, 1994), 343, 374.
15. Wharton to Monsieur Faitout, October 9, 1919, Yale.
16. A receipt for garage rent of 33.50 francs a month paid to Monsieur le Comte J. de Segonzac, October 17, 1919, Yale.
17. Wharton's secretary ("pr. Mrs. Wharton Secretaire") to Mlle Cahen, October 21, 1919, Yale.

    A letter from Wharton to Monsieur de Poessac of November 28, 1919, must have been occasioned by the almost monthly reminders from the persistent Mme Cahen that she had not received her promised medals. The *Ministère de la Guerre* replied on December 1, 1919, telling Wharton that the medals would not be distributed to individuals until several months after the general announcement. Being caught between demanding individual charity workers and the inevitable bureaucratic delays after the war was annoying and draining for Wharton. A letter to Madame Antoinette Cahen of 8 rue d'Anjou, of March 19, 1920, shows that Wharton was still trying to straighten out the matter of the medals for her workers.
18. Wharton to Monsieur J. Reinach, December 23, 1919, Yale.
19. Wharton to Winifred Power Schroeder, October 27, 1919, Yale.

    On the same day Wharton wrote to Dr. F. Konechowsky, (in translation), ". . . because I know that Madame Tyler is like me, and that the tranquillity of the country is necessary when she is tired," Yale.
20. Wharton (per secretary) to the American Library Association in Paris, October 30, 1919, Yale.
21. Wharton to Mrs. Stern, the director of the *Oeuvre de l'Enfants en la Famille*; Wharton sent her annual subscription of 250 francs, November 3, 1919, Yale.
22. Wharton sent a check for $35 to Mrs. Rider (in charge of work for the blind) of the American Library Association "to enable you to reproduce one of my short stories for our blind soldiers. I have the pleasure of enclosing herewith $35 for the purpose, and beg to leave the choice of the story to you," November 6, 1919, Yale.

    A letter of April 20, 1920, from the American Library Association's disbursing officer, says that they have set her story "The Debt" in Braille and are returning a balance of $2.60.
23. Wharton to Madame Salambier, secretary to Mrs. Wallace at the Embassy of the United States in Paris, December 24, 1919, Yale.

24. Wharton to Miss Lee, November 12, 1919, Yale.
25. Wharton to Mrs. Nichols, November 12, 1919, Yale.
26. Wharton received three checks ("165 frs. for your charities, 2,510 frs. for Children of Flanders, and 1,763 frs. for American Hostels") on December 24, 1919, Yale.
27. Wharton's secretary to Oscar Lichtenberg of Princeton, New Jersey, November 28, 1919, Yale.

    Mr. Lichtenberg had sent her $15 a month since the beginning of the war.
28. Wharton to the Lincoln Trust Company of 7 Wall Street in New York, January 9, 1920, Yale. She closed her account with Hanover National Bank and moved her holdings to Lincoln.
29. A letter from the law firm of Middlebrook and Borland in New York of April 7, 1920, regarding a deed of trust, Yale. This involved the formal and legal resignations of Berry and Mr. Edgar as trustees of her trust property.

    A letter to Wharton from Edward J. Hancy of the law firm of Cadwalader, Wickersham & Taft of November 5, 1920, Yale, states:

    "You will recall that during the past several years the United States Trust Company, holding a mortgage for $150,000 covering No. 14 West 23rd. Street, has required the payment of the entire rent to be applied on its mortgage and, therefore, neither Mrs. Jones nor her daughter Mrs. Farrand received any income from that property. During the same period the rent of 737 Broadway has been at a very reduced amount so that after paying the interest on the mortgage covering that property and the taxes and the repairs the Trustees were, at times, unable to meet all the charges. During that period you advanced $780 to the trust in order to meet the deficits in the trust income."

    Now, he says, the trust is in better shape since rents have increased. He asks her if she would like that money returned. "I am glad to say to you that there has been a very desirable increase in the rental of 737 Broadway, as you will no doubt be advised by letter through the Lincoln Trust Company."
30. Wharton to Chère Mademoiselle, February 2, 1920, Yale. The letter in translation specifies: "I have sent today chapter XXVIII, and at the same time I have received from you chapters XVI and XXVII, which have been retyped. Remark throughout in chapter XXVII, the numerous wrong

letters which I have corrected in red pencil. It is necessary that literary copies be 'letter perfect', because a small error may change the sense of a word or a phrase. — Here now is what I would like to do. Send me TWO COPIES of XXVI and XXVII corrected, but also send me as quickly as possible the XVIIIth. After this send me two copies because we are in a hurry, and if the changes are not too numerous, I will do them here with a pen."

31. Jean Duprat to Chère Madame, February 20, 1920, Yale.
32. Wharton in a letter with no salutation from St. Brice, June 30, 1920, Yale.
33. Wharton to Mrs. Herbert, May 20, 1920, Yale.
34. Wharton to Mrs. Benet in answer to a request that she write an appeal for a charity on whose board she had agreed to serve, May 28, 1920, Yale.
35. Wharton acknowledging a contribution of 52,223.80 francs from the Rhode Island Committee of Edith Wharton's War Charities, August 7, 1920, Yale.
36. Stanley Cooperman, *World War I and the American Novel* (Baltimore: Johns Hopkins University Press, 1967), 19-20.
37. Ibid., 41.
38. Ibid., 97.
39. Cynthia Griffin Wolff, *A Feast of Words: The Triumph of Edith Wharton* (New York: Oxford University Press, 1977), 407. In her appendix, "The Dating of the 'Beatrice Palmato' Fragment," Wolff has persuasively argued that "the fragment was written in 1918 or 1919."
40. Judith Sensibar in an insightful essay on *A Son at the Front* has explored the homoeroticism in the novel. See her "'Behind the Lines' in Edith Wharton's *A Son at the Front*: Re-Writing a Masculinist Tradition" in *Wretched Exotic: Essays on Edith Wharton in Europe*, eds. Katherine Joslin and Alan Price (New York: Peter Lang, 1993), 241-256.
41. Paul Fussell in his chapter "Soldier Boys" in *The Great War and Modern Memory* (New York: Oxford University Press, 1975), 270-309.
42. Edith Wharton, *The Marne* (New York: D. Appleton and Company, 1918), 22-23.
43. Ibid., 23.
44. Ibid., 33-34.
45. Ibid., 58-60.
46. Edith Wharton, *A Son at the Front* (New York: Charles Scribner's Sons, 1923), 128-129.
47. Ibid., 171.
48. Ibid., 171.

49. Ibid., 187-188.
50. Ibid., 229-230.
51. Ibid., 255.
52. Ibid., 258.
53. Ibid., 314.
54. Ibid., 325.
55. Ibid., 333.
56. Ibid., 366.
57. Edith Wharton, *The Mother's Recompense* (New York: D. Appleton and Company, 1925), 12.
58. Wharton to Beatrix Farrand, October 21, 1930, Yale.
59. Wharton to Max Farrand, October 19, 1930, Yale.

BIBLIOGRAPHY

PUBLISHED WORKS

Adam, Pearl H. *Paris Sees It Through: A Diary 1914-1919*. London: Hodder and Stoughton, 1919.

Albright, Alan. "American Volunteerism in France" and "The Legion of American Friends and Allies in the Great War," in *Les Américains et la Légion d'Honneur: 1853-1947*, ed Véronique Wiesinger; 124-127, 134-137, Chateau de Blérancourt: Musée national de la Coopération franco-américaine, 1993.

Aldrich, Mildred. *A Hilltop on the Marne*. London: Constable and Company, 1916.

Ammons, Elizabeth. *Edith Wharton's Argument with America*. Athens: University of Georgia Press, 1980.

Asselineau, Roger. "Edith Wharton—She Thought in French and Wrote in English," in *Wretched Exotic: Essays on Edith Wharton in Europe*, eds. Katherine Joslin and Alan Price, 355-363, New York: Peter Lang, 1993.

Auchincloss, Louis. *Edith Wharton: A Woman in Her Time*. New York: Viking, 1971.

Barnard, Charles Inman. *Paris War Days*. Boston: Little, Brown and Company, 1914.

Bellringer, Alan W. "Edith Wharton's Use of France." *Yearbook of English Studies* 15 (1985): 109-124.

Benstock, Shari. *No Gifts from Chance: A Biography of Edith Wharton*. New York: Charles Scribner's Sons, 1994.

———. *Women of the Left Bank: Paris 1900-1940*. Austin: University of Texas Press, 1986.

Berenson, Bernard. *Sketch for a Self-Portrait*. New York: Pantheon, 1949.

Bremner, Robert H. *American Philanthropy*, 2nd ed. Chicago: University of Chicago Press, 1988.

Buitenhuis, Peter. "Edith Wharton and the First World War." *American Quarterly* Fall (1966): 493-505.

————. *The Great War of Words: British, American, and Canadian Propaganda and Fiction, 1914-1933*. Vancouver: University of British Columbia Press, 1987.

Burlingame, Roger. *Of Making Many Books: A Hundred Years of Reading, Writing and Publishing*. New York: Charles Scribner's Sons, 1946.

Canfield (Fisher), Dorothy. *The Deepening Stream*. New York: Harcourt, Brace and Company, 1930.

————. *Home Fires in France*. New York: Henry Holt and Company, 1918.

Carter, Susanne. *War and Peace through Women's Eyes: A Selective Bibliography of Twentieth-Century American Women's Fiction*. New York: Greenwood Press, 1992.

Chanler, Mrs. Winthrop. *Autumn in the Valley*. Boston: Little, Brown and Company, 1936.

Chapman, John Jay. *World War I*. Vol. 8 of *The Collected Works of John Jay Chapman*. Reprint. Weston, MA: M and S Press, 1970.

Clarke, Ida Clyde. *American Women and the World War*. New York: D. Appleton and Company, 1918.

Clough, David. "Edith Wharton's War Novels: A Reappraisal." *Twentieth Century Literature* 19 (January 1973): 1-14.

Cohn, Jan. *Improbable Fiction: The Life of Mary Roberts Rinehart*. Pittsburgh: University of Pittsburgh Press, 1980.

Coolidge, John Gardner. *A War Diary in Paris, 1914-1917*. Cambridge, MA: Riverside Press, 1931 (privately printed).

Cooper, Helen M., et al., eds. *Arms and the Woman: War, Gender, and Literary Representation*. Chapel Hill: University of North Carolina Press, 1989.

Cooperman, Stanley. *World War I and the American Novel*. Baltimore: Johns Hopkins University Press, 1987.

Curti, Merle. *American Philanthropy Abroad: A History*. New Brunswick, NJ: Rutgers University Press, 1963.

David, Daniel. *The 1914 Campaign, August-October, 1914*. Bryn Mawr, PA: Combined Books, 1987.

Davis, Richard Harding. *With the Allies*. In the series *The War on All Fronts*. New York: Charles Scribner's Sons, 1919.

Davison, Henry P. *The American Red Cross in the Great War*. New York: Macmillan Company, 1919.

Dryden, Elizabeth. *Paris in Herrick Days*. Paris: Dorbon-Aine, 1915.

Dulles, Foster Rhea. *The American Red Cross: A History*. New York: Harper & Row, 1950.

Dwight, Eleanor. *Edith Wharton: An Extraordinary Life*. New York: Harry N. Abrams, 1994.

Edel, Leon. "Walter Berry and the Novelists." *Nineteenth-Century Fiction* 38 (March 1984): 514-528.

Elshtain, Jean Bethke. *Women and War*. New York: Basic Books, 1987.

Everett, Susan. *The Great War*. Greenwich, CT: Dorset Press, 1980.

Fenton. Charles A. "Ambulance Drivers in France and Italy: 1914-1918." *American Quarterly* 3 (1951): 326-343.

———. "A Literary Fracture of World War I." *American Quarterly* 12 (1960): 119-132.

Ferrell, Robert H. *Woodrow Wilson and World War I, 1917-1921*. New York: Harper & Row, 1985.

Ferro, Marc. *The Great War 1914-1918*. New York: Military Heritage Press, 1989; earlier editions Gallimard, 1969, Routledge and Kegan Paul, 1973.

Fields, Anne Marsh. "Writing a War Story: Edith Wharton and World War I." Ph.D. diss., University of North Carolina at Chapel Hill, 1992.

Flanner, Janet. "Dearest Edith." *The New Yorker*, March 2, 1929: 27-28.

Fosdick, Raymond B. *The Story of the Rockefeller Foundation*. New York: Harper & Row, 1952.

Fowles, Edward. *Memories of Duveen Brothers*. London: Times Books, 1976.

Fussell, Paul. *The Great War and Modern Memory*. New York: Oxford University Press, 1975.

Gaeddert, Gustave R. *The Boardman Influence, 1905-1917*. Vol. 3 of *The History of the American National Red Cross*. Washington, D.C.: The American National Red Cross, 1950.

Gaines, Ruth. *Helping France: The Red Cross in the Devastated Areas*. New York: E. P. Dutton, 1919.

Gamson, William A. *The Strategy of Social Protest*. Homewood, IL: Dorsey Press, 1975.

Garey, E. B., et al. *American Guide Book to France and Its Battlefields*. New York: Macmillan Company, 1920.

Garland, Hamlin. *Afternoon Neighbors: Further Excerpts from a Literary Log*. New York: Macmillan Company, 1934.

Gide, André. *The Journals of André Gide*, vol. 2, 1914-1927. Translated and annotated by Justin O'Brien. New York: Alfred A. Knopf, 1951.

Gilbert, Sandra M., and Susan Gubar. *Sexchanges*. Vol. 2 of *No Man's Land: The Place of the Woman Writer in the Twentieth Century*. New Haven, CT: Yale University Press, 1989.

Ginsberg, Lori D. *Women and the Work of Benevolence: Morality, Politics, and Class in the Nineteenth-Century United States*. New Haven, CT: Yale University Press, 1990.

Gordon, John Steele. "What We Lost in the Great War." *American Heritage* (July/August 1992): 80-91.

Halsey, Francis Whiting. *The Literary Digest History of the World War*. 2 vols. New York: Funk and Wagnalls Company, 1920.

Higonnet, Margaret Randolph, et al. *Behind the Lines: Gender and the Two World Wars*. New Haven, CT: Yale University Press, 1987.

James, Henry. *Henry James and Edith Wharton, Letters: 1900-1915*, ed. Lyall H. Powers. New York: Charles Scribner's Sons, 1990.

Joslin, Katherine, and Alan Price, eds. *Wretched Exotic: Essays on Edith Wharton in Europe*. New York: Peter Lang, 1993.

Kennedy, David M. *Over Here: The First World War and American Society*. New York: Oxford University Press, 1980.

Lamont, Thomas W. *Henry Davison: The Record of a Useful Life*. New York: Arno Press, 1975; originally published by Harper & Row in 1933.

Lauer, Kristin O., and Margaret P. Murray. *Edith Wharton: An Annotated Secondary Bibliography*. New York: Garland, 1990.

Leach, Nancy R. "Edith Wharton's Unpublished Novel." *American Literature 25* (November 1953): 334-353.

Lewis, R.W.B. *Edith Wharton: A Biography*. New York: Harper & Row, 1975.

Lewis, R.W.B. and Nancy Lewis, eds. *The Letters of Edith Wharton*. New York: Charles Scribner's Sons, 1988.

Lockwood, Preston. "Henry James's First Interview: Noted Critic and Novelist Breaks His Rule of Years to Tell of the Good Work of the American Ambulance Corps." *New York Times Magazine*, March 21, 1915, pp. 3-4.

Longstreet, Stephen. *We All Went to Paris: Americans in the City of Light*. New York: Macmillan, 1972.

Lubbock, Percy. *Portrait of Edith Wharton*. New York: D. Appleton and Company, 1947.

MacDonald, Charles B. "World War I: The First Three Years," "World War I: The U.S. Army Overseas" in *American Military History*, 358-380, 381-404, Army Historical Series, General Editor Maurice Matloff. Washington, D.C.: United States Army, 1969.

Marbury, Elizabeth. *My Crystal Ball: Reminiscences*. New York: Boni and Liveright, 1923.

Mariano, Nicky. *Forty Years with Berenson*. New York: Alfred A. Knopf, 1966.

Marshall, S. L. A. *The American Heritage History of World War I*. New York: American Heritage Publishing Company, 1964.

Maxwell, William Quentin. *Lincoln's Fifth Wheel: The Political History of the United States Sanitary Commission*. New York: Longmans, Green and Company, 1956.

Mellow, James R. *The Charmed Circle: Gertrude Stein and Company*. New York: Avon Books, 1974.

Méral, Jean. *Paris in American Literature*. Translated by Laurette Long. Chapel Hill: University of North Carolina Press, 1989.

Mitchell, Percy. *The American Relief Clearing House: Its Work in the Great War*. Paris: Herbert Clarke, n.d.

Morse, Edwin W. *The Vanguard of American Volunteers: In the Fighting Lines and in the Humanitarian Services, August 1914-April 1917*. New York: Charles Scribner's Sons, 1922; originally published 1918.

Nevius, Blake. *Edith Wharton: A Study of Her Fiction*. Berkeley: University of California Press, 1953.

New York Committee of the Edith Wharton Charities, *Report of Edith Wharton's War Charities in France* (1916).

Plante, Patricia R. "Edith Wharton and the Invading Goths." *Midcontinent American Studies Journal* 5 (Fall 1964): 18-23.

Price, Alan. "The Composition of Wharton's *The Age of Innocence*." *Yale University Library Gazette* 55 (July 1980): 22-30.

———. "Edith Wharton at War with the American Red Cross." *Women's Studies: An Interdisciplinary Journal* vol. 20, no. 2 (Spring 1991): 120-131.

———. "Edith Wharton's War Story." *Tulsa Studies in Women's Literature* vol. 8, no. 1 (Spring 1989): 95-100.

———. "The Making of Edith Wharton's *The Book of the Homeless*." *Princeton University Library Chronicle* 47 (Autumn 1985): 5-21.

Pryor, Elizabeth Brown. *Clara Barton: Professional Angel*. Philadelphia: University of Pennsylvania Press, 1987.

Rinehardt, Mary Roberts. *The Amazing Interlude*. Garden City, NY: Doubleday, Doran and Company, 1929; first published by George Doran Company, 1918.

Sait, James E. "Charles Scribner's Sons and the Great War." *Princeton University Library Chronicle*. 48 (Winter 1987).

Samuels, Ernest. *Bernard Berenson: The Making of a Legend*. Cambridge, MA: The Belknap Press of Harvard University Press, 1987.

Sarolea, Charles. *The Anglo-German Problem* (American edition). New York: G. P. Putnam, 1915.

Scharff, Virginia. *Taking the Wheel: Women and the Coming of the Motor Age.* New York: Free Press, 1991.

Schlesinger, Arthur M. *Political and Social Growth of the American People 1865-1940.* New York: Macmillan Company, 1941.

Schneider, Dorothy, and Carl J. *Into the Breach: American Women Overseas in World War I.* New York: Viking, 1991.

Sensibar, Judith L. "'Behind the Lines' in Edith Wharton's *A Son at the Front:* Re-Writing a Masculinist Tradition" In *Wretched Exotic: Essays on Edith Wharton in Europe.* eds. Katherine Joslin and Alan Price, 241-256, New York: Peter Lang, 1993.

Seymour, Charles, ed. *Into the War.* vol. 3 of *The Intimate Papers of Colonel House.* Boston: Houghton Mifflin Company, 1928.

Simpson, Colin. *Artful Partners: Bernard Berenson and Joseph Duveen.* New York: Macmillan, 1986.

Smith, Jane S. *Elsie De Wolfe: A Life in High Style.* New York: Atheneum, 1982.

Steinson, Barbara J. *American Women's Activism in World War I.* New York: Garland, 1982.

Sutherland, John. *Mrs. Humphry Ward.* Oxford: Oxford University Press, 1990.

Tehan, Arline Boucher. *Henry Adams in Love: The Pursuit of Elizabeth Sherman Cameron.* New York: Universe Books, 1983.

Tuchman, Barbara W. *The Guns of August.* New York: Macmillan, 1962; Bantam, 1976.

Tylee, Claire M. *The Great War and Women's Consciousness: Images of Militarism and Womanhood in Women's Writings, 1914-1964.* Iowa City: University of Iowa Press, 1990.

Updike, Daniel Berkeley. "Notes on the Press and Its Work." In *Updike: American Printer and His Merrymount Press.* New York: American Institute of Graphic Arts, 1947.

Walsh, Jeffrey. *American War Literature: 1914 to Vietnam.* New York: St. Martin's Press, 1982.

Weintraub, Stanley. *A Stillness Heard Round the World: The End of the Great War, November 1918.* New York: Oxford University Press, 1985.

Wharton, Edith. *A Backward Glance.* New York: D. Appleton and Company, 1934.

———. *The Collected Short Stories of Edith Wharton,* 2 vols,. ed. R.W.B. Lewis. New York: Charles Scribner's Sons, 1968.

———. *Fighting France: From Dunkerque to Belfort.* New York: Charles Scribner's Sons, 1915.

————. *French Ways and Their Meaning*. New York: D. Appleton and Company, 1919.

————. *The Marne*. New York: D. Appleton and Company, 1918.

————. *The Mother's Recompense*. New York: D. Appleton and Company, 1925.

————. *A Son at the Front*. New York: Charles Scribner's Sons, 1923.

————. *Summer*. New York: D. Appleton and Company, 1917.

————. *Xingu and Other Stories*. New York: Charles Scribner's Sons, 1916.

Wharton. Edith, ed., *The Book of the Homeless (Le Livre des Sans-Foyer)*. New York: Charles Scribner's Sons, 1916.

Winter, J. M. *The Experience of World War I*. New York: Oxford University Press, 1989.

Wiser, William. *The Great Good Place: American Expatriate Women in Paris*. New York: W. W. Norton Company, 1991.

Wolff, Cynthia Griffin. *A Feast of Words: The Triumph of Edith Wharton*. New York: Oxford University Press, 1977.

MANUSCRIPTS, CORRESPONDENCE, AND ARCHIVES

The Edith Wharton Papers, Collection of American Literature, The Beinecke Rare Book and Manuscript Library, Yale University, New Haven, Connecticut. *Contains published and unpublished letters to Mary Cadwalader Jones, sister-in-law and close friend of Wharton, published letters and unpublished letters to Gaillard Lapsley, published and unpublished letters to Sara Norton, and The American Fund for French Wounded Weekly Bulletin, 1917-1919, in the Gertrude Stein Papers.*

The John Work Garrett Library, Evergreen House, John Hopkins University, Baltimore, Maryland. *Contains unpublished letters from Wharton to John Work Garrett, career diplomat, and his wife Alice Garrett. Also letters to John Garett's mother and to D'Arcy Paul. There is one undated and unsigned letter from Egerton Winthop to Edith Wharton on how to read and take notes on a difficult scientific book.*

The Hoover Institution for War, Revolution and Peace, Stanford University, Stanford, California. *Contains the letters and papers of Brand Whitlock.*

The Houghton Library, Harvard University, Cambridge, Massachusetts. *Contains an unpublished letter to John Jay Chapman, unpublished letters to Barrett Wendell, published and unpublished letters to Theodora Bosanquet, published and unpublished letters to William Roscoe Thayer, unpublished letter to Josephine Preston Peabody Marks, unpublished letters to Ethel Derby in the Theodore Roosevelt Papers, unpublished letters to Theodore Roosevelt in the Theodore Roosevelt Papers, unpub-*

lished letters to Corrine Roosevelt Robinson, sister of Theodore Roosevelt, in the Theodore Roosevelt Papers, unpublished letters to Elizabeth Gaskell Norton; unpublished letters to Mr. and Mrs. Whitney Warren.

The Lilly Library, Indiana University, Bloomington, Indiana. Contains published and unpublished letters to Elisina and Royall Tyler in the Tyler Papers.

National Archives, Washington, DC. Contains the papers of American Red Cross, Commission to Europe, Transportation Department.

The New York Public Library, New York. Contains the papers of The American Fund for French Wounded. Archives. Manuscripts Division.

The Pusey Library, Harvard University, Cambridge, Massachusetts. Contains the Royall Tyler Papers, Harvard University Archives.

Rare Book and Manuscript Library, Columbia University, New York, New York. Contains the business correspondence of Dorothy Canfield Fisher in the Paul Reynolds Papers.

Rockefeller Archives Center, Pontanico Hills, New York. Contains unpublished letters from Wharton on the establishment of an organization to fight tuberculosis in France. Rockefeller Foundation History: Source Materials. Volume 8, and minutes, letters, and cables related to the founding and operation of Rockefeller Foundation's Commission of the Prevention of Tuberculosis in France.

The Scribner Archives, Special Collections, The Princeton University Library, Princeton, New Jersey. Contains published and unpublished letters between Wharton and Charles Scribner and members of the Scribners firm, especially related to the creation of The Book of the Homeless.

Villa I Tatti, Harvard University Research Center for Italian Renaissance Studies, Settignano, Italy. Contains published and unpublished letters from Edith Wharton to Bernard and Mary Berenson and their letters to Wharton.

CONTEMPORARY NEWSPAPERS

Chicago Tribune (European edition), 1917-1919.
New York Herald (Paris edition), 1914-1919.
New York Sun, 1915.
New York Times, 1914-1919.

INDEX